CONTROL RELATIONSHIPS BETWEEN AMERICAN CORPORATIONS AND THEIR EUROPEAN SUBSIDIARIES

ROBERT J. ALSEGG
AMA RESEARCH STUDY 107

Control Relationships Between American Corporations and Their European Subsidiaries

Robert J. Alsegg

American Management Association, Inc.

338.74
A 461

ROBERT J. ALSEGG was born and educated in Vienna. After studying law and economics, and graduating with a doctorate from the University of Vienna, he went into the field of international trade. The first 15 years of his business career were devoted to the production of films in Germany, Austria, and Italy, and their distribution throughout the world, and to the import and export of fountain pens, mechanical pencils, lighters, and similar items throughout Europe. When war broke out in Europe, Dr. Alsegg came to the United States and joined Clairol Inc. as export manager. After World War II, he developed the company's international business, first by selling products through local distributors and licensees, then by establishing wholly owned subsidiaries—for semimanufacture and later for full manufacture—in Central and South America, Europe, South Africa, the Far East, and the Pacific. A few years ago, Dr. Alsegg retired from Clairol after 25 years of service. He is also the author of AMA Research Study 95, *Researching the European Markets,* published in 1969.

International standard book number: 0–8144–3107–0
Library of Congress catalog card number: 74–152035

Contents

Basis and Limits of Research   1

1   Some Observations Regarding Corporate–Subsidiary Relation-
    ships in Europe   6
    Findings and Conclusions–The Human Factor–Support Relation-
    ships–Delayed Decisions from Corporate Management–Group Meet-
    ings–The Subsidiary Manager–The Shifting Profit Center–Reorganiza-
    tions

2   Many Problems and Some Solutions Relating to Organization of
    European Subsidiaries   41
    Oldtimers and Newcomers–Organizational Problems of European Sub-
    sidiaries–The Regional Office–Regional Staff and Support Services–
    The Role of Corporate Staff Departments

3   Some Successful and Unsuccessful Methods of Communicating   66
    Information, Methods, and Channels–Manuals–Reports: A Contro-
    versy–Visits and Conferences–Language: Overcoming a Fundamental
    Obstacle

4   Tight Versus Loose Control Relationships   98
    Variables in Control Relationships–Control Versus Autonomy–Strict
    Control of Subsidiaries–Loose Control of Subsidiaries–Tight Versus
    Loose Controls–Headquarters' Views on Responsibilities

5   Control of Key Areas in Subsidiaries   142
    Strategic and Tactical Decisions–Financial Control–Forecasting–Ex-
    penditures–Local Financing–Accounting–Pricing–Advertising–Per-
    sonnel Matters

6   Product-Related Control Affecting Subsidiary Operations   184
    Product and Process Uniformity–Sources of Supply–Problems of Local
    Production–Quality Control–Research and Development

Basis and Limits of Research

In UNDERTAKING the present research project, the author was aware of certain basic difficulties; they not only increased considerably but also became more apparent as the study progressed. One of the most conspicuous was that very few patterns or rules could be detected that govern international management relationships and their infinite variety. The type of industry, the age of the company—particularly the age of its international operations—the company's size and structure, its historic development and experience, its leading personalities, and several other factors all influence the functioning of a corporation's international organization, but the general direction of the many crosscurrents is unpredictable. An official of the U.S. Department of Commerce told the author that two companies in the same industry, though they are the same size, have the same resources, make exactly the same products, and have plants and headquarters near each other, may have entirely different systems of control over and relations with their foreign subsidiaries—and yet be doing equally well abroad.

Another research problem is the absence of accepted yardsticks for measuring and determining the degree of centralization and control. The author saw journalistic attempts to classify corporations according to "tight," "intermediate," and "loose" control of their foreign operations, as indicated by the corporations themselves; to group them statistically by such categories as consumer goods, industrial products, and defense industries; and then to draw conclusions from such flimsy and unscientific data.

A further problem is the constant change in the international structure of many American corporations; this makes it difficult for the observer to find a point of reference from which to study, inquire, and analyze. Other research problems arise from tendencies in some companies to minimize or distort facts that would otherwise create an undesirable image. Such companies do not want the researcher to see their international operations as they are, but rather as, in the opinion of management—or the public relations department—they should be, or at least should appear to be. For example, there is frequently a great difference between legal and actual control and relationships. A foreign subsidiary may legally depend on its board of directors, to whom local management submits an annual report; but actually the subsidiary manager reports weekly to and is in daily contact with regional or corporate headquarters, and it is from that source that he gets his detailed instructions.

A similar obscurity can result from overrating the organization chart. Though a valuable help to a better understanding of corporate structure and units, it does not always accurately and fully portray actual relationships. For reasons of greater clarity and better appearance, only some, if any, of the multiple dotted lines are indicated. Then, too, identical straight lines between upper and lower management levels may mean different things even within the same corporation. Moreover, formal or technical relationships established by company policies and directives are seldom exactly the same as actual living relations between personalities. There are also the old forms of management relationships still on the books as contrasted with new patterns evolving in response to changed conditions.

Some corporations emphasize their multinational character and try to convey a transnational image; others stress that they are and remain everywhere American companies. But this does not mean that the former are decentralized or loosely controlled or that the latter are under tight central management. These terms must be used carefully. Centralization is usually taken to mean strict control from the top; but decentralization does not necessarily diminish control. Often, it merely means that control is shifted from a higher level to the one below (regional or area). It can also signify a reorganization whereby control is shifted from a geographic basis to a product or functional one.

These various difficulties were taken into consideration when selecting the research methods for the present study. The three principal methods were: (1) literature, (2) a survey through a questionnaire, and (3) personal interviews. Each of these methods presented both shortcomings and advantages.

1. The literature on the subject consists of several books on international management and numerous magazine articles. Some of the books suffer from a noticeable lack of empirical or practical knowledge, and in this rapidly changing field they are also subject to rapid obsolescence. Magazine articles, on the other hand, are frequently written on the spur of the moment and therefore tend to be superficial. Occasionally, books and articles are not entirely objective and impartial, but are colored by present or past business interests, personal opinions and impressions, even sometimes by outright bias and prejudice.

2. In April, 1968, a four-page questionnaire was mailed to presidents or international vice-presidents of 660 companies selected from several directories listing U.S. corporations with foreign operations. The answers to the questionnaire were in a few cases shaded by misunderstandings or different uses of the same term. Furthermore, general questions do not always fit a particular industry or company since, as mentioned previously, few universally accepted practices and patterns exist. Therefore, some respondents found that several or most questions were either inapplicable or irrelevant to their organization. In a few other instances the filled-in questionnaires revealed certain highly subjective viewpoints or a public-relations deference to the latest fads in international business administration (and some are greatly respected, if not always observed).

3. Personal interviews were by far the most satisfactory research method for the present study, as they are in a good many other projects. This viewpoint was shared by the American secretary of an American chamber of commerce in Europe that frequently conducts surveys both through questionnaires and by interviews. He said that the same company executive may give one answer in written form, but quite another verbally. Not that one will be correct and the other false, but rather the oral response is usually more frank, specific, and to the point. The secrecy factor, which often inhibits written responses, makes the personal interview even more desirable. Yet interviews have their drawbacks: Many of the participants had no up-to-date theoretical knowledge of the problems in question (although this was certainly compensated for by their pragmatic knowledge and wide expertise). And a few were not completely free of subjective impressions and dislikes, or the impact of particular experiences concerning companies, countries, or special problems.

From April through October- 1968, the author conducted interviews with 172 executives in 153 European subsidiaries, affiliates, and regional offices of 127 different companies. The time available did not permit a greater number of interviews, but the author attempted to obtain a good cross section of industries, markets, and corporate structures. Several additional interviews were conducted in the American headquarters of industrial corporations and consultants.

The prudent interviewer should always be on guard against personal opinions and colored factual statements, but the author found these in only about 6 percent of his interviews. The older and higher ranking the participant, the franker and more objective was his response. A highly subjective viewpoint, an exaggerated description, or a soft-pedaling of facts sometimes had to do with the fact that the participant had insufficient experience with other companies to make valid comparisons. Overcritical attitudes engendered by years of friction, frustration, and dissatisfaction could also be observed. Most frequent was the desire to maintain personal pride and prestige, when the unmitigated facts could detract from them.

Thus while subsidiary managers and one or two regional executives told the author that they enjoyed "complete independence" or "great autonomy," questions on specific activities soon revealed that such statements had to be taken with a grain of salt. Many activities were rather strictly controlled either by the regional office or by corporate headquarters; or else this alleged autonomy was severely restricted by frequent detailed reporting requirements. Occasionally there was a tendency on the subsidiary level to paint a rosy picture of local decision-making powers or to claim a greater authority than apparently existed, while on the regional level of the same corporation an opposite opinion was expressed.

Frequently, both levels used such euphemisms as "consultation, recommendations, suggestions, discussions," "inducing or convincing local management," "arriving at a consensus of opinion or unity in action," "advice, guidance, assistance, coordination," to sugarcoat and disguise "orders, instructions, directions and command." Top management, though fond of military terms—such as "line and staff," "field force," "objectives," "headquarters," "strategy and tactics," even "outposts" and "beachheads"—often uses and encourages euphemisms when speaking of controls.

A particular case of face-saving in the interest of national pride was evident in the French subsidiary of a very large U.S. corporation. A new American general manager had recently been sent over to "assist" the French president, and the latter's assistant emphasized that it was the French president himself who had asked corporate top management for the new general manager to introduce American standards in production and management. Actually, the decision was made in the United States because of the subsidiary's poor performance. The new manager's words were "for closer coordination." Moreover, the assistant to the president claimed that responsibilities are about equally divided between the French president and the American general manager, while actually the president now takes care only of legal, external, and representative duties, all other activities being under the general manager's exclusive jurisdiction. This was an illustration of a most delicate situation with important economic and political ramifications due to the country involved, the national sensitivity of the particular industry, and the size of the American corporation and its French operations.

When for prestige reasons a local manager tries to convey an impression of greater power than he actually has, he can create a difficult and even dangerous situation when third parties become involved. This is particularly true for important clients or suppliers with contractual rights or obligations, lawyers, accounting and advertising firms, consultants, and government agencies—especially in the case of disputes, new agreements, or the interpretation, application, or modification of existing contracts.

This problem can be further complicated by the fact that in many cases the subsidiary manager is, at the same time, the European equivalent of an executive vice-president of the local company (*administrateur délégué* in France and Belgium, *amministratore delegato* in Italy, *Prokurist* in Germany, Switzerland, and Austria). According to almost all continental European laws the legal position, functions, and privileges of this title are strictly circumscribed and cannot be restricted or abridged by the company. Whatever they do or sign under these legal provisions is valid and binding. A Spanish lawyer stated that the external or legal powers of such a manager must be clearly distinguished from his internal or actual authority under company manuals, job descriptions, or directives, with the former having precedence in court, before government agencies, or in public. Some corporations therefore prefer to vest such powers in an older and completely trusted executive at the regional office or even one at corporate headquarters, even though he may not be as accessible as might be desired. Other companies nominate their local lawyer (member of an American international law firm) or auditor to this position, but such men, though more accessible, may lack the necessary intimate knowledge of the business operations. Where the subsidiary manager has this important title and function, he must be in every respect trustworthy or strictly supervised or both if unpleasant occurrences are to be guarded against.

These are exceptions, however. Many executives of U.S. companies abroad may disagree with and dislike restrictions placed on their freedom of decision by higher management levels, but few are the executives who are not fully aware of them, or would try to create a false impression in their business dealings.

1. Some Observations Regarding Corporate-Subsidiary Relationships in Europe

IT HAS already been mentioned that the prevailing viewpoint regarding control relationships of U.S. companies with their European subsidiaries seems to be that generalizations are impossible. One executive summed up the situation as follows:

> There is no general pattern regarding the degree of control, even among corporations of the same size and industry. There isn't even a pattern regarding the areas or functions that are controlled. Control relationships depend on a great many variables, such as corporate history and tradition, structure and development, and personalities of top executives and their backgrounds. Therefore each company develops its own way of conducting its international business. Identical ideas and intentions in two subsidiaries can lead to dissimilar patterns because of differences in business environment, and similar, or even the same, methods can produce quite divergent results due to different attitudes prevailing at a given time.

The variables that affect control relationships also include: size and importance of subsidiary and market, age of subsidiary, distance from headquarters, organization and legal form of subsidiary, its operations, type of environment, and stability of conditions in the host country. Equally important are the qualifications of the subsidiary manager, in particular his personality, length of international experience, and the confidence he inspires in his superiors. The parent company's size, age, and growth have little influence on its control relationship with European subsidiaries. Large established companies may impose much or little control on local groups; similarly, young and aggressive companies may provide strict control or give their subsidiaries extensive autonomy.

Because of the tremendous number of variables, U.S. companies are seldom able to implement strictly uniform policies regarding control of their European subsidiaries. Even where it is possible for the companies to exercise absolutely rigid control, it is unwise for them to do so. Absolute autonomy of foreign subsidiaries is equally undesirable. Both extremes are unrealistic for companies operating in distant countries where conditions are unfamiliar and continually changing.

FINDINGS AND CONCLUSIONS

In the course of this study, some facts became apparent. One of the most obvious was that companies with highly centralized organizations tend to tightly control their foreign operations. Also, companies in certain industries lean heavily toward centralized control for some very specific reasons—drug manufacturers because they require consistency of product; cosmetics and photographic equipment manufacturers because they have achieved great uniformity and their local markets vary little; and oil processors because they require worldwide coordination of exploration, production, shipping, and storage. In industries that have no small or medium-size firms, companies exercise relatively rigid control, especially in highly competitive markets such as Europe.

Manufacturing subsidiaries are usually more tightly controlled than marketing units because production more readily lends itself to centralized direction, and engineers and technicians adhere more firmly to standards and regulations than do salesmen. However, the European executive of a toilet goods company said that his headquarters exercises control over subsidiaries "in order to maintain an identical company image and uniform product appearance and quality, as well as rigid conformity to corporate policies in marketing and promotion." He explained that strict centralization is possible and advisable because differences between various markets are not very deep and are more and more minimized by consumer education.

The one area in which an overwhelming majority of multinational companies are centrally controlled is finance. Most companies strive for uniformity in financial reporting, budget preparation, accounting, statistics, and forecasts. Consistency of sales reporting is also considered important, as are two aspects of personnel policies: executive appointments and compensation. Sources of supply are often also strictly controlled by the home office. In some companies, administrative procedures and systems are regulated. Control is required to achieve uniformity related to product lines in these areas: product identity, package, label, name and trademark, literature, and advertising.

Subsidiaries that have a wide range of products and a variety of markets tend to be more autonomous than those with uniform products and markets. Companies that have only one or two large subsidiaries in Europe rather than a number of smaller ones also tend to exercise little control. In one large diversified corporation, a trend toward ever increasing local autonomy was explained by the many different product groups, each with its own international organization, and by the size of the operation, which had many thousands of employees overseas.

Companies give more autonomy to subsidiaries situated far from headquarters, in countries that have unfamiliar socioeconomic conditions, unstable political conditions, or stringent legal requirements regarding business operations, expansion, imports, exchange, and personnel. The legal form of a company's European operations is an important factor. Joint ventures usually have considerable local autonomy, especially in countries where foreign ownership is restricted to 50 percent or less.

Autonomy is frequently retained by newly acquired subsidiaries that continue to manufacture their old product lines under their former management. It is also common among large subsidiaries that have many years' experience, elaborate organizations, extensive functions, and numerous staff members. Autonomous subsidiaries often conduct independent research, develop products for their own markets, determine product introduction, arrange local advertising, and select marketing outlets. One local executive commented that while theoretically all subsidiaries in his company are equal, in practice the large one with the most important market carries more weight.

Several participants pointed out that controls are seldom constant; they are usually either changing or evolving. During an early stage companies may have light controls; as they grow and become more centralized they have increasingly heavy ones; then, when additional growth brings decentralization, they may relax surveillance of divisions and subsidiaries. Some companies undergo several control–autonomy swings during their history.

Of the 127 companies whose European subsidiaries and other units were visited by the author, approximately 40 percent imposed strict control, 40 percent had loose control, and 20 percent had control that was intermediate, flexible, undeterminable, or in the process of being changed.

Nevertheless, a trend toward stricter control is seen by a number of European subsidiary managers and other experts, while a trend toward autonomy is claimed by some headquarters executives and authorities such as professors of business schools. The author concurs with the former opinion, since he believes that people who are not actually involved in a situation sometimes confuse what they consider to be desirable with what is actually happening.

Several developments have contributed to increased control of European subsidiaries by many American companies. The reason most often mentioned by executives is the development of jet transportation, transatlantic telephone, and Telex. A second important reason is the constant growth of European subsidiaries since World War II; prior to that time most of them were small and isolated from both the parent company and each other. A third factor favoring centralization and strict control is the development of the Common Market, which has resulted in the elimination of tariffs and, in turn, the relocation of plants and the reorganization of distribution and marketing. A fourth reason for the adoption of strict controls is that the performance of many subsidiaries has been unsatisfactory. Frequently this is caused by the subsidiary manager's lack of competence and is a particularly difficult problem since highly qualified international executives are scarce.

In forward-thinking companies, authoritarian management has been abandoned for consensus reached by mutual discussion and participation. The latter approach tends to be associated with the behavioral sciences and reflects individualism and specialization, while authoritarianism is based on economic theories, particularly on growth and planning, conformism, uniformity, and standardization. Nevertheless the outstanding characteristic of both is that they are conditional. Autonomy is often granted only as long as certain conditions prevail.

Some Generalizations about Control Relationships

As a result of discussions with 172 executives, managers, and experts, the author concluded that six generalizations can be made about the control relationship between U.S. corporations and their European subsidiaries.

1. *Control is exercised in the same way and degree as long as conditions and situations remain relatively constant.* Therefore, many companies adopt controls that are conditional or situational. They establish reasonable limits, then within that framework modify their controls as required to meet various conditions and situations. For example, a company may retain several basic responsibilities, delegate several others to its regional office in Europe, and let the subsidiaries handle the rest. But if it finds that major market changes have occurred and it needs to modify its production or marketing, management changes must be made, and these may well alter the company's control relationship with the regional office and subsidiaries.

When top management uses a pragmatic approach it is more sensitive to special situations and conditions. It either makes quick changes and fast decisions or it permits its subsidiaries freedom to make them. As one manager in Milan commented, "We adjust our controls to local conditions because we are a practical company."

2. *Strict control is imposed only as long as required.* The developmental stage of a subsidiary is an important factor. Newly established subsidiaries have to be nurtured. They have special needs, such as extensive market studies, large expenditures for capital equipment, and wide-scale recruiting. After a subsidiary is established and its manager has proven himself competent, the parent company often relaxes its hold and permits greater freedom. Similarly, a well-established subsidiary may have controls imposed on it for a short period of time because the subsidiary manager resigns, the competitive situation deteriorates, or some other change occurs.

3. *Control is determined by management confidence.* The degree of subsidiary control is often determined by how much confidence corporate executives have in local managers. Loose control should therefore always be accompanied by careful selection of managers and staff members abroad. Some companies have less confidence in nationals than in American managers who are familiar with company products and policies; but an increasing number prefer nationals because they are more knowledgeable about local people, organizations, and conditions. Regardless of their nationality, outstanding subsidiary managers are difficult to find.

4. *Control depends on the subsidiary's success.* Closely related to the confidence of corporate executives is the degree of success achieved by the subsidiary. As long as the subsidiary is making money and functioning smoothly, the parent company may give it freedom. This was confirmed by a number of subsidiary managers, one of whom said: "As long as we show a profit according to our forecasts and adhere to the general rules and directives, we can do pretty much as we think best." If a subsidiary loses money and has difficulties, the company investigates, assists and advises, and then, in all likelihood, imposes tighter controls.

5. *Control is dependent on methods.* From the standpoint of subsidiary managers, the way control is exercised is often more important than the extent of control. If the methods are not reasonable and useful, they will not be effective. For example, established limits of authority and special authorizations seem to be useful to most parent companies and subsidiaries, and so are budget controls. However, few international executives are satisfied with their company's reporting systems; most consider them exaggerated and limited in value.

6. *Control requires two-way relations.* Some of the most effective control methods—and, at the same time, brakes against excessive autonomy—are the face-to-face variety. Some of the methods preferred by subsidiaries are meetings between U.S. and foreign executives, product managers, and technicians; special sessions with staff specialists from headquarters and regional offices; and conferences of European managers. Most meetings and

conferences are multipurpose. At the same time that they disseminate information to the subsidiary, they provide feedback to the company. Meetings and conferences are used to inform, teach, advise, assist, consult, coordinate, and control. Above all, if they are conducted properly, they can save companies considerable time and effort.

Major Problems in International Corporate Relations

In interviewing executives at home and abroad, the author quickly discovered that certain problems severely block relationships between executives of U.S. corporations and their European subsidiaries. Here are some of the most critical problems.

1. *Headquarters' lack of knowledge about conditions abroad.* Most U.S. companies with foreign subsidiaries have at one time or another underestimated the importance of social, cultural, economic, and political conditions abroad. Many companies are still not well informed about such conditions.

"It is difficult to explain to the parent company that conditions in Europe are different from those in the United States, especially in marketing and personnel relations," said the American controller of an Austrian affiliate. "Fortunately our headquarters does not interfere in these activities and lets us go our own way, so these things don't matter so much in our company." But other subsidiary executives complained that they had serious problems because corporate executives lack understanding of the many differences between the United States and European countries, and between various European countries. They said that headquarters fails to identify fundamental consumer and market characteristics, to appreciate European traditions, and to recognize European resistance to certain American management techniques.

For these reasons, many companies are unable to make sound decisions regarding their European subsidiaries. More specifically, they cannot determine the degree of autonomy or control that should be given a subsidiary, and when they do exercise strict control they encounter resistance. In general, local managers will accept strict control without grumbling only when they know that decisions from headquarters are based on thorough knowledge of European conditions.

2. *Disregard of human factors.* Many American companies overlook the importance of human relations in their international operations. They overestimate the importance of management programs and techniques, especially those relating to the marketing function. Young American managers, new to the European scene, frequently have a kind of missionary spirit; they believe they are bringing enlightened management to foreign countries, but fail to realize that they have much to learn about them.

Executives at U.S. headquarters often have too little contact with managers of foreign subsidiaries. Even though many of them visit several times a year, they have too few meetings with local staff members and spend too little time with them. Local managers feel they are not truly supported by corporate management. These factors cause misunderstandings and misconceptions at home and the loss of goodwill abroad.

3. *Delays in decisions from headquarters.* One of the loudest and most frequent complaints made by subsidiary managers and others—suppliers, customers, agents, lawyers, accountants, and consultants—was that corporate decisions are made far too slowly. Delays in receiving important, and even urgent, decisions from headquarters cause companies to miss many opportunities. Worse, such delays sometimes result in irrecoverable financial losses.

Strangely enough, this problem seems to be compounded by improvements in air transportation, overseas air mail, telephone, and Telex. As these become faster and immediate communication becomes easier, procrastination in decision making seems to increase rather than decrease. The problem is particularly acute when no regional office exists or when it is vested with little decision-making power.

4. *Cumbersome reporting systems.* Participating managers complained that entirely too many reports had to be sent to headquarters, that everybody sends reports to everybody else and nobody reads them, and that the situation gets worse every year. Most local managers said they want fewer reports and ones that are shorter and easier to fill out.

Although reporting systems usually reflect the size of a company, reporting requirements are often as rigidly uniform and quantity as voluminous for the small subsidiary as the large one. An Italian manager with 20 office employees said that he prepares more than 50 reports a year— approximately the same number prepared by his company's British and German subsidiaries, which have three times as many employees. Very few of the participating executives defended their companies' voluminous and frequent reporting requirements.

5. *Lack of knowledge about immediate situations.* The extent to which reports are read and followed by appropriate action is another matter. The ever increasing volume of reports makes it impossible for corporate executives involved in international decision making to read all of them. Furthermore, when executives do read reports, they tend to minimize the significance of the facts presented.

Even when corporate executives visit subsidiaries they usually spend too little time studying the local situation and the business at hand. The result is that they often rely on advice from outsiders or make hasty decisions based on superficial knowledge.

The other side of the coin is that some subsidiary managers also disregard facts that seem unrelated to their specific situation—sometimes because they are uninformed about company policies, sometimes because they are uninterested. Occasionally they ignore new situations because they are worried about their own positions.

6. *Low level of credibility.* Corporate executives tend to disregard local managers' recommendations—in addition to the facts on which they are based—and at the same time demand more information. As a result, in highly centralized and controlled companies, local managers have to resort to persuasion and salesmanship to get their messages and ideas received at headquarters.

Another aspect of the problem is that some local managers doubt the soundness of decisions made by headquarters executives, even when they have few apparent reasons to question them. Frequently local managers are uninformed about situations responsible for these decisions—in which case headquarters may be at fault—but at other times the managers simply cannot concede that a corporate executive is better informed or better qualified than they to make decisions regarding operations abroad. Often local managers are unable to understand the global considerations that influence headquarters decisions.

7. *Poorly qualified subsidiary managers.* In the opinion of many experts, the most acute problems of U.S. corporations with foreign subsidiaries stem from their selection of subsidiary managers. An international lawyer who is a member of an American law firm in Brussels said this: "A major reason for the failure of some American companies in Europe is mismanagement caused by unqualified local managers. Few companies send their best men overseas; they keep them at home and the men prefer staying there. In addition, companies seldom select the best men when they hire nationals as subsidiary managers."

This condition is more prevalent in companies with newly established subsidiaries. It is probably also more prevalent in companies that are highly centralized since most highly qualified international executives prefer working for companies that grant extensive autonomy. An American executive in London summarized this situation as follows: "Companies that centralize all authority at headquarters have to be content with second-best managers and bureaucrats rather than aggressive, imaginative executives."

THE HUMAN FACTOR

Management relationships within corporations are not between men and materials or between people and products, but between people and people. In large companies this fact may be obscured, but in no way lessened, by the importance given to impersonal organizational forms. The emphasis on people is, or should be, even stronger in multinational corporations and in their overseas business, where differences among company personnel, customers and suppliers, agents and officials, are much greater but less known, less measurable, and less predictable than at home. Yet, in the opinion of many executives of U.S. companies abroad, Americans as well as Europeans, the human factor is often neglected or misunderstood, and practically always underestimated by management in the home office. The widely discussed communication gap is only one of various contributing factors; the real cause lies deeper—in sociopsychological attitudes.

In interviews with American executives in Europe the problem came up in two negative ways: general criticism and specific complaints.

"American companies," said an American subsidiary manager in Lisbon, "overestimate marketing and make a mythology out of it. They generally neglect human relations in their dealings with employees and customers alike. Everything is standardized and computerized and the human element is lost." He pointed out that in the United States key men can and frequently do leave their company, taking positions elsewhere, but abroad this escape route is less often available because changing jobs is difficult. This is true despite the shortage of qualified key personnel. This manager also had a personal complaint: His company did not recognize and did not compensate him for all the losses he suffered and sacrifices he made when he was transferred to Portugal from another continent.

By contrast, another local manager seemed to be quite happy with his company, for which he has been working 30 years—first in Latin America, later in the United States, and now in Spain. But he too commented that the human factor is frequently neglected in American companies, particularly in their foreign operations, where it is of paramount importance. As he put it: "The best organized company, with the best equipment and the best products, is not good enough without the enthusiastic cooperation of carefully chosen and well-trained employees." This is exactly the position that was taken by the Italian manager of a subsidiary in Milan, who said that although he has been enjoying a close rapport with his superiors in New York, he believed that human relations could be greatly improved. The lack of knowledge of European conditions at the home office and the resulting desire for strict uniformity were described as the greatest handicaps.

Almost the same words were used by the Canadian deputy manager of a Swiss subsidiary. He, too, stressed the loss in goodwill, image, and prestige that results when the human element is overlooked, and he too mentioned the hardships for American executives and their families when moving from one country to another. Several key men in European subsidiaries said it is ironic and inconsistent that U.S. corporations put so much emphasis on the right type of organization, when they are so prone to discharge, or at least transfer, the local manager when something goes wrong. Also, while many companies greatly restrict the decision-making authority of the subsidiary manager, they make him responsible for failures. Most corporations insist on an exaggerated and time-consuming reporting system whereby every detail is supposed to be communicated back home, yet they blame local management for lack of success.

A member of an American law firm that operates internationally observed that there are no sure patterns of success in multinational structure and organization, personalities being more important than organization charts. If two companies in the same industry and of the same size have different degrees of success in international business, he suggests one should first look at their overall executive personnel policies. And the manager of an American association in Brussels commented that often management relationships in a large corporation work smoothly not because, but in spite of, the organization chart, manuals, job descriptions, and so forth, simply because the people have been working well together for many years. He suggests that if one or the other is being replaced, the second-in-command can take over and continue; most likely he is the one who did the real work anyway. Although the author does not fully agree with this oversimplification, this opinion again focuses attention on the importance of personalities over systems.

This was vividly brought home in a subsidiary where an unhealthy atmosphere prevailed. The company had gone through numerous reorganizations accompanied by changes in location and key personnel. Morale seemed to be very low. There was a tendency to tighten even more the already strict control, adding more intermediate levels in the chain of command, more and more regulations, and more and longer reports, including both regular reports and those done in response to numerous special requests. As the manager put it: "Everybody in Paris, London, and America writes to everybody here at the subsidiary and asks for information without doing anything with it but justifying his department's existence and need for increased personnel." Furthermore, personal visits from America are rare, and so are meetings. There is little contact, let alone a friendly spirit between higher and lower management levels. The subsidiary manager, with five years of employment, is the oldest European executive in years of service.

A prominent member of the American business community in London said this: "Generally, American companies put too much emphasis on technical knowledge when selecting a key man in Europe, but if the man does not know how to handle people, how to convey his knowledge to them, and thereby put it to best use, then it is of no great value to him or to his company." Many subsidiary managers would add to this that the company should also let the man they have selected do the best he can and give him a chance to develop and demonstrate his abilities.

Many headaches on the part of the company and heartaches on the part of its employees are caused by misinformation, misconceptions, and misunderstandings. This, of course, applies mostly to American newcomers in the European business. An executive of an advertising firm with a long and varied counseling practice tried to find some of the deeper causes, commenting: "Americans had the experience of the melting pot of their European immigrant groups, which resembles a fruit cocktail, where the original colors and flavors are more or less preserved and are still faintly different—but the whole is one dish. Therefore, Americans often transfer this experience to Europe—but we resemble, rather, a fruit basket, in which each is a separate and different entity with its own size, shape, and taste." Later he added these thoughts:

> It really does not matter too much whether or not a corporation has a regional office or where, as long as the people who run the international operations, whoever they are and wherever located, are intelligent and open-minded, and have international expertise and enough authority to do their job. In the past, too many of these men were sitting in London or Paris with their eyes and ears turned to America and their back toward Europe. Even today, some young Americans sent over by their companies have a kind of missionary spirit instead of knowledge of the environment. However, missionaries are no longer appreciated, not even in Africa—though progressive Europeans like to use American products and to adopt American methods.

A refreshing contrast to the unhealthy atmosphere described previously was provided by the Frankfurt area office of a business machines and computer manufacturing company. Two young executives, both in their early thirties, discussed the situation there. One was the applications manager and acting regional manager; the other was director of customer engineering. Operations began only five years ago; technical qualification requirements for managerial positions are high and take priority over other considerations, which is understandable and common in this extremely technical industry. Therefore, the company's policy of employing as many nationals as possible has not yet been implemented. It was frankly admitted:

> We made plenty of mistakes and learned the hard way. We did not know the intricate European preferences and prejudices. We found out, for

instance, that you had better not send a German supervisor to Switzerland or Austria. We learned that you cannot put a clause in a contract that the law of the state of Minnesota will rule in the interpretation of the agreement in case of disputes. We had legal counsel, sure, but sometimes we thought they exaggerated and just did not always believe them.

The two young Americans quickly discovered that "when you ask a German junior executive to call you by your first name, he is horrified." Yet when a young German comes back from several weeks' training in America, he is used to the idea, which means, as one of the executives put it, that there is then "the necessity of distinguishing between those who are Americanized and those who are not."

Appointing the Subsidiary Manager

Among the reproaches most often voiced in Europe against American companies is that they frequently appoint the wrong men to managerial positions, or men who have only technical qualifications and lack other equally important prerequisites. In the past, close relatives of top executives have in many cases been sent to Europe either because they wanted to go to exciting places like Paris or London, or because this was the only way to get rid of them at home, or to let them gain experience. This would have been less damaging if these young men had been made assistants to knowledgeable managers, but often they took the top position without proper preparation or background. Some of them have learned the hard way through trial and error, but others have come back after a couple of years without being any wiser and often blaming everybody but themselves for failing. Few of the established companies in foreign trade commit this grave mistake nowadays, but many of the newcomers do.

Another problem is that first-class executives often refuse to go to smaller markets. The result is that these subsidiaries are frequently staffed with second-best managerial talent or with men who left the corporate headquarters all too willingly to get away from it all. These are the discontented, the frustrated, the forgotten geniuses, the hard-to-get-along-with. Such men seldom find the right contact with their local associates, whether Americans or Europeans, and they are bound to have unpleasant and unsatisfactory relationships with headquarters. One of the first men the author interviewed said: "You want to know how relations are between American corporations and their subsidiaries? The answer is simple: They are bad." Sometimes this may be the fault of headquarters, but often the local man can rightly be blamed. It is recognized even by the most critical observers of American corporations, however, that Americans are always willing to admit their mistakes and to learn from them.

The Problem of "No Return"

A widely discussed complaint about the majority of American corporations operating abroad is the problem of "no return"—that for an American executive returning home after several years of foreign service there is no place to go. Often there is no vacancy in the international department commensurate with the seniority and rank that the repatriate has reached. He is simply given a title and shifted to some domestic department, where his long years of foreign experience, including the knowledge of languages and markets, is wasted. The reorganization trend along product group lines magnifies this danger because it de-emphasizes the special foreign know-how formerly considered essential and because it operates under the assumption that the international business is neither as special nor as difficult as the people in the international division say it is.

Some able executives shy away from foreign assignments because they are afraid to lose touch, to forgo the personal contacts with important members of management at home, to become forgotten men, bypassed when new opportunities open up or when promotions are due. Therefore, they try either to avoid a position abroad altogether or to make sure they stay no longer than three to five years.

Some American executives in Europe have a tendency to make frequent trips back home, to call the corporate president on the telephone more often than necessary, and to bypass intermediate levels just so they can maintain personal contact. In this connection an advertising executive in Geneva made an interesting remark. He said that too much autonomy for a subsidiary manager, however desirable it may seem to him at the time, can backfire in the long run because it increases the dangers of losing contact and widens the gap between the cautious people who stayed home and the daring ones who went abroad. It is not only the danger of losing close personal communication that faces the executive abroad; in some corporations he is also to some extent out of touch with policy changes, new technical developments, and new research projects. Though many companies require an extensive and constant flow of information from the subsidiary to headquarters, not too many respond in kind. A great amount of independence for the local manager will almost certainly mean even less information going back to him. The executive who enjoyed less autonomy abroad may find it easier to readjust to life with the parent company upon his return.

Some subsidiary managers interviewed seemed very apprehensive about the problem; others—a small minority—have lived abroad for ten years and longer and said they did not intend to return home until retirement; still others said that in their corporation the difficulties had been overcome. If the company is very large and has been in the international business successfully for many years, and if its foreign business forms a substantial part (35 percent or more) of the total volume, chances are good that satisfactory solutions have been worked out. A growing international business will create more positions in international work at home. Even the product-group organization slowly finds out that in one way or another real international experts are needed. A carefully established plan to keep the foreign executive alerted to developments back home, to maintain his close contacts with all facets of the company's life and growth, will be of enormous help. Above all, he must feel that the international business is an integral part, not an outlandish offshoot, of the corporation—and here the product-group organization may very well pay off. There is, of course, one way to minimize this problem: appointing as many European nationals as possible to key positions abroad. Indeed, this solution is being used increasingly by more and more American companies.

To what extremes, however, the neglect of the personal and personnel questions can lead is illustrated by the following case.

CASE BRIEF

A medium-size manufacturer of industrial equipment has subsidiaries in Britain, Belgium, and several other European countries. About two years ago it was felt that the growing European business required a headquarters nearer these subsidiaries and the company's licensees, and, following the general trend, the company decided to establish a regional office in Brussels. It already had a Latin American office and a Far East office. Of necessity, some regional functions had formerly been assigned to the London subsidiary, but now the new Brussels office was to exercise full control over the subsidiaries and give them the necessary technical support.

The move to Brussels was carefully planned and prepared long in advance. The preparations included selecting the location, arranging office space and office equipment, and establishing communication with divisional and corporate headquarters in the United States. It was determined exactly which responsibilities were to be assigned to Brussels. The only matter completely overlooked was personnel. Practically at the last moment it was decided that a key man from England was to go to Brussels temporarily; for three months, he and a secretary were the only people in the new regional office. They were unable to cope with even its most basic functions. The regional director and a product manager later arrived from America—after they had finally been chosen. Further, the company grossly underestimated the difficulties in acquiring the necessary local staff, such as engineers and office help. It followed the traditional method of putting advertisements in local papers, a method that is never very effective in Europe. Some essential technicians were still missing up to a year after the opening of the office. Needless to add, the losses in vital customer service, in goodwill and prestige, in supervision of and assistance to the subsidiaries, were incalculable.

Another kind of failure to understand the human factor and the different conditions under which business is conducted in various countries lies at the root of all the difficulties in this situation:

CASE BRIEF

A Southern textile manufacturer bought a factory in the English midlands, intending to produce goods not only for the British market but also for export to the European continent. It seems, however, that he was completely ignorant of British labor conditions. There was no union in his American firm, and he wanted none in England. But after a short time he had a strike on his hands. When he tried to keep the plant running with nonunion women, the workers in the plants that supplied the raw materials threatened to strike, and thereby forced the suppliers to stop deliveries.

The dispute understandably attracted wide and unfavorable publicity. When American officials tried to offer their assistance, the manufacturer replied: "I don't care whether I lose a million dollars, and I don't care about public relations and political implications. I won't have it." He finally had to liquidate—and he did lose the million dollars. Thus ended his experience with his first European subsidiary.

Since bad examples, even though they are few, always get wide attention, it is perhaps not surprising that many Europeans are convinced of the existence of American "business arrogance." The European secretary of an American chamber of commerce in a smaller country that is definitely pro-American and not exposed to communist or Gaullist influences told the author that in his opinion most American business leaders are convinced of the absolute superiority of *all* their methods, not only in production and marketing, but also in organization. Most Europeans concede American superiority in technology and management, but have reservations in some other areas, notably regarding the human element. To this area belong the following: the tendency toward uniformity and the desire to impose American methods and approaches without proper consideration of local differences, rash and erroneous judgments concerning European countries and peoples, whirlwind tours resulting in superficial information and hasty observations, and a "Father knows best" attitude. The chamber of commerce secretary added, however, that a remarkable change for the better has been slowly taking place since about 1960. This has been due principally to closer contacts between American and European businessmen, to the presence of a greater number of European executives in American companies (some of whom have been promoted to important positions in the home office), and to the success of European industries in foreign countries, often in competition with American companies.

SUPPORT RELATIONSHIPS

Many subsidiary managers talked about burdensome control relationships, but only a minority of them really complained about them. By contrast, while relatively few local executives indicated a lack of support from regional or corporate offices, all of them were strongly critical of such conditions. It seems that neglect is harder to bear than control; local management resents an uncaring attitude on the part of headquarters much more than excessive attention. The latter course may occasionally cause rebellion; the former, however, creates something worse—frustration and apathy.

"We feel like outcasts," or "We do not really belong to the family," or, in milder form, "Top management focuses its attention on the domestic business," are typical expressions of such feelings. Ordinarily, this situation is characteristic of the initial stage of a corporation's foreign business, when the international division has to fight for recognition and for every bit of help it can get from the production division or the product groups and from many staff departments. Later, as business abroad develops favorably, often to the surprise of certain corporate executives, the home office's negative attitude changes gradually—in some more internationally minded companies faster than in others. Yet larger markets with greater potentials and faster growth frequently receive much more attention from top management than the smaller subsidiaries in poorer countries. It is like supporting only those children who have already shown an ability to support themselves.

Support and Control

All this does not exist—or no longer exists—in those corporations that have had experience in multinational trade. They have developed support relationships with their foreign subsidiaries that accompany and supplement their control relationships. In fact, these relationships often grow and diminish together: They are both stronger when the local unit is young and needs more assistance and advice than during the later stages of its development, when it can supply its own services in many fields without regional or corporate help.

At the beginning, the subsidiary needs support in many areas of activity, such as installation of machinery, production procedures, technical training, marketing, merchandising, and distribution. In most activities three phases can be distinguished: the first, when corporate personnel actually perform local functions; the second, when headquarters delegates act more and more as instructors; the third, when these technicians have only supervisory duties. At this time, the support is gradually and in various degrees transformed into control, but the two can never be clearly separated. Many specialists who assist or advise a local unit are not allowed by their regional managers to interfere in local operations or to veto the subsidiary manager's decision. They can only report back to regional management or to their corporate staff department. Nevertheless, local decisions are often influenced or modified by higher management levels. Thus the fact remains that any kind of assistance may result in additional or increased controls.

Support is usually given by the regional office or, where none exists, by the international division. In large organizations, the regional office frequently has its own traveling support staff and can, if necessary, rely on the assistance of corporate product groups and functional departments. In other cases, the regional office transmits designs, plans, outlays, formulations, models, directions, and so forth, these having been either prepared by its own technical staff or received from corporate departments. It is always much better if such information is available at the European office, because if it originates at offices, plants, or laboratories in the United States and is forwarded without adaptation, it may be expressed in terms not readily intelligible to European staff members of the subsidiary or to its clients. A company giving technical assistance for the manufacture of compressors, turbines, and other machines sends designs for such installations to the customers of its subsidiaries through a regional office in Brussels without converting them into the metric system. This has to be done by the client himself—which reflects an almost incredible lack of service and salesmanship on the part of the parent company in general and its regional office in particular.

If technical advice is furnished directly by a product group or by the production department at U.S. headquarters, this service is often completely independent of the European office or the international division. Support and control relationships in these instances are separated, although sometimes they overlap and conflict.

Nontechnical assistance, especially assistance involving marketing and promotion, is frequently supplied by the regional office through product managers. Indeed, this is often regarded as one of the regional office's most important activities. When an American executive took over his duties as new regional manager in Frankfurt, one of his first actions was to appoint several product managers with broad marketing experience and specific knowledge in their respective product lines. It was their task to advise local managers how to market their products better and to scout for new sales opportunities in each line. This is particularly useful because subsidiary managers often have a tendency to adopt set ways in their handling of marketing, distribution, and promotion, and to continue the traditional pattern as long as it produces satisfactory results.

There is always a danger of conflict between the subsidiary's general and marketing managers and higher-level product managers, since they frequently represent two different backgrounds and schools of thought. The former are market-oriented, the latter product-oriented, and this signifies a considerable difference. The European manager mentioned earlier, therefore, strictly forbids his product managers to impose their point of view on local management and reserves for himself the final decision in any dispute. There may be reasons for not following the advice of the specialist in this instance as in others—reasons that escape their understanding because they are not fully familiar with local market conditions.

Support by Neighboring Subsidiaries

This danger can be practically eliminated if the specialists do not come from the regional office but from a neighboring subsidiary. In such a case, a support relationship exists between the supplying large subsidiary and the receiving unit in a small neighboring country (Germany–Switzerland and Austria; France–Belgium, Western Switzerland; Sweden–Denmark, Norway). If such assistance is made available regularly, a careful program should be worked out by the regional office or by the parent company that is similar to an international aid program to developing countries. The question always arises as to whether the type, amount, and direction of support should be determined exclusively by higher corporate levels or influenced by the needs of the receiving unit and the desires of the supplying subsidiary—which certainly does not want its own operations to be adversely affected. It will nearly always have to be reimbursed for its expenses, either by the parent company or by the assisted subsidiary. In a few companies, the planning of aid and support is left entirely to bilateral negotiations between the subsidiaries concerned. This may strengthen or strain mutual relationships and may or may not work out to the satisfaction of local, regional, and corporate managements.

Whatever the methods employed, it takes goodwill and team spirit to avoid the creation of a feeling that there are, within the corporation, first- and second-class citizens. Such attitudes and impressions are particularly dangerous in the changing European economic environment, where favorable and unfavorable market conditions may shift the center of gravity from one country to another. This has been evidenced over a number of years by divergent business climates in Great Britain, France, and Italy, as well as in several of the smaller markets.

DELAYED DECISIONS FROM CORPORATE MANAGEMENT

Some years ago, there was no fast air traffic, air mail, telephone, or Telex service between Europe and America, and local subsidiary managers or regional offices had to make many decisions that just could not wait several weeks. Now, although immediate responses by higher management levels back home are *technically* feasible and therefore often required, decisions as a rule are made much more slowly than in the old days. The technical-communications gap has been closed, but an organizational gap has been opened, mostly in companies whose management is still inexperienced in the international business, at least at the top.

This inexperience causes an overcautious attitude, a reluctance to make decisions for fear they will be wrong. And, since the problems to be decided become more complex as European business expands, some companies seem never to catch up. The American method of making, or at least preparing, decisions in committees frequently makes it necessary to wait until all the executives concerned are present—that is, back at headquarters from their constantly increasing travels. In some corporations, especially in those that are newcomers to worldwide business, the old attitude of considering the international division the stepchild of the company still lingers on, as does the attitude that all problems facing the corporation abroad are so much more difficult than domestic problems that they have to be handled with much greater care. In fact, in a few American enterprises, domestic decisions involving hundreds of thousands of dollars are frequently made within a few days, while foreign decisions of much smaller volume and less far-reaching consequences may take many weeks.

Some delays can be eliminated when the international division or corporation becomes stronger, better staffed, and vested with greater authority. Another step in this direction is an independent European regional organization, but even then some delays are hard to overcome. The reorganization of the international business along product-group lines, which has been popular in recent years, has not always reduced delays, because while the lines may have been shortened and the interest in the international business increased, there is again the problem of inexperience and uncertainty on higher levels.

The long delays in reaching final decisions are felt and criticized, particularly by the foreign partners in joint ventures and affiliates, and by the European staff of newly acquired firms. They are not familiar with the various reasons for delays, and little effort is normally made to explain the situation to them. The European associates cannot understand long delays and complain that many advantages of the new association are thereby upset and many disadvantages magnified. The national members of the local board of directors are usually available on short notice, but representatives of the American corporation may have to come from the United States or from another country. This makes delays inescapable. Moreover, the American members or their delegates often do not have full authority and have to refer important questions back to headquarters, which causes even greater delays.

Decision Making on the Regional Level

The question of lack of authority on the local and regional levels is indeed the crucial one. The problem of avoiding or creating delays is used by friends and advocates of a regional setup, as well as by its adversaries. There can be no doubt that the mere number of levels or links in the chain of command—subsidiary, area and regional offices, international division, and corporate management—each with its line and staff organizations, causes delays even when communications are by Telex and telephone and all executives can be reached immediately, which is seldom. This lengthy chain can only be shortened in two ways: (1) through bypassing some of the intermediate links, (2) by ending the chain of command in as many instances as possible at lower levels.

To some subsidiary managers a regional office means just the opposite: It means adding a new link and thereby causing further delays. This can be particularly annoying when a new regional office, or one that has been transferred to another city, has not been planned and organized with the necessary care and foresight. Often the new office suffers in the beginning from a shortage of experienced personnel and staff members. In the Italian subsidiary of a specialized machinery manufacturer where design and technical assistance to the industrial customers are of prime importance, the new European headquarters was for several months so poorly staffed that technical information that previously had been forthcoming from the United States within a few days took weeks and even months. These delays applied even to routine matters, where no top-level decisions were involved.

In other cases the regional office may have all the necessary staff, but not sufficient authority. It is a letter box, and subsidiary managers feel they could do better and certainly work faster without it. They have to route all requests and reports through it and receive answers and approvals the same way. Even though the fault may very well lie somewhere else, they blame the regional management for delays.

However, the author found that such negative attitudes toward regional headquarters were in the minority. By far the greater number of local managers with whom this question was discussed thought that a regional office expedites and accelerates decisions—at least routine ones. To be sure, this opinion was particularly strong where a regional office did not yet exist and was therefore looked upon as the cure for many ills; but it was also voiced in cases where regional headquarters had been abandoned or pulled back to the home office.

Even in a very old and large European subsidiary of a major household appliance manufacturer, the local manager welcomed the newly established London headquarters organization. He said that not much had been changed as far as his own responsibilities were concerned, but that he expected faster action from London than he had had from New York because, among other things, it would be easier to explain to a European regional office why certain local conditions require quick decisions. A similar view was expressed by both the Austrian and Spanish subsidiaries of a giant oil company with new European regional headquarters (rather distant from both countries). Here too the author was told that this was a big step forward, because it brings decision making nearer (both geographically and psychologically) to the subsidiary. Furthermore, the splitting of this European organization into two separate product-group offices, one for oil, the other for chemical products, which report directly to their product groups in the United States without an international division, was described as expediting the flow of requests and inquiries in one direction and of approvals and replies in the other.

The necessity of giving the regional office sufficient authority was stressed by several local executives. One subsidiary and area manager put it this way: "A substantial part of the international division's responsibilities should be transferred to a European headquarters, and it should have the power to make its own decisions in normal activities without referring back to New York. Otherwise, it is just one more intermediary level and delays decisions even longer." The question of whether and how to divide authority is still being discussed in this corporation, and, according to the executive interviewed, the international division seems to be reluctant to relinquish part of its responsibilities. "Of course, it is true," continued the local manager, "that some of the advantages of being closer to the field are balanced by the disadvantage of being farther from top management, product divisions, and various important staff departments. It is not easy to find the best middle way."

A similar view was taken by a paper company's subsidiary manager who thought that the regional office of his corporation is essentially useless, that it only delays and complicates everything. He said:

It would be different if New York would delegate more power to the region, but this is unlikely because the mentality at the home office is not such that they would give up their prerogatives. And even if they wanted to do this, it is doubtful that they really could, because only in New York do they have all the necessary information in such important matters as supplies and prices. They often have to consult the mills in the United States and Canada from which most shipments are made.

In a few cases the VP residing at European headquarters is at the same time the international manager or "manager of international operations" and from his European office directs *all* matters of international trade including (sometimes) foreign manufacture. He usually has greater authority than a regional manager and can make independent decisions—provided again he has not only the title, but also the full function of foreign operations manager.

It should be noted that opinions and approaches as discussed here did not appear to have any connection with whether the local managers were Americans, citizens of the host country, or third-country nationals.

GROUP MEETINGS

Where subsidiaries enjoy wide autonomy, visits by regional and corporate executives with the local managers are often the principal management control measure. General directives from top management can then be translated into the language of everyday routine; questions and objections from the local managers can be answered and clarification given on doubtful points. All this is more easily done in a meeting than by written instructions, which somehow always look like orders to be obeyed. The same instructions given in a meeting can be couched in more diplomatic language and made to sound like recommendations arrived at by mutual consent. A few corporations actually modify their directives in certain matters—for example, marketing, distribution, promotion, packaging—in accordance with suggestions made by the subsidiary managers and their experts and openly discussed during the meeting. The representative of corporate management may have the authority to make the recommended changes himself, after telephone conversation with headquarters, or he may transmit them personally to the higher level, with the amended instructions or "recommendations" being issued later to the local unit. It of course takes special skill to conduct such meetings successfully, but this skill becomes more and more a prerequisite for effective international management.

An engineering firm's Dutch subsidiary manager reported that regular meetings are held in London for all local managers with the VP–Europe as chairman, but that it does not diminish the authority granted the subsidiaries in several areas. In an optical company, by contrast, the large British and German subsidiaries report directly to American headquarters, while all other, smaller local units are under the jurisdiction of a European regional office. Nevertheless, common meetings of *all* subsidiaries are held at this office. Yet if directives are to be issued, they must come from a key executive of the U.S. home office.

Promoting Unity

European management meetings are particularly valuable for promoting coordination among subsidiaries that have different organizations or backgrounds. Some may be old and experienced, others young and inexperienced; some may have been established originally by the U.S. corporation, others by acquisition; some are wholly owned, others majority controlled; some handle all products of the parent company, others only a selected line. To equalize operations in spite of these differences may be difficult, but it is also necessary up to a certain point for corporate planning and comparison, as well as for investment and budget policies.

Meetings will both demonstrate how far unification efforts can go and help eliminate conflicts and competition among subsidiaries. The temporary American adviser of a food company's Spanish affiliate noted that thanks to regular European meetings his corporation—which operates exclusively through majority controlled affiliates—can sometimes get across its ideas on new products and its suggestions for improvements in production, promotion, and administration. The food industry is known to be subject to local preferences and taboos, and some local managers are extremely reluctant to try new approaches. "But at European meetings," as one participant observed, "nobody wants to stay behind or bear the stigma of being old-fashioned and against progress."

In the United States, heated arguments between departments and personalities are commonly settled by the time-honored truism, "After all, we're all working for the same company." But this sort of company spirit is not born overnight. In new company units it must be instilled through patient persuasion, indoctrination, and practice. European meetings are an ideal battleground for promoting a common spirit, for fighting subsidiary-nationalism and isolationism. At these meetings corporate representatives can point out that the company does not wish to harm legitimate national business interests, but rather wants to further them—and anti-American propaganda can be answered with facts and figures. A corporation cannot expect to obtain wholehearted cooperation and teamwork without giving something in return, and the meeting provides the ideal opportunity for that. An exchange of personnel in middle management is also sometimes discussed and made possible during European conferences, where junior executives can meet with their present and potential superiors from various countries on a comparatively informal basis. Such exchanges contribute greatly to a growing pan-European frame of mind within the corporation and, ultimately, to a truly transnational spirit.

Developing the International Mind

The basis for developing the international mind so essential in the multinational corporation is a steady flow of accurate information and a mutual understanding between corporate management and its local units and between individual subsidiaries. Both aims can well be served by a thorough dissemination of news, question and answer sessions, and debates. It can be argued that the exchange of information can be accomplished just as well or better in print, or writing, and certainly at lower costs. In fact, budget figures and sales statistics are better communicated in written form (as anyone knows who has ever had to follow a treasurer's oral report on receipts and disbursements), but figures always need comments and explanations, and these can best be given in person. No American sales manager relies solely on his bulletins and memoranda to the sales force, knowing that he can never reach all his men this way. He has to supplement mail information by regular sales meetings, which usually have stronger and longer lasting impact, especially when modern audiovisual aids are used.

European management meetings are an attempt to extend and adjust this American managerial tool to the European environment through familiarizing local European managers with its benefits and inducing American executives to make the necessary modifications to fit international operations. At the Brussels regional office of a synthetic fiber corporation, the regional marketing manager emphasized that the regular meetings of subsidiary general and marketing managers made it possible "to discuss all our problems in an informal setting without taking notes" and that this replaced many reports. He referred to these meetings as the real "dynamo" of his company's European organization. The general manager of an American advertising firm's French subsidiary pointed out that in his company biannual meetings of all subsidiary managers in New York replace much reporting, which thus can be kept at a minimum. There can be little doubt that these executives attend meetings with much greater enthusiasm —and therefore probably also with better results—than they write or read reports!

An executive in another industry and another country declared that regular meetings of all local managers keep them in close and useful touch with regional headquarters in Paris and with one another. He added: "It is only natural that at these meetings every subsidiary manager tries to report his successes rather than his failures, but criticism of regional and corporate actions is freely made." In fact, it is easier and requires less courage to criticize headquarters orally and backed up by a sympathetic group of fellow critics than in a letter. Enlightened management should welcome such complaints, which, if nothing else, clear the air. Self-criticism, on the other hand, is a rare commodity on all management levels, and personal visits are the only practical means of discovering certain shortcomings.

Who, in addition to the local executives, is usually present at group meetings? If they are held at the home office, the president of the corporation may attend the opening session to say hello, but he will normally leave the chair to the VP–International. If the meetings are held in Europe, the top executive of the international division may attend once or twice a year, but at other occasions the regional manager will take over. When the meetings are on a rotating basis, the manager of the host subsidiary may chair some or all sessions held in his country. Similarly, the meetings of production, marketing, and other second-level executives are chaired by the international or regional department head.

There is one notable exception to this pattern: The president and chairman of the board of one major corporation, accompanied by his staff, personally attends all European meetings, held monthly at Brussels regional headquarters. The general managers of larger subsidiaries and their seconds-in-command also attend all meetings; managers of smaller units participate every three months. More than 100 persons are present, and the meetings last two full days. The various plant and staff directors have their own separate sessions, with their counterparts from the home and regional offices. The participants exchange information, discuss problems, hear complaints and suggestions, and arrive at decisions. When the subsidiary manager returns home, he feels that the decisions he has to carry out are the results of a consensus, not orders imposed on him by top management. And he knows the reasons for these decisions.

THE SUBSIDIARY MANAGER

Perhaps there is no problem in international operations with as great a potential for success or disaster as the choice of a subsidiary manager. Yet it is often treated casually. As the VP–Europe of an old and very successful corporation remarked: "Yes, it is quite true that some U.S. companies do not use their best men in Europe, and they have to pay for it. *We* send very few men from America to Europe, because we use mostly nationals, but when we assign an American to an important position overseas, he is the best qualified person we have available."

Several executives in established companies shared this view. As one put it:

> Where do American companies, especially those which are new in Europe, make their biggest mistakes? First of all, in the selection of the key men they send over. They mostly select them from their own ranks and therefore they have little or no international, let alone European, experience. If product knowledge and familiarity with company policies are really so important, they should send a team consisting of one product specialist and one international expert.

An executive of a U.S. accounting and consulting firm fully agreed:

> The managers sent over from America are often—especially in inexperienced American companies—not the best-suited people. They get their job because they are of European origin or speak the language (at least so they claim) or they just volunteered and nobody else wanted to take the risk, or maybe they had a good record as district sales managers in New England or Texas. All this does not necessarily qualify them for the difficult task that awaits them if they are to start a new subsidiary or take over a new acquisition.

Why do newcomers so often prefer less qualified people from within than highly experienced men from without? First, because in the opinion of most experts they overestimate the special technical or organizational requirements, the company spirit, the home office atmosphere, the old personal connections, and the advantages of "belonging"—important as they are for good management relationships. Second, and this has created a good deal of resentment, they do not trust outsiders who come from another corporation, perhaps even from a different part of the United States, and another industry, people who are imbued with other managerial concepts and attitudes. They often reject, instead of welcoming, different men with new ideas. The result is a parochial spirit, an inbreeding of old thoughts and wrong approaches, a closed corporate mind and a lack of flexibility.

If the local manager is to overcome these difficulties, which include his own shortcomings, he will require the utmost cooperation of his superiors. All decisions handed down by higher levels, especially the rejection of proposals, should be fully explained as to their reasons and aims, lest the local executive feel he is an object of corporate management, not a part of it. Even the most painful restriction of local freedom of action is more bearable when the reasons that prompted the interference are known, though they may not be shared or fully understood at lower levels.

In subsidiary–headquarters relationships, however, explaining the reasons behind headquarters actions not only has salutary psychological effects for the local manager, but also encourages him to abandon parochial approaches and to think in global corporate terms.

Delegation of Responsibilities

Delegation of responsibilities and explanations for decisions should be pushed below the subsidiary level. In large organizations this will avoid the danger of local autocracies being formed that prevent initiative on the lowest level and concentrate too much power in the hands of the subsidiary manager. This process of widening the base of decision making must, however, be undertaken with great caution. In some large corporations it leads to constant bypassing of intermediate levels by allowing subsidiary managers to contact the home office directly without notifying the regional office and by allowing subsidiary staff members to go over the head of local managers. This undermines the authority of the executive who has been bypassed and can result in general confusion. It leads to fragmentation of authority.

A regional manager who frequently mediates—or meddles in—disputes between subsidiary managers and their staff members may eventually not educate any of them, but instead antagonize them all. In a very large and well-organized corporation, on the other hand, many national subsidiaries have their own branches throughout their market and their control is modeled after the pattern of relationship to higher levels. It is, in fact, a valid test for successful relationships if those established between a higher and intermediate level can be applied, with appropriate modifications, to the relationships between the intermediate and lower echelons.

Regardless of whether the delegation of certain powers is part of a development program for subsidiary managers, is performed in emergencies only, or is conceived of as a special privilege for outstanding local executives, these delegated powers must be clearly separated from those retained by the delegating higher level as well as from those normally and permanently assigned to local management. If this distinction is not made, the result may well be uncertainty and vacillation, which are worse for local management than the strictest controls.

Length of Stay

The subsidiary manager's length of stay and his return were stressed by many as being of great importance. In most European subsidiaries, the general manager and other key executives stay three to five years, rarely longer. Some companies have a policy of shifting their higher executives around frequently, not only within Europe but also to and from other continents and to and from the home office. They do this especially with their most capable international executives to expose them to diverse circumstances and situations and thereby develop their versatility and usefulness. In such companies being transferred often is considered a sign of confidence and a prerequisite for promotion.

Executives of subsidiaries that are new acquisitions are practically never moved out if they are nationals who have been previously employed by the acquired company when it was still independent. But Americans who have been assigned to these acquisitions or affiliates as coordinators or assistant managers may be given a similar position in another new acquisition after they have successfully integrated the firm into the corporation's worldwide network.

There is undoubtedly a connection between a company policy favoring frequent shifts of key personnel and tight centralized control. A subsidiary manager who has been in his position for a good many years naturally acquires—by intent or by acquiescence—great authority, especially if he has been highly successful. Furthermore, he has acquired seniority and will not easily yield to orders from a younger regional manager or heed the advice of lower ranking staff members in the international office. When he retires, a complete change may take place. The corporation, or more precisely the regional or international manager, may reverse the policy—or extend an already existing policy to the subsidiary in question—so that henceforth a subsidiary manager will not be left in his local position so long as to make him dominant, inflexible, and uncooperative.

THE SHIFTING PROFIT CENTER

Many local executives have been quoted here as saying that they enjoy a certain autonomy as long as the subsidiary makes an adequate profit. In many company directives the subsidiary's profit is mentioned as its primary objective and raison d'être; the local P&L statement is nearly always the most important report to be submitted by local management. "Every subsidiary is responsible for its profits" is printed in bold letters in a leading soap manufacturer's international manual. "My autonomy," said a local manager in an electronics company, "is predicated on the principle that I must produce a profit and act accordingly."

In modern business language this is commonly called the principle of the local profit center. Sometimes an adequate and, if possible, increasing market share is considered as important as growing profits if not more so, at least in the short-range view. Headquarters may not always be as inquisitive as it should be, and local managers who feel that they do not get all the support and assistance from higher echelons that they would like, sometimes concluded their remarks with the observation that the home office seems to be satisfied if the profits remain stable and the volume increases. The fact is, as one manager said: "We could actually do much better—*if* our suggestions were followed more often and more thoroughly."

Other subsidiary executives point out that they are inhibited from acting as profit centers, not only because of acts of omission, but because of positive actions on the part of top management. In some cases, local managers acknowledge that there are good reasons for such actions at the top, which may not be to the advantage of one particular subsidiary, but are dictated by global considerations in the best interests of the entire company. In other cases, the subsidiary manager either does not understand or is not aware of these overriding reasons. However this may be, the principle of a local profit center has been sidetracked. In a real profit center, management should do everything that furthers the single objective of attaining higher profits in a short or long period and avoid doing anything that would hamper these efforts, regardless of outside influences. Global corporate aims are to be regarded as "outside" if the subsidiary is rightly called a profit center. If corporate interests deter or prohibit local management from acting independently to achieve its own objectives, the term "profit center" is no longer fully warranted.

A true, unlimited local profit center is impossible without full autonomy. And as the once unrestricted autonomy of foreign subsidiaries gave way before the expansion of the multinational corporation, the profit center began to shift to area or regional management, to the international division or corporation, to the product group, or, in some instances, to the entire company represented by top management. This development requires careful examination of responsibilities delegated to local units or higher levels for the following functions.

1. *Pricing.* Independent pricing authority is rarely given to subsidiaries, but without such power local management cannot take full advantage of the sort of competitive position that might make higher prices and thereby greater profits possible or, on the contrary, that might make lower

prices advisable if the sales volume is to be increased. However, a price reduction may hurt neighboring subsidiaries, and price increases are often contrary to the policy of corporate uniformity.

2. *Supplies, export, import.* In order to reduce costs, an independent businessman purchases his merchandise where he can obtain it at lowest prices, in the best selling quality, and at the most favorable terms. This privilege is denied to most marketing subsidiaries. Company interest may require purchases from manufacturing subsidiaries that have higher production costs or are located in countries not favored by low tariffs or low transport costs in the country of the purchasing subsidiary.

For historical reasons, a Swiss subsidiary still has the right to buy component parts for its local assembly from noncompany sources in its own country. It uses this privilege to great advantage, but the subsidiary manager sees ominous signs that in the near future he will be forced to import all these parts from a company plant in Germany at higher cost, due to tariff and transport disadvantages. He fears the company will want to assure full production at the German factory and thereby keep down its production costs—and that the Swiss subsidiary will have to pay the bill.

On the other hand, a manufacturing subsidiary could increase its profits if it had the right to export freely. This is naturally almost never permitted, nor is selling to the company's other subsidiaries without approval. Obviously, such arrangements would create chaotic conditions in a corporation with several plants that are located in different countries and manufacture competing products.

3. *Production.* A plant that is an independent profit center would produce those items that offer the best local marketing potential, but a subsidiary factory has to comply with company rules concerning uniform models and standards. Recently, production in the Common Market has been frequently concentrated where it will be most economical, but most economical for the European business as a whole. And this is not necessarily identical with the best interests of one particular subsidiary, especially the one where manufacturing has been discontinued.

4. *Product selection.* A major task of the local manager is convincing headquarters that certain new items are not suitable for local markets and that they will not produce a satisfactory profit. Almost equally important for the local business may be continuing to sell old products the company wants to discontinue, even though they are still profitable in certain markets.

5. *Uniformity.* Whatever the necessity or advantages of strict uniformity for the corporation, it is more often than not in conflict with the immediate profit potential of the subsidiary and sometimes with long-range

local business interests. Uniformity usually saves money for corporate operations as a whole, but it is frequently rather expensive for the smaller subsidiary.

6. *Long-range policy.* A man responsible for a profit center in an American corporation should endeavor to strive for long-range accomplishments, but normally a local manager does not stay long enough in the subsidiary to see these results through—or to get credit for them. Consequently he is tempted to achieve short-term successes, an approach that runs counter to corporate policy.

7. *Key personnel.* The hiring of qualified staff members involves considerable expense, which may not be warranted during the initial stage of a new subsidiary. If the manager is responsible for the P&L statement, he should also have the right to determine how many people in higher brackets are to be engaged and for which specific jobs. However, local managers seldom have this authority. A part of their budget is thereby predetermined.

8. *Budget.* Income according to valid forecasts and expenditures necessary to attain these goals is, or should be, an essential part of the management of a profit center. Budget proposals always need headquarters approval, which in itself does not necessarily violate the principle of a profit center. However, discussions and consultations between subsidiary and regional office or the parent company usually precede the presentation of final budget figures, and during this time all kinds of pressures and influences are brought to bear on local management. And here the considerations may be not the limited interests of the subsidiary, but rather pan-European or global interests, which inevitably infringe on the self-determination of a profit center.

9. *Expenditures.* Many of these could be substantially reduced if local management had its way. The parent company usually insists on employing, wherever possible, the local branch of the same big American auditing company, law firm, advertising agency, and customs brokers. Yet while they have the home office's confidence, give excellent service, and assure uniformity of standards and methods, they are often much more expensive than smaller, local outfits, and many subsidiary managers wonder whether the better service is worth the much higher costs. Yet they can hardly refuse to employ these firms, especially if the local manager is a citizen of the host country and wants to avoid any suspicion of basing a recommendation on friendship or personal preference.

There are other expenses that could be reduced. Many U.S. companies do not check closely on telephone and Telex costs, which are sometimes unnecessary and could be replaced by air mail. Yet these expenditures, at least in part, are charged to the subsidiary. Also, travel expenses are often inflated and not to the direct benefit of the local unit.

10. *Local financing and investments.* These are nearly always decided by the corporate or divisional controller, and the subsidiary manager is often not even consulted. When a local executive recommended ˜purchasing twice as much acreage as was necessary for building a new factory, on the theory that whether or not it was needed for future expansion it was always an excellent investment, he was told: "We are not in the real estate business." Even reinvesting profits in expanding local facilities may have to be postponed, when the money is needed for building a new plant or warehouse in another country where it would be more expensive to borrow capital locally. Tax reasons frequently dictate the direction of profits and investments, which may result in a clear corporate saving, but operate to the detriment of the local profit picture.

11. *Helping younger and smaller neighboring colleagues.* Larger and older subsidiaries are often asked by regional or home management to do this—for example, by sending specialists, giving technical assistance, providing component parts, and sharing packaging and advertising materials. They are seldom fully reimbursed for all their costs—and even if they are, their executives often feel that they could have used their material and manpower to greater advantage for their own business. Usually, higher management levels point out that this is done for the overall corporate business and in the true company spirit. This does not change the fact, however, that it is not in line with the autonomy of a true profit center.

It is quite different, of course, if the other local unit that receives regular assistance is a sub-subsidiary of the helping neighbor. In this case, the smaller unit forms part of the larger profit center and increases its profit balance after an initial buildup. The trouble is that when business begins to develop favorably, the parent company sooner or later decides to detach the younger member of the family and make it independent.

It should be emphasized that most of the reasons for parent company interference with local decision-making authority in violation of the autonomy that the notion of a real profit center implies are quite justified under the aspect of pan-European or worldwide corporate objectives and policies. The misleading term "profit center" should then no longer be used, however, at least not without restrictive qualifications. These restrictions would make it clear that under the circumstances local management cannot be held fully responsible for all items that enter the P&L statement.

The profit center principle could be restored only if a corporation were to establish on its books a compensation account by which each subsidiary would be credited for expenses incurred by higher level instructions for corporate, regional, or other subsidiaries' benefits and interests. On the other hand, benefits received from other subsidiaries would have to be charged fully at the real costs caused to the supplying unit. This would be similar to service, license, or patent fees charged by some corporations to their foreign subsidiaries.

The tricornered relationships between the home office and supplying and receiving subsidiaries are sometimes quite complex, particularly if they have been allowed to grow without planning or regulations.

CASE BRIEF

Both the American plant and the large French subsidiary of the same corporation had been supplying the other European units for an extended period of time. There was never a clear guideline as to who was to supply whom with exactly what types of merchandise. Naturally, the French manager tried to divert as many orders as possible to his factory to increase his business volume. He was interested in his own profit and loss statement and frequently pointed out the favorable tariff and shipping conditions from France to other continental markets, especially within the Common Market. He could not understand that tax considerations and other reasons made it advisable at times to make shipments from the United States and to absorb any cost differential. He was a marketing man; overall financial thinking was alient to him.

Finally, the company, intent on getting its own views across without losing the excellent local executive, commissioned an American law firm in Paris to draw up a formal detailed agreement between headquarters and subsidiary. The negotiations were as between independent and unfriendly parties. All these difficulties could have been avoided if a clear understanding had been reached at the start of the French operations as to where local autonomy ended and when corporate objectives and policies had preference. It would have also helped a great deal if these overall aims had been explained to the subsidiary manager and he had been made to realize that he is not only in charge of a profit center, but at the same time a member of a multinational corporation whose interests come first.

REORGANIZATIONS

Many U.S. corporations have reorganized their European operations in recent years. Some have done so several times. Their principal reason is usually either dissatisfaction with performance over a period of time or the conviction that better results can be achieved. One international lawyer described the situation as follows: "The frequent reorganizations usually result from failures and shortcomings that are first laid at the doorstep of local management. The company corrects these inefficiencies by dismissing the executives held responsible. If that doesn't help, the successors are given new guidelines and directives, and finally, if this too proves ineffective, new organization forms are substituted for old ones."

Other experts express the need for reorganization in different terms; they say that from time to time companies believe that they must modify their operations to meet changed conditions. An advertising executive explained: "The basic reason for reorganizing is that companies have to adjust to changing business opportunities. Later some of them recognize that they have underrated or overrated certain changes or that they did not take the correct steps. This results in a second reorganization."

A few critical observers contend that the frequent reorganizations are in part due to an American propensity for change and experimentation, for trying out new and unproven things, which may or may not lead to new discoveries and, if not, can easily be discarded.

Some other reasons why U.S. companies reorganize their European operations are:

- Acquisition of a number of European companies.
- Merger with another American corporation or joint ventures with European companies.
- Expansion and establishment of new subsidiaries.
- Personnel changes in the company's top management.
- Market and product changes that result in greater emphasis on product divisions.

Reorganization along product lines is also caused by an increased volume of foreign business and the inability of a company to resolve constant infighting between various groups. Growth and divergent developments result in efforts to split centralized divisions, departments, and offices at the international, regional, and functional levels. The desire for better control and accountability, on the other hand, results in attempts to unite and consolidate operations.

Most local and regional executives interviewed for this study were unenthusiastic about reorganization. They mentioned innumerable disadvantages: lowering of morale, uncertainty among customers and other groups, disruption of distribution, lateness in order processing, slowdown of production, and delays in many types of important decisions. One regional executive stated: "I consider the frequent reorganizations that have occurred in recent years one of the biggest mistakes of American top management. It takes two or three years to make all the necessary adjustments before a reorganization can be digested. During this time much goodwill is lost, many business opportunities are ruined, much prestige is jeopardized, and a good deal of personal hardship is created."

Time after time, executives emphasized two problems: neglect of the human factor, which is so important for profitable, efficient business operations, and the exaggerated valuation of forms, charts, systems, and patterns.

The most enthusiastic evaluation of reorganization came from consultants, lawyers, and bankers. One banker referred to it as a sign of vitality. And a consultant added this: "Reorganizing means keeping pace with developments. How else would companies have achieved the transition from exporting finished goods and selling them through agents to full production and marketing through wholly owned subsidiaries?"

The hard fact of life in overseas operations is' that too many companies just sail with the wind instead of investigating the consequences of rash decisions.

2. Many Problems and Some Solutions Relating to Organization of European Subsidiaries

MULTINATIONAL companies are subject to constant changes. Newly established subsidiaries grow as their markets develop and they expand their operations. The countries in which some subsidiaries are situated suffer from revolutions and economic crises that may have long-lasting effects, while the host countries of other subsidiaries stabilize their government and their economy. Experienced local managers are promoted or retire, while young and untried executives are learning and increasing their status within the corporation. Also, the de facto exceptions granted to some subsidiaries and some managers under one chief executive may be radically curtailed under a new company president or vice-president—international. These factors and many others shape the structure and control relationships of foreign subsidiaries.

OLDTIMERS AND NEWCOMERS

Company age is an important factor in management relationships between parent company and subsidiaries. The age referred to here is not the number of years that have passed since the corporation was founded, but rather the time that has elapsed since it established its first European branch, subsidiary, or major distributor. A very old U.S. company that moved into Europe only recently must for the purpose of this study be considered a newcomer, because in its foreign business it can and usually does make just as many mistakes as a young company.

Similarly, an American company with many years of experience in

Latin America must still be regarded as a neophyte in Europe. Its Latin American knowledge helps only to a limited extent; in fact, in some important aspects of European management this onesided foreign experience actually hurts. Some American companies had agents, distributors, and subsidiaries in various Latin American countries for years before they opened their first office in Europe. Consciously or unconsciously they transferred views and opinions based on their Latin American experience to Europe—after all, both belonged to the international division and both were foreign business ventures. Such an attitude can lead key men in the international division to ignore the profound differences in practically all aspects of marketing and production between Latin America and Europe.

A somewhat similar situation existed when U.S. corporations with many years of business experience in the Middle East first entered Europe as sellers or producers. The European regional manager of an American corporation, who was born and educated in Europe but worked for many years for his company in South America, said that he had to learn many things afresh and to unlearn others after being transferred to Paris. "Some things," he commented, "were easier in Latin America for me, because there I could do them one at a time. We had more time to organize ourselves. Nobody at the top expected us to have a complete continental organization ready within a few months. We had time to grow."

Errors of the Past

The author was told by many experts, both inside and outside old established American corporations, that their European organizations work much more smoothly than those of more recently arrived companies. As one executive put it: "Sure, we made our mistakes, but that was 40 years ago." Another manager commented: "I have had 13 years' experience in Europe. American companies now make fewer mistakes than 10 years ago, but they certainly repeat some of the very same errors which I made then and which my company made at the turn of the century. Times have changed; some of the errors of judgment have remained basically the same." The majority of the old established companies manufacture industrial goods: electrical equipment, machinery, and office machines. But there are also a few producers of consumer goods among them, such as photographic equipment, automobiles, even food. Most are very large corporations, but some medium-size companies also date back to the early twenties. The majority established marketing subsidiaries, and later, manufacturing ones; some acquired existing plants. If they had to reorganize and adjust themselves to changed conditions, they did so gradually because they had learned to be flexible.

One large corporation was prior to World War II a holding company that had acquired many European plants; it was satisfied if they showed a profit. It did not matter that they often competed with each other in the export markets. There was no overall planning of production or marketing. All this was completely changed after the war, but it could be achieved without major upheavals because the corporation had profited from its 80 years of European experience. A reorganization could, for example, be accomplished by dividing a national unit into two or more separate subsidiaries or by detaching a particular local department, such as the subsidiary's export department, and organizing it as a sub-subsidiary of the local unit.

The heavy machinery manufactured by one U.S. corporation was first exported to France a hundred years ago, later assembled locally, and finally produced locally. The French subsidiary has existed since the beginning of the century. Needless to say that nothing remains of the old models, but the company name and brand are still the same and a "spirit of internationality" has developed, as the French manager termed it. The American headquarters understands European production, marketing, and administrative problems; the men in the international division have lived with them all their life. The important difference between these oldtimers and most newcomers is that in the established corporations the European subsidiary or regional manager does not need to explain basic principles or differences to the U.S. home office. Usually the people at headquarters have had working experience in Europe and know many of the problems firsthand. It is sufficient to tell them what has changed, and they accept such information much more readily than executives and staff members of new companies.

Stability and Business Volume

All this gives the experienced European operations a stability that is so often missing with the newcomers, which have to learn through trial and error, and which frequently have an urge to experiment with people and structures. Moreover, there is normally less rivalry and infighting between domestic and foreign operations, and therefore less cause for "global integration." In fact, most old established companies still have their geographic pattern of organization, supplemented by dotted-line relations with functional and product departments. It seems to work smoothly because the executives on both sides have been used to working together—and not against each other. This does not mean that they do not sometimes institute structural changes. They may even decide to pull back a regional office from Europe to the United States, but the various subsidiaries are so thoroughly familiar with company procedures and so steeped in company tradition that they are much less affected than a newer organization is.

An important characteristic of the established American companies in Europe is that their international business in general and their European business in particular are significant when compared with their business in the United States. Foreign sales range from about 30 percent to 100 percent. A typical case is that of a machinery manufacturer whose European business is 70 percent of the total international business, which in turn has now surpassed the domestic production and sales volume.

The first foreign subsidiaries of U.S. corporations were established in England in the 1880s, followed a few years later by subsidiaries in France, Belgium, and Holland, and later still in Germany, and Italy. During both world wars their operations were usually interrupted, but resumed soon after the end of hostilities. Business developed in Latin America, the Middle East, and the Far East usually much later.

It could be assumed that a company that has been operating in the same country and city for 40, 60, or 80 years shows signs of old age or symptoms of immobility and petrification. Nothing could be further from the truth. Living and working through two major wars and many smaller armed conflicts, as well as through several political, social, and economic revolutions, the oldtimers of American industry in Europe had to remain alert, flexible, and vigorous if they were to survive. They did.

ORGANIZATIONAL PROBLEMS OF EUROPEAN SUBSIDIARIES

It is next to impossible to classify the European subsidiaries of U.S. corporations in several broad categories with common denominators, because in addition to the manifold differences of their parent companies—such as industry, size, structure, international organization, and historic development—the subsidiaries vary in their own way. The impossibility of categorizing the subsidiaries makes statistical analysis all but useless and comparisons extremely difficult. Yet a study of control relationships can only proceed if the patterns and conditions of one unit are compared with those of another.

To determine these relationships as well as possible, the first question in an interview with a subsidiary's general manager had to be: To whom do you report? The question seems simple, but the answer was often not. A typical reply was the following:

> In routine business matters, such as administration and personnel, to the regional manager in Brussels; but for major decisions, to the international division in St. Louis; and in all questions relating to production,

to the respective product groups, some of which have their own representatives in Brussels, others not. Furthermore, we have informal lateral contacts with other European subsidiaries, as well as with certain Latin American subsidiaries [for example, in Mexico] with which this country [Spain] has favorable trade agreements. The lateral connections outside of Europe, however, go mostly through international staff departments at U.S. headquarters.

In another case, the international division has line functions only for Latin America (there are no subsidiaries in the Far East, nor is there a regional office in Europe), while the European subsidiaries report directly to the chairman of the board with the international division acting in an advisory staff function. However, sub-subsidiaries in smaller European markets report through the subsidiaries in the neighboring larger countries to which they belong. The control exercised by the chairman of the board is understandably loose.

By contrast, in an Italian subsidiary, requests for promotional and certain other funds exceeding $100—which includes most such requests—are sent first to the vice-president of the international division, then to the proper corporate staff department "and numerous other executives," then to the VP of the product division, and finally to the chairman of the board. Since this is a fairly large company, the subsidiary must follow up by making certain that its request for expenditures does not get stuck somewhere during this lengthy process. Theoretically, the local manager reports to the head of the international division, and knows that the last O.K. on his request for funds will be that of the chairman of the board. But the real decision will be made somewhere in between by a staff officer, and the subsidiary manager usually has only a faint idea who, for each particular instance, that might be. Moreover, final approval comes only after the item has been discussed in a financial committee meeting under the chairmanship of the controller. Here, the original request is presented with either favorable or adverse comments by an intermediate staff member who, to get the necessary background information, has probably discussed it informally with other executives prior to the meeting. Under such circumstances, can it really be said that the local manager reports to the vice-president of the international division?

In addition to this multiple reporting and complex lines of requests and approvals, it has become the rule rather than the exception in larger subsidiaries for local staff—such as the plant and sales managers, the treasurer, and personnel manager—to correspond directly with their counterparts at regional and corporate levels. They are usually required to send copies to the general manager of the subsidiary or the regional office, but since contacts are more and more via telephone and Telex, this rule no longer safeguards the authority of the local manager, if indeed such authority exists.

On the other hand, many a subsidiary has suffered—and still suffers—from the complete separation and isolation of the international division from the various domestic executives (which the reorganization along product-group lines is designed to cure). And even within the international division itself lines of authority are not always observed, demarcation lines between line and staff functions are not clearly drawn, and the responsibilities of local managers are not respected—because of expediency, or neglect, or ignorance of their importance. The result is that subsidiary executives do not feel secure and protected, and therefore not really responsible for failure. Several subsidiaries reported that this condition has now been corrected, or is being changed for the better, but usually it was pointed out that there is still room for improvement, and that often vested intracompany interests stand in the way of wider reforms.

Both before and after a reorganization, general confusion is quite common. One Dutch subsidiary "normally" reports to its company's office for the Benelux countries in Antwerp. But from there communications may be channeled to headquarters in New York or, especially in matters concerning a formerly independent product division, to Chicago, or to a new regional office in Southern Europe (when industrial products are involved), or to the former European office in Switzerland (consumer goods). Sometimes lines go to other European subsidiaries for supplies to be shipped by them. Though these communications should go through an export department in New York, more often than not they go directly to such sources of supply in England or France. Moreover, all this is being constantly changed and rearranged. Not surprisingly, the local manager stated: "It is so confusing that when I have an order which is not strictly routine I sometimes really don't know myself who handles it and where—that is, to whom I should send it with the hope of speedy attention."

At higher levels these problems are frequently conceded, but explained or excused with such phrases as "this is the price we must pay for bigness," or with such statements as: "We are in the process of changing all this. Come back next year and you will see." This, of course, is of little consolation to local management, which must live through it—and which sometimes gets blamed for the unfavorable consequences.

Solving Organizational Problems

It must be emphasized, however, that many corporations have solved their organizational problems—and before the problems grew almost too big to be solved. They refused to permit lines of communication to become entangled and confused, and had the foresight to adjust their structural patterns to their needs at the right time. Typical is one company that is still growing and gradually converting its European outlets from distributorship or licensing arrangements to wholly owned subsidiaries, but that already has a fully organized geographic and product organization for its international operations. Its costs are relatively high now, but will result in substantial savings later. An international division in New York makes product managers responsible for the marketing and promotion of their lines and for maintaining liaison to the product groups. The division also has a general production manager, a VP for legal and administrative matters, and a treasurer, all under an international president who is a corporate VP. Similarly, the regional office in Europe is headed by a vice-president, with a production and a marketing manager who also handles advertising. Lines of command are strictly observed, responsibilities are separated, and no interference by one line or staff department in the activities of another is tolerated. The local managers know exactly whom to look to for instructions, advice, and support. If and when a new department is created and takes over functions previously handled by someone else, the change of responsibilities is immediately spelled out and no residue or overlapping is allowed to result from such an expansion.

In another corporation, a much larger and older one, the responsibilities are equally clear. The general managers of the many European subsidiaries, their production and marketing directors, treasurers, and other staff executives all report to the European office in Geneva in all matters of administration, finance, marketing, personnel, and promotion. In production, pricing (as distinguished from marketing), R&D, factory building and equipment, they report through Geneva to various product groups in the United States. Even though this is a more complex organization, it still runs smoothly because responsibilities are strictly defined and respected.

Exceptions from the Norm

A successful international organization does not mean that everything and everybody must conform in all matters to one general norm. On the contrary, exceptions are necessary; in many far-sighted companies, the right to make them is granted to local managers as part of their authority. A subsidiary manager in Germany related that while most decisions are made by the regional office in London and practically all communications go to London, in some exceptional cases, reports can go to New York (with copy to London). The wishes and opinions of important customers regarding new or improved products, for example, are sent to the R&D center in New York.

In a company with two European regional offices (London and Holland), the local manager in Brussels is required to report to Holland, except in purely technical matters. Then he can consult corporate headquarters and, should he need products not made by continental subsidiaries but only in England or America, he can order through an export department in the United States.

Many corporations separate the export business—meaning the shipment of orders from America—from their regular foreign operations, which consist of manufacturing abroad. Sometimes the export department also handles shipments from one subsidiary to another, but where such shipments move exclusively within Europe, the export department frequently is attached to the regional office. Therefore the local manager has no special leeway in his lines of communication.

There is, of course, an inherent danger in granting to local management exceptions to the established line of reporting. Such privileges can easily be abused and thereby compromise the authority of the regional office (or international division or product group or whatever). Exceptions are therefore sparingly given, usually being proportionate to the trust earned and the experience gained by the local manager.

Reuniting Foreign and Domestic Operations

The desire to reunite the foreign and the domestic operations, which have grown too much apart, has led not only to product-group reorganizations but also to less spectacular, less radical, and sometimes more smoothly working compromise solutions that are usually preferred by subsidiaries. One consists simply of making the vice-president in charge of the international division (or president of the international corporation) simultaneously a corporate executive vice-president. Thus, ideally, he can create a bridge between the organization at home and operations abroad, eliminate rivalries, insure cooperation, and give the foreign subsidiaries the priceless feeling of really belonging to the family and not to a somewhat alien sideline.

Another expedient sometimes used successfully is to separate from the regional office new subsidiaries that still have growing pains and problems of their own, and to put them directly under the jurisdiction of the international division at corporate headquarters. This protects their individual needs, which may be quite different from those of the older subsidiaries, as may their background and development. They are perhaps new acquisitions or joint ventures, and consequently they may have different product lines, may not yet fit into the existing European organization, may not yet have been "absorbed" and, in fact, may not yet be adjustable. Unless the regional office is accustomed to such situations, it may not be able to handle them correctly—that is, to educate the new subsidiary slowly and to make it part of the family. This is no reflection on the abilities of the regional manager, who otherwise may very well be an excellent executive. However, it stands to reason that he will normally object to special status for a local unit, and fail to recognize its advisability.

Such an arrangement usually means greater support from the home office, but it also means stricter control. It works only as long as a special liaison officer at the home office watches over it continuously. It also represents a transitional stage, and sooner or later the subsidiary must be brought into the European organization. Unfortunately, simply because of inertia, its special status is quite often prolonged beyond the point of usefulness.

Similarly, sub-subsidiaries that are controlled not only legally, but actually, by the larger subsidiary to which they belong, mostly for historical reasons, should not be frozen in second-class status. Otherwise, this can easily cause inferiority feelings in their management, and resentment against the manager of the controlling subsidiary.

The author visited such a local unit in Switzerland. This unit had always been a subsidiary of a German company and had been purchased with it prior to World War II. During the war, however, it naturally became quite independent and continued to do business successfully even while the German firm was inoperative. After the war, the parent company, an American firm, put the Swiss unit back under the German subsidiary. The latter, meanwhile, was considerably expanded. This, in the eyes of the Swiss management and personnel, was agreeable as long as the manager of the German subsidiary was an American sent over from the home office. But when he was later replaced by a German, resentment began to build up, resentment compounded by the new manager's efforts to exercise stricter control over the Swiss firm. As the Swiss manager summed it up: "The new man in Frankfurt wants to earn his spurs with the parent company, which the former American manager did not need to do, because he had already earned them in the States." All reporting is done exclusively to Frankfurt and goes from there in condensed form to the home office, a useful and widely practiced method, but one that in this case only adds to the discontent. The local manager in Switzerland sees signs pointing to an eventual detachment from Germany, and impatiently looks forward to the day when his subsidiary will report directly to the American firm's international division.

A Product Group Crosses Organization Lines

An equally difficult and delicate situation, though an entirely different one, arises where one product division is partly within and partly outside the corporation's regular European organization. In a company making various measuring instruments and other electronic products, the computer division has a separate European office in London, while the other product groups have two common regional offices, in London and Frankfurt. However, the separation does not reach down to the subsidiary level. Instead, the computer division uses the existing local units and has in each of them its divisional manager and staff with a continental marketing director in Frankfurt. These local computer managers are under the jurisdiction of the subsidiary manager in administrative matters, but otherwise report directly to the marketing manager in Frankfurt and to their regional office in London.

It was explained that the special requirements of the computer industry in leasing, service, replacement, training, marketing, and distribution make this separation desirable, while on the other hand, the computer division is still too young and too small to warrant separate subsidiaries in all markets and can use the valuable support of the older European network. However, goodwill, tact, and diplomacy are needed to prevent conflicts of interest, friction, and other consequences of divided authority. The company tries as a matter of general policy to be flexible and to avoid rigid uniformity because of product diversity.

Another diversified corporation takes, or has taken until now, a somewhat different approach. This is one of the large oil companies, with several product and functional divisions. The chemicals division is subdivided into various product groups, such as fertilizers, pesticides, and industrial chemicals. The fertilizer group is organized in a domestic division and two international divisions, one for Latin America and the Far East, the second for Europe. The other product groups work through joint ventures and affiliates. There are two separate research groups, one for the oil business, the other for the chemicals divisions. Except for this common research, the various product groups have practically no connection with each other, and their European organizations are so entirely separate that their executives know very little about what their colleagues are doing, even in the same country. Since they also have different company and product names, they appear as independent enterprises. While this certainly prevents the confusion of authority and the mutual interference that so often plague other corporations, it also leads to an uneconomical duplication of offices, services, and manpower.

Another oil company, a somewhat smaller one, found itself in a similar situation some years ago when it acquired several chemical companies. At first, each company continued its domestic and foreign operations undisturbed by the merger. One worked exclusively through agents; another worked with affiliate companies ranging from minority participations to majority controlled companies; the third had a well-established network of subsidiaries. Until recently, all these licensees, affiliates, and subsidiaries reported to their respective product divisions at three separate locations within the United States, but a new American headquarters building for all chemicals divisions (now united in a single separate corporation) is under construction, and a united international division will be created. It will take a long time and strenuous efforts to unify the diverse local units, and no doubt subsidiary managers, directors of affiliate companies, and independent agents are looking to the future with mixed feelings.

The problem of finding a way to avoid duplication of facilities and the creation of parallel organizations in several countries, while still maintaining separation between different product groups with unequal requirements, was solved by one corporation in an original way. Its geographic organization in Europe consists of a London office that covers the United Kingdom and Scandinavia, a subsidiary in Bonn that handles Germany, and a regional office in Brussels that has a dual function: It takes care of the rest of Europe and has administrative jurisdiction over London and Bonn. At the same time, however, each of the three offices is responsible for a different product group: London for aircraft, Bonn for weapons, Brussels for electronics. In technical matters, London and Bonn report directly to their product divisions at home. Moreover, financial reports, forecasts, budget proposals, and requests for large-scale assistance also go directly to the product groups. When one of the three offices receives invitations to bid or negotiate or wants to offer products that are not its immediate responsibility, it requests help from the appropriate subsidiary, which then dispatches the required talent. Thus, if the British subsidiary wants to sell electronic equipment, it would be responsible only for marketing and for financial arrangements, but Brussels would provide the technical expertise.

Production and Marketing

Where a plant and a sales office exist side by side, the question arises as to whether they should be under the general management of one executive or should form two separate and equal subsidiaries. In the first case, the general manager is usually in one of two positions: Either he has a technical background and is assisted by a competent marketing manager, or he is himself a marketing man who leans heavily on the plant or production manager. Sometimes, however, he may be an administrator or financial expert, and he will need production *and* marketing specialists at his side. In any event, the unity of production and marketing in one subsidiary is preserved, and reports, except sometimes in purely technical matters, go via the general local manager to higher levels. The other solution is the formation of two separate units. This eliminates many but not all personal difficulties, because this solution is feasible only if the plant is of considerable size, and of course it will then need administrative and financial talent and accounting, tax, and personnel experts if it is to be run efficiently. One corporation in the synthetic fiber industry has a network of marketing subsidiaries in several European countries, but only one plant. This is located in Belgium, as is the regional office, which exercises direct supervision over it. Product managers attached to the European office form the liaison between the plant and the marketing subsidiaries.

A canning company imports all items to be sold in Europe from its plantations and canning plants in the Pacific. It therefore has only marketing subsidiaries in Europe. Once the amounts of yearly deliveries to Europe have been determined by corporate top management on the basis of regional forecasts and available sources of supply, the European general manager corresponds directly with the production managers at their Pacific locations. These plants, however, are under the jurisdiction of the Pacific regional manager located at American headquarters. The author asked why under the circumstances the Pacific units are not more closely linked organizationally to the European region, to which they export over 90 percent of their produce. The reply was that the VP–Europe and all of his staff are marketing men, while the executives of the Pacific region (as well as those in Latin America) are production-oriented, and therefore far better qualified to supervise plantation and canning operations.

THE REGIONAL OFFICE

The regional office seldom remains unchanged. It is either strengthened and expanded, or weakened and restricted. It may be divided into geographical areas, along product-group lines, or according to functional departments; conversely, it may be pulled together and its divisions unified. Sometimes it is moved from one location to another; at other times it is pulled back to headquarters; occasionally it is abandoned altogether.

There are many types of regional offices in Europe. They range from the huge headquarters office headed by a vice-president and staffed with hundreds of employees to the one-man office occupied by a regional manager and his secretary. A fully staffed regional office can be a replica of the international division at home. The regional manager or vice-president has line authority, while the various staff and service departments provide support functions.

Staff executives serve in an advisory or consulting capacity and when one finds something wrong with the subsidiaries in his area of activity, either on the basis of written or telephone communications, or during frequent personal visits, he will bring it to the attention of local management. Yet it was several times pointed out that staff executives can only make suggestions, not issue orders. Such orders come exclusively from regional management and they are usually couched in diplomatic terms, as recommendations or consultation. The regional manager may actually act more as a mediator between his own staff executives and subsidiary managers than as a field commander.

The thinking behind this way of exercising regional control is that while the regional staff executives know more about their various specialties than anyone else involved, subsidiary managers and their staffs know the local situation better. The regional staff can compare the performance of various local units; the subsidiaries have more experience in the application of corporate policies and directives. However, exactly as at the home office, staff executives, unless strictly controlled by a strong regional manager, tend to increase their power and convert suggestions into orders. In turn, this tends to create strong dotted-line relationships between local and regional staff executives. They communicate directly with each other, bypassing, at least in routine matters, subsidiary and regional managers. Indeed, as business volume and day-to-day communications increase, this is inevitable. The result is that only major questions or real conflicts are referred to the regional manager for mediation.

Regional Growth

Usually, regional offices have to "grow" into stronger positions and acquire more authority gradually. However, there are exceptions—as when several European area offices may already exist and the corporation feels the need of supervising and coordinating them through a strong regional office because their operations can no longer be effectively controlled from U.S. headquarters.

It would be wrong to assume that strengthening the European regional office represents any trend among American corporations in general or in any industry or type of business in particular. While some large companies have recently established, reestablished, or enlarged and fortified their European offices with greater authority, resources, and responsibilities, others have gone in the opposite direction. If a generalization may be attempted, it could perhaps be stated that strong regional offices—those that have initially been established with sufficient authority and are headed by a strong personality—have a tendency to grow even stronger, while very weak regional units get weaker as they cannot effectively function, and eventually disappear or become useless. In between are moderately effective regional or area units whose development is touch and go, depending mostly on their own managers and their superiors.

Sometimes there will be an overgrowth of the European headquarters to a point where it has more employees and is more powerful in decision making than its next higher management level, the international division. This can cause deep conflicts and a power struggle that may lead to a splitting of the foreign operations into two or more equal international divisions. In some cases, however, such a prolonged conflict ends with the resignation of the European manager—or else with his promotion to the position of VP–International or corporate executive vice-president, in which case he will exercise strong influence on European affairs from the home office. The resignation, promotion, or retirement of the European manager, as well as of other international and corporate executives, will cause important changes of organization and authority in a surprisingly large number of companies, while in other instances they are the consequence of such changes.

The common thinking on the part of the experts interviewed was that European regional offices can be very valuable—if they have enough decision-making authority. They were also agreed that this value is not readily apparent in dollars and cents.

One factor that now works heavily in favor of a European office and that is beginning to influence the economy-minded corporate executives of the financial department is the growing computerization of local accounting, statistics, reporting, forecasting, and budgeting. With rare exceptions, local computerizing is impossible—because of lack of adequate facilities or excessive costs. In most cases, it must be done on a multinational basis and therefore means that computer centers have to be established. While in some cases this has been done without involving regional headquarters, it usually leads to a strengthening of the European office, where one exists, and, where one does not, to its establishment or reestablishment, at least on a limited basis.

The man who manages a British subsidiary that is independent of the company's continental regional office in Brussels, and who can therefore observe the situation with detachment, remarked that regional offices should be confined to support and coordinating activities and be prevented from getting a dominant role. He thought that pan-European coordination of procurement (especially in raw materials), coordination of exports from one subsidiary to another, and standardization of systems and procedures (particularly in production, uniformity of quality, and similar efforts) are worthwhile and profitable activities for a regional office. But he felt that such activities should not interfere with the subsidiaries' day-to-day operations.

Regional Control of Local Units

If the subsidiary was formerly strictly controlled by the international division and had few responsibilities of its own, the new regional office will take away little authority from local managers, because it cannot divert power where hardly any power existed. By contrast, where control of local units by the home office has been slight and considerable authority has been left to the subsidiaries, it is likely that the new European office *will* take away a sizable portion of these local responsibilities.

Several subsidiary managers hinted that if they have to live under strict control from superior management levels, they prefer this control to be exercised by a European office rather than by the home office. There are a number of reasons for this attitude.

First of all, an absentee landlord or a faraway manager is usually more objectionable than the resident owner or administrator. At the same time, a redress of grievances can be obtained more easily and more quickly from a superior who lives and works nearby and is in constant touch with developments. The regional manager who lives in Europe usually has attitudes and viewpoints closer to those of local management, and he shares part of its criticism of "the people back home." Also, the personnel and executive staff at regional headquarters is often predominantly European or has previously worked in subsidiaries, while in most corporations only a tiny fraction of staff and personnel at the international division and even fewer among corporate staff members have ever worked in Europe. Finally, the subsidiary manager and his staff executives may very well be called to work in the regional office, and at a future time one of them may even become regional manager, but only in exceptional cases do local executives, especially European nationals, reach the top positions at the home office.

If a home-office decision displeases the local manager—and naturally this occurs often enough—he will probably ascribe it to lack of knowledge and understanding of local conditions; if the same thing happens with decisions by the regional office, the subsidiary executive may simply explain it by a divergence of opinion and evaluation of facts. As the European countries slowly draw closer together, anything that originates within Europe will tend to be considered more or less a family affair, but anything that emanates from the United States may well take on a flavor of alien domination.

On the other side of the ledger, the nearness of the regional office and its greater familiarity with local situations permits regional executives to exercise closer control. They may do it more diplomatically, more intelligently, in a less uniform way, with greater regard for local differences, but for all these reasons they may also do it with greater and longer-lasting impact.

In many cases, a tendency could be detected among subsidiary managers to play down the role of a regional office and to emphasize the autonomy of the subsidiary. This rather subjective view was in contrast to a tendency among other subsidiary managers to complain about too much authority being exercised by regional executives, and with still a third opinion—that regional headquarters should have more and home offices less control. The third attitude seemed to represent the majority.

REGIONAL STAFF AND SUPPORT SERVICES

Quite a few American corporations operating in Europe have found a middle way between the indirect method of organization, where a full-fledged regional office performs most line and staff functions and thereby links the subsidiaries with the parent company, and the direct method, where the subsidiaries are in immediate contact with the international division, product groups, functional staff departments, or top management. In this intermediate type of organization, one or several small offices —or sometimes traveling executives, staff members, and technicians—supervise or give staff support to the subsidiaries in certain well-defined activities. Some of these supervisors or staff people report to the international division or to the product groups in the United States, others to staff departments.

Among the activities performed by these groups of specialists are:

- Coordination among subsidiaries.
- Coordination among several product groups operating independently in Europe.
- Liaison between subsidiaries and various staff departments at the home office.
- Assistance in marketing.
- Coordination of sales and exports or of production.
- Finance and auditing.
- Advertising.
- Procurement.

son with affiliates.

e, customer service.

elp in computer programming.

n which these fragmented regional organizations
first grows out of a situation where the corpora-
egional office in Europe and is hesitant to estab-
essity of providing support or supervision in some
ccurs after the disbanding of a full regional office,
reorganization. It is likely that certain functions
k or, if they were, had to be reestablished on a re-
y solution is then often remnants or outgrowths of
anization, with many features eliminated, some re-
e added. The advantages of the new system are:

es, fewer personnel, reduced expense.
and adaptability to changing conditions.
p between the regional specialists and their coun-
osidiaries.
nflicts between subsidiaries and full regional offices,
the subsidiary is old, large, and important and its
ranking executive.
subsidiary in fields of activity where help is most
ested.

acks of the fragmented regional offices are:

of communication and liaison between different spe-
arly if they have no offices or are stationed at distinct

are too much on their own, and therefore are not suffi-
ed.
specialists to overvalue their particular area of ac-
efore to lack perspective.
overestimate specialized technical knowledge and un-
e importance of being familiar with local conditions.

antage is that often the distinction between staff and
against line functions becomes blurred. On the other
anagers are inclined to take only that advice or support
requested and with which they agree. Without a re-
back him up, the specialist or technician may find it

difficult to get his ideas across or his suggestions accepted. Un
diplomatic skill—which, of course, should be a prerequisite fc
he may be considered a creature of the home office at the subs
and treated with suspicion. As in so many other instances in t
tional trade, professional excellence, while of fundamental imp
not enough to obtain results.

Organizational Forms

As indicated in Figure 1, several specialists may perform
service. For example: several technicians, each delegated from a
ing to different product-group divisions; or two marketing s
representing the international division, one for the northern, th
the southern area of Europe; or various advertising experts, son
for larger subsidiaries, another for all the smaller ones. The con
ter usually serves only a limited area. The liaison man may re
international division, or directly to an executive vice-president
president of the corporation. This liaison man may very well ha
line relationships with some or all of the other regional dele
specialists. In some cases—for example, in technical assistance—th
ship of the specialist to the local production or plant manager,
control, or to technical development, may resemble a straight-lin
even though the local managers are not subordinates of the spec
of equal rank.

In fact, the type of organization discussed in this section is
result of rivalries and infighting between the international div
product groups, and various staff or functional departments—as
reorganization plans. Such disagreements frequently exist also
subsidiaries and home office departments, and some corporatio
that a fragmented regional organization offers a better solution t
a weak regional office without real authority or one that is too s
has too much power over local units. The regional delegates or
are therefore a compromise solution born of practical requirer
a pragmatic philosophy. But all 27 executives throughout Eu
discussed this subject with the author seemed to be pleased wit
port they receive from regional specialists. Some, to be sure, beli
at some time in the future this loose system would be replaced b
ually grow into a full-fledged regional office.

It should be noted here that a fragmented regional organiza
not necessarily mean less control. In some corporations it only n
tight control is exercised directly by the international division, o
uct groups, or by functional departments from the home office.

Figure 1.   Organization Chart Showing Relationships Between Corporate Departments and Divisions, Fragmented Regional Offices, and Subsidiaries.

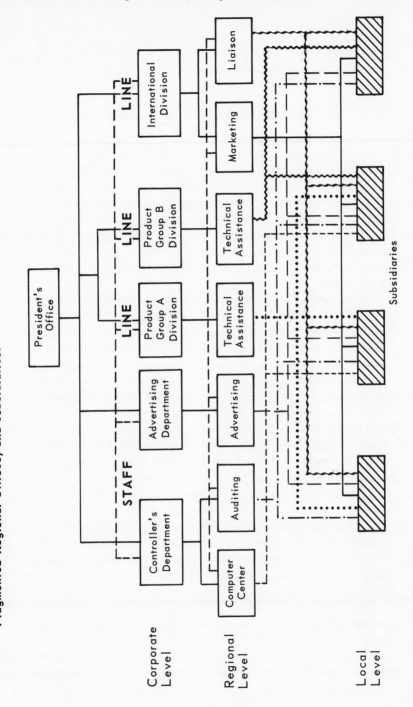

cialists delegated by a corporate department normally act as trouble-shooters and help the subsidiary, but they also report back to the home office. Sometimes a reprimand or sterner measures may follow for the subsidiary's having gotten into trouble in the first place.

THE ROLE OF CORPORATE STAFF DEPARTMENTS

A staff department can be defined as a group of specialists under their own executive head who make their expertise available to other departments. It is not always completely clear whether the staff department's "advice" must be followed or whether it can be modified by the transmitting line department. This depends on general company policies as specified in manuals and directives, and these policies may be different for various staff departments and various categories of advice. Also, higher corporate mediation or arbitration may be provided in important cases of disagreement.

Where staff department advice is usually followed by the other departments because of corporate directives or superior staff knowledge, it has frequently become accepted practice for the staff executive to send a copy of the advice directly to the subordinate level (regional office or subsidiary) and the original to the superior department (international division), or even vice versa. Originally, this was chiefly intended to shorten the line and quicken the transmission, but often the hidden purpose was to establish direct communication between corporate staff departments and lower levels and to create a dotted line of secondary command. Whatever the real or supposed purpose, the result has frequently been considerable confusion among employees at lower levels as to the identity of their true superiors. Moreover, visits from staff department executives followed. At first, they were occasional and more or less private; later, they became regular and official. And they are not always cleared with the line department. For example, staff department members visit their counterparts in regional offices or subsidiaries without notifying the international division or the regional or local manager. The dotted line grows less dotted and straighter, the influence of the staff department increases, and the lines of command may become hopelessly snarled.

The dotted-line relationships between corporate staff departments and lower levels are described in Figure 2. This simplified chart has many possible variants.

1. International is an independent corporation. It has its own staff departments and communicates only occasionally with some important cor-

Figure 2. Organization Chart Showing Relationships Between Staff Executives in Corporate Departments, Regional Office, and Subsidiary.

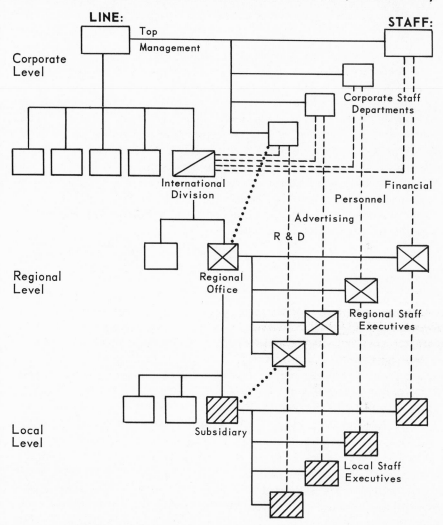

porate staff departments, perhaps finance and advertising, or research and development.

2. The international division has been disbanded. The various product groups or top management deal directly with regional offices.

3. There is no resident regional management. The international division or the product groups are in direct contact with subsidiaries.

4. The subsidiaries, or the smaller ones among them, have no staff officers. Straight and dotted lines go to the local manager.

5. Some staff functions are represented only on higher levels. Therefore, dotted lines connect higher staff echelons directly with local or regional general management.

6. Some subsidiaries and some regional offices have fewer staff departments or officers than others. Dotted lines therefore go either to local and regional staffs or to their general managers.

In many companies much infighting and many rivalries with damaging consequences have resulted from multiple lines of divided authority. They have had to be resolved by strong decrees from top management, sometimes in favor of the international line organization, sometimes in favor of certain powerful staff departments. The final solution in very large corporations is either the creation of separate staff departments within the international division (or corporation), or else the reorganization of international operations along product or functional lines. In the latter, the international division disappears or itself becomes a staff or service or coordinating department, and straight and dotted lines are reversed.

The Controller's Office

In practically all larger companies, the controller's office exercises what amount almost to line functions. It does not give advice; it gives orders that must be followed, at least in major matters. The reasons are obvious: Important financial decisions cannot be left to the international-division management, unless it is completely self-sufficient (and then has its own financial organization). Direct communications with regional and subsidiary managements are often deemed desirable, and unified action throughout the corporation is essential. Since international managers must follow the orders of the controller and have learned that an appeal to top management to reverse one of his decisions very seldom brings results, they may actually prefer to be relieved of the duty to transmit such financial orders—usually limitations and restrictions—to lower levels, and thereby to share the onus of an unpopular decision. Also, the expertise of the corporate financial executives is generally recognized, though their actions may not always be appreciated.

The Legal Department

Another staff department that in most corporations has achieved a dominant position is the legal department. But in the opinion of many international experts it is much less qualified to exercise these powers internationally than it is at the domestic level. The fact is that the corporate legal department usually insists that all contracts that are more than routine and all other legal matters occurring abroad be referred to it, even though it can hardly ever do anything more than refer these matters back to foreign counsel. The viewpoint and aims of the corporation can be adequately explained to the foreign lawyers by the subsidiary manager or, if he should be inexperienced, by the regional manager, or as a last resort by the international division, and this is exactly what usually happens. But in most larger companies the foreign lawyer is required to discuss the matter further with the corporate legal department and to obtain its final approval for whatever course of action he suggests. With very few exceptions the members of the legal department have no foreign legal expertise, and their knowledge of the laws of, say, Minnesota or New York is of little use. In fact, the company lawyers more often than not fail to comprehend the extent to which various European law systems differ from American law, and the local lawyer abroad frequently must go to great lengths and must waste valuable time explaining it to them. Also, any attempt by the corporation to unify or equalize its own legal procedures, forms, or technicalities is doomed to failure.

Many U.S. corporations, however, deal with international law firms that have headquarters in America and have their own affiliates or correspondents in major European countries. This is an excellent method for handling legal problems overseas, but even in this case the corporate legal department normally clings to its prerogatives. In the eyes of foreign executives, as well as European lawyers, this frequently complicates and delays matters. The usual way is for the subsidiary or regional management where the problem originates to transmit it to the international division. From there it is channeled to the corporate legal department, then via the law firm's U.S. headquarters or nearest American office to its foreign affiliate, which in the meantime has already been contacted by the corporation's subsidiary.

An executive of a chemical corporation's Spanish subsidiary put this in simple terms: "Routine agreements are concluded by me with the help of local lawyers; but important contracts, such as those for large continuous orders or with government agencies, must be sent to the corporate legal department for review and approval, and in this case the Spanish lawyers correspond directly with them." This sounds simple enough, but where do "routine agreements" end and "important contracts" begin? And who decides what is "routine" and what is "important"?

Several international lawyers reported that as a precaution they nearly always contact the corporate legal department by sending it memos describing conversations with local executives or copies of correspondence with them. The lawyers will then either proceed unless they hear from headquarters or ask for instructions.

When the subsidiary manager visits the local lawyer and requests legal advice, many lawyers will ask whether or not headquarters should be informed. Say the matter to be discussed is the case of a subsidiary employee who was discharged and now threatens a lawsuit for compensation under local laws, with which the corporate legal department is normally unfamiliar. The subsidiary manager may declare that such matters are his responsibility and that consequently there is no need to inform headquarters; but he may not be aware of the extent of such claims. The conscientious local lawyer, especially if he is affiliated with an American law firm, will want to avoid future recriminations and therefore will use his own judgment as to whether or not to inform the legal department at headquarters. This, however, may be taken by the local manager as an insult to his status, and a strained relationship between him and the local lawyer may follow. A local attorney told the author that as a result of just such an incident, one subsidiary manager now takes small routine matters to another lawyer.

Members of a worldwide American law firm make it a practice to send copies of all correspondence and memos regarding conversations with their client subsidiaries to the law firm's U.S. headquarters or to the American office nearest the corporation's home office. This has the advantage of providing a complete file, one that enables the corporate legal department to get quick information on any pending matter.

In tax matters, both the corporate legal department and the controller's office usually have to be consulted. There is seldom disagreement, but some tax matters can be settled on the regional level if the regional office is authorized and equipped to handle them and if no basic policy decisions are involved.

Other Staff Departments

Similarly, patent and trademark matters are normally the domain of the corporate legal department or of a special patent and trademark department because these problems are worldwide and must be decided in principle in a unified and centralized way. Here, too, technicalities are left to local specialized attorneys. The regional office usually has a watchdog role. In rare cases, it assumes wider functions if some corporate trademarks are registered only in and for European countries. However, most U.S. corporations try to avoid such situations.

Among other staff departments that have a tendency to invade, as it were, the sphere of authority of the international division and to communicate directly with its subordinates is advertising. Here, too, their knowledge is mostly domestically oriented and therefore, in the opinion of international experts, less than suitable for foreign advertising problems; here too most of the actual work, beyond setting corporate objectives, is done by an agency that, it is to be hoped, has its own foreign branches. If so, subsidiaries and regional offices will be able to consult and communicate directly with them.

3. Some Successful and Unsuccessful Methods of Communicating

CONCERN about information and communication was expressed by executives participating in the questionnaire survey that preceded the interviews in Europe and America. Prevailing communication problems were described in much stronger terms by executives who were visited. They made one fact clear: If companies are to establish and maintain sound relations with their foreign subsidiaries and affiliates, they must improve their communication.

Distance was cited as a major cause of problems. For example, one executive stated that his company's major difficulties are geographical distance and lack of actual first-hand knowledge, and another complained that distances cause time lapses in taking action.

Problems regarding differences between American and European environments were also mentioned by participating executives, one of whom specified a lack of "bilateral appreciation and understanding of cultural, economic, social, and other differences." A common complaint was the lack of understanding between persons in headquarters and subsidiaries or between Americans and Europeans. One respondent commented that "traditions are an obstacle to change," as are "overseas management attitudes toward new management techniques." Lack of qualified local managers was cited as both a cause and an effect of communication problems.

INFORMATION, METHODS, AND CHANNELS

Survey participants were asked: "What types of management information are communicated to corporate headquarters by the foreign offices on an irregular, ad hoc basis, either directly or through regional offices abroad?" The respondents were given a choice of six specific boxes: production process changes, equipment replacement, need for capital, expansion opportunities, legal and tax problems, and political developments. A seventh box was added with the description "Other."

While the majority of participants checked all or most of the six types of information listed, only a few added "other" information and only one mentioned "market conditions." This is in marked contrast to the subsidiary and regional managers contacted in Europe, who nearly all stressed the importance of funneling market information to the home office. Why this discrepancy?

While some corporations may use the services of American or European market research organizations, and most companies probably study bulletins and newsletters on economic and business conditions published by banks and specialized institutes, the author believes that these companies also frequently receive such information from their own people in the field. If this did not come to mind when an international executive filled out the questionnaire, it can only mean that he did not place too much importance on these reports from his local units—and this demonstrates a serious communication gap, not in structure, personnel, or organization, but in purpose and intent.

Some answers, of course, were vague and all-inclusive—such as "any other pertinent data" or "any critical problem." "Acquisition opportunities" were also indicated, and these are often the task of special foreign area representatives. One reply was particularly interesting: "Possible conflicts with domestic or other subsidiaries' operations and policies." It seemed to point the finger at a serious difficulty in some corporations, where the geographic or functional limits of responsibilities are not clearly enough defined, so that intrusions into each other's territory or sphere of activities occur.

Reverse Flow of Information

To the question "What types of management information are communicated from corporate headquarters to the foreign offices?" respondents supplied what they considered their most important or most frequently transmitted information. Perhaps significantly, some listed what might be regarded less as information than as management control measures—policy directives, inventory and credit control, quality standards, and similar checks and instructions.

"Suggestions on procedures and various other forms of guidance," as one answer had it, would also seem to refer to directives rather than to mere information. And "technical assistance," however valuable it may be, equally does not constitute information in the strict sense of the term. It is fair to assume that a corporate or international headquarters that does not provide substantial information to its foreign units has not yet recognized the enormous value of adequate *mutual* information. One corporation answered the question thus: "Very little." And indeed, the author found an unsatisfactory relationship between the home office and subsidiaries in Europe.

This, however, is an exceptional case. Many companies replied that of prime importance among their home-office-to-subsidiary communications were such vital transmissions as "corporate objectives and plans," "policies and objectives," and "goals and procedures"—information designed to acquaint the foreign managers with the corporation's overall strategy.

Many respondents stressed the necessity of advising their overseas units of new products and other changes and developments in production, know-how, and techniques. Some also said they advised their foreign offices of new developments in organization and management as well as changes in policy and key personnel.

Participating executives were also asked to indicate the methods and channels most often used to communicate management information between headquarters and the foreign offices, and to specify which were most important. Most respondents listed letters first, then memos and reports. Manuals or other directives were the third choice. As to channels, the overwhelming majority of participants in the survey listed mail first, but they also answered yes to the additional question: "Have these methods and channels been modified during the past decade?" They indicated a growing use of telephone, cable, and Telex, as well as an increase in meetings, conferences, and visits.

Visits can be considered a comparatively new channel as well as a new method of exchanging mutual information. Letters and mail as principal methods and channels of communication were largely ignored by the participants in interviews, probably because they are so much taken for granted.

MANUALS

Manuals and directives are often considered routine. While 40 or more executives discussed with the author reports and meetings, and over 30 talked about information and visits, only 10 found something to say about manuals. As methods of conveying policy information, manuals exist in most fairly large companies. The importance attached to them, however, varies.

A Portuguese subsidiary manager considered them indispensable:

"Manuals are necessary to insure uniform procedures in production, marketing, accounting, and many other activities." In fact that is the way his corporation has achieved a high degree of uniformity. But an American executive in Germany whose company is in a service industry saw cause and effect differently. "Our business is practically identical everywhere," he said, "with very few and small differences. Because of this uniformity, strict overall guidelines could be established and followed by the subsidiaries without their giving up the autonomy granted them by top management." He felt that except for rare instances, the local manager would have no occasion to make decisions not covered by the guidelines.

Yet it is obviously important to know what to do in such a case, particularly in an emergency. The treasurer of a subsidiary in the automotive industry put it guardedly: "In practically all matters, manuals with strict procedural instructions must be followed. But there are sometimes local variations in their application which are necessary due to different or unforeseen conditions." An executive in the office-equipment industry was more specific. He explained that his corporation has a "thick book of directives for every conceivable occurrence. But the book explicitly states," he pointed out, "that no instruction should ever prevent or excuse the local manager from taking action in an emergency that is dictated by sound business practice, provided he explains his reasons for such an action as soon as possible." He added his own tagline: "and provided it was successful." The author was reminded of a parallel in military history. In the 18th century, the Austrian empress Maria Theresa instituted an order that was to become the highest military decoration in the Austrian army. It was awarded for a gallant and successful action performed without or even against orders. If the action was unsuccessful, however, the officer was subject to court martial. Or as another subsidiary manager said: "If you violate the company's regulations, but are successful, nothing will happen. But if there is any failure or misfortune, however slight, they will throw the book at you and cite chapter and verse."

The young assistant to a large oil company's Spanish subsidiary manager voiced the opinion that guidelines are a protection for the local executive—as long as he follows them carefully, he can avoid both taking risks and having to ask for permission in each important matter. Many experts would characterize this as an example of corporate bureaucratic thinking that takes refuge behind a protective wall of regulations as a substitute for independent judgment and initiative. A timid local manager who is afraid to make decisions of his own can either use the book of procedures as a shield or follow the example of a subsidiary executive in Paris who admitted that he seldom referred to the manual, but rather discussed matters almost daily by telephone or Telex with his area manager because his company "encourages such discussions." He obviously does not want to take any chances either, but at least he asks for approval to go beyond the manual when he deems this necessary.

Some manuals are specifically designed to define the authority or to limit the decision-making power of local executives. They are therefore the basis for more or less centralized management control. Most of the European executives who discussed manuals with the author had this type of manual or job description in mind.

None of the respondents was really concerned about the "written statement," if any, in which his authority was circumscribed. In many cases, such granting or restriction of authority seemed to be pragmatic rather than "statutory." This lack of precise definition of authority, let alone its written codification, can lead to difficult situations—costly, time-consuming, and destructive of morale.

REPORTS—A CONTROVERSY

All companies require their domestic and foreign offices, departments, branches, subsidiaries, affiliates, licensees, and agents to submit regular reports at periodic intervals. Few experts would question the necessity of doing so, but many assert that there is too much required and that it is required too frequently.

Participating executives were asked in the questionnaire, "What management reports are submitted to corporate headquarters by foreign offices at regular intervals?" Were they "submitted monthly, quarterly, biannually, or annually?" The following reports were itemized: sales reports, sales forecasts, capital budgets, operational budgets, income and expenses, profit and loss statements, balance sheets, funds reports, progress reports, and competitive activity. Most respondents checked all these reports as being regularly forwarded by their foreign offices to headquarters. Sales reports, P&L statements, balance sheets, and funds reports are usually required monthly; sales reports and funds reports, sometimes weekly; forecasts and budgets, mostly annually or biannually; forecasts, sometimes quarterly. In a few cases, sales, income and expenses, and profit and loss are reported monthly *and* quarterly or quarterly *and* annually, or even at three different time periods. Many local managers consider too frequent and too voluminous reporting a great burden on themselves and their staff members and they normally do not mince words about it. It is therefore strange that headquarters, with its larger staffs, does not always see fit to alleviate this burden by itself compiling quarterly statements from monthly figures or annual summaries from quarterly reports.

Only funds reports were sometimes omitted in the replies, and it is safe to assume that they are included with other financial statements, such as balance sheets. Competitive activity reports were also omitted by one or two participants; in fact, some companies consider this as ad hoc information to be sent in by local units when something worthwhile occurs.

On the other hand, quite a few "other" reports were added in the spaces provided in the questionnaire, such as "cash flow" as a separate financial report, and "capital appropriations and expenditures," which apparently supplies an exact check as to whether and when such appropriations have been spent as intended. Several more detailed forecasts were also indicated in addition to the ones already printed in the questionnaire: "profit and loss forecasts," "long-range capital forecasts," "five-year business plans," or "plan projections." No doubt many companies require such forecasts, but they may include them with annual sales forecasts and budget suggestions.

Other special reports mentioned by some respondents were "annual salary reviews," reports on "income tax liability," "insurance," and "advertising budget," which most corporations include in other financial reports. One corporation listed in addition to practically all the foregoing a report on "quality control"; this seems to be separate from the ad hoc information if the quality of one batch or production unit has been found unsatisfactory. All in all, American corporations require a lot of reporting from their overseas units. The loud complaints, then, if not always completely justified, are at least understandable.

The Critics Speak

A few years ago a cosmetics manufacturer's European regional office conducted a time and cost study and found that 25 percent of the time of *all* its executives, plus all the time of several employees, went into reporting. Because the corporation considered other activities more productive, reporting has now been reduced to essential matters, mostly concerning financial operations and sales.

In an important machinery and electronics corporation the regional office's deputy director was very outspoken—perhaps because he had resigned and was soon to join another company. He described the reporting system as "insane," with an enormous amount of unnecessary reports required of the subsidiaries at much too frequent intervals—some of them daily! Some of these reports, he contended, are never read by anyone, much less acted upon, which creates a feeling of frustration among those who make the reports. According to this man, it started naturally enough with the controller's office, where financial reports are of course needed. But the people at the home office could not understand certain facts and figures caused by outside influences, such as different legal and tax situations, or economic conditions over which the subsidiary had no control. Therefore, the controller's department demanded more and more detailed reports. The marketing and sales department followed soon afterward with much too complicated report forms—forms based on domestic operations and often not fit for overseas use. The result was that the marketing and sales departments were also unable to understand the filled-in forms and also asked for more details. Thus reporting snowballed to incredible proportions.

The regional executive contended that vested interests within the company bureaucracy prevent the simplification and restriction of this reporting "craze," now long overdue; it would be necessary to appoint a man with sweeping powers to reduce reports to manageable size. As it is, some entire departments at headquarters keep busy receiving, classifying, and filing reports without doing anything of real value with them.

Another executive talked of a more positive experience. In his younger years he worked in the home office of one of the largest chemical corporations, where, among other duties, he had the task of gathering and distributing the numerous reports sent in from subsidiaries all over the world. He soon discovered that, in keeping with Parkinson's Law, all departments had a tendency to ask for ever more reports. Moreover, a review revealed that most department heads read only a small fraction of the reports. In fact, they just could not have studied all of them in toto, even if they tried. Therefore, top management decided to weed out what was not necessary—and that was a great deal. But this executive stressed that such reviews must be repeated from time to time, because the weeds grow again. At regular intervals a high executive should be charged with carefully checking reporting—including forms, procedures, and volume—with a view toward eliminating every report that cannot be proved necessary.

An American advertising executive, whose views are similar, recently conducted an interesting experiment by stopping the mailing of detailed reports to a large client's home office. He felt that the procedure had grown to unwarranted proportions, that it cost too much money, and that nobody in the corporation wanted to be charged for it. For four months the absence of these reports went unnoticed.

A rather discontented subsidiary manager described the reporting situation in his company simply in these terms: "Everybody must report to everybody and it gets worse every year; nobody is doing anything with our reports except justifying his own existence and the need for more staff." These remarks were echoed by many other local managers, and some added that the ever increasing quantity and volume of reports made it virtually impossible for anyone at the home office to read them—except perhaps third assistants who have no say in decision making. This was frequently cited as one of the reasons why the regular study of reports and suggestions for action based on them should be delegated to a regional office. The other reason was that a regional office is also much better qualified to understand these reports and to take the right action warranted by them.

Some extreme cases are worth mentioning: In an alcoholic beverage company, local managers had to mail cash and sales reports twice a week, which, most experts will agree, does not make sense at all. In a cosmetics company, monthly forecasts and projections are required of all subsidiaries, which is, to say the least, of doubtful value.

In Defense of Reports

In practically all other questions the author found divergent opinions and has recorded them in the present study. But only three or four out of more than forty respondents defended the policy of voluminous and frequent reporting requirements. One, an American bank executive, said that he hears a lot of grumbling about too much reporting from the managers of local client subsidiaries, but he shrugged it off as "quite natural" and something they have to live with. A German subsidiary manager declared himself strongly in favor of extensive and unified reporting in multinational corporations. He claimed that with a modern American accounting system most reports consist only of secretarial work, plus perhaps two or three days per month of his own time for comments and remarks. He does not consider this too much. He thinks that detailed reporting is essential in a large corporation such as his, employing 100,000 people throughout the world and operating through hundreds of separate units under the jurisdiction of several product divisions, whose activities must be coordinated and consolidated to work out overall objectives and policies. The basic question, however, remained unanswered: whether an overextended reporting system in a giant corporation overburdened with a deadweight of unnecessary details furthers, or handicaps, or just does not influence the preparation and execution of corporate aims and strategies.

Some smaller and less tightly centralized companies are satisfied with financial reports, such as monthly cash and profit and loss statements, biannual balance sheets, annual forecasts, and budget proposals, plus regular sales reports. But many, especially larger corporations, feel that this bare minimum is not sufficient to really know what is going on overseas and to act accordingly. The amount, volume, and frequency of reports are therefore geared to the size of the corporation and its international operations, their diversity and complexity, the management control pattern prevalent in the organization, the corporation's historic development, past experiences, successes, failures, and reorganizations, and the personalities at the top.

Reporting by Small Subsidiaries—The Problem

But while the reporting system usually reflects the size of the corporation or at least its European operations, it is not, in the majority of companies, adjusted sufficiently to the size and potential of the local unit. In other words, reporting requirements are frequently rigidly uniform whether the subsidiary is large or small. An American subsidiary manager in Lisbon considered this an enormous burden for his and most other U.S. companies in a small market like Portugal. There simply is no relationship between his sales and resources and those in the large European countries, where the corporation has a multimillion-dollar business. Still, he asserted, reporting cannot be changed in accordance with the size of the business. That it cannot is due to the requirements of uniform statistics, accounting, comparisons, and control, particularly in a business with a multitude of product lines. While this makes the reporting even harder in a small local unit handling most of these products, in some of the big markets the different lines are divided among several subsidiaries.

An Italian manager related that with only 20 office employees he has to prepare a total of more than 50 reports a year. Meanwhile, the much larger subsidiaries in England and Germany, each with a staff three times as large as his, meet exactly the same requirements, which they can easily handle. Putting smaller figures in the reports does not diminish the amount of work necessary to compile and to explain them. It may even increase the need for commenting on them. This executive has made many suggestions for simplifying the reports, but so far without avail, because the home office insists on uniformity. Yet, interestingly enough, a breakdown of sales by areas within Italy is not required in his company. The manager feels this would be useful because of the great differences between North and South.

In Austria, another of Europe's smaller markets, a very large corporation's national manager disagreed with the contention that smaller subsidiaries should be allowed to send fewer and less detailed reports to headquarters. And he disagreed even though reporting in his company is extensive and encompasses all possible categories. His solution is simply to attach fewer and less voluminous comments to the reports.

The Solution

By contrast, an American executive in Switzerland contended that initially only those reports that help a subsidiary in its activities should be required. Later, as the local business grows, other, more amplified reports can be added, but they should still be tailored to local needs and resources. This would avoid saddling a young subsidiary with duties so burdensome they may very well contribute to an unfavorable balance sheet. Or as the executive asks: "What is the use of painstaking reports if there is not enough business to report on?"

Many corporations have failed to realize that it makes good sense to alleviate the heavy reporting burden for their smaller and younger subsidiaries, especially new acquisitions, and thus to help them get in or stay in the black. The easiest way to accomplish this in spite of general uniform procedures is to allow the small subsidiary to submit reports less frequently —such as quarterly rather than monthly. This makes a major difference for sparsely staffed units, a difference perhaps not readily realized by the home office staff. This reduced frequency may apply only to some less important reports while those basic for accounting, production, and marketing may be required monthly from *every* local unit. Furthermore, less frequent reporting in some or all categories may be coupled with shorter and less complex report forms. But such changes require a broad-minded attitude, one that is lacking in many corporations, especially in middle management.

A large chemical corporation's regional marketing manager in Zurich told the author that his company has uniform reporting as far as frequency is concerned, but that it allows its smaller subsidiaries to use simplified forms. These are so reduced in size that "a secretary can fill them out in half a day each month." Moreover, small local units can employ outside auditing help for their financial reports. It is clear that in this company flexibility is the rule. Another enlightened American corporation requires a smaller subsidiary to report detailed sales only for a few fast-moving items; it can lump all others together under "miscellaneous." For these latter products, comments and explanations, as well as forecasts and programs, may also be reduced. The local manager added that he is convinced that with a minimum of goodwill, similar, if not identical, solutions to this thorny problem could be found in other corporations. The important thing, he said, is to get rid of an "accounting mind," to recognize the broad principle of maximizing profits, and to balance it against the usefulness of compiling, tabulating, and comparing a mass of more or less relevant figures.

A young regional executive in Germany frankly admitted: "We have not solved the problem of our smaller subsidiaries being overburdened by too many and too frequent reports, except that by the very nature of their larger business volume, the more important local units have to file more voluminous reports."

Asked if there was any difference in reporting on the part of large manufacturing subsidiaries and reporting as done by smaller production or assembly plants, an automobile manufacturer's local manager said this:

> Theoretically there is no difference, but in practice if a small plant is a
> day behind in its production schedule it means a few dozen cars for the

home market only. By contrast, in one of the large factories it means several hundred cars, including exports to other European countries, and that makes a lot of difference in sales, distribution, transport, components, raw materials, and consequently in programs and financial matters. Furthermore, the larger plant produces a wider variety of models, styles, and colors and is required to report in greater detail. To be responsible for the production of a thousand cars a day cannot possibly be the same as for a hundred cars.

The flexible approach to this very important problem was summed up by the VP–Europe of a gigantic electronics corporation: "We tailor the reports to the volume and facilities of our subsidiaries. Therefore, they are not the same for large and small units except in financial matters. Like all our policies this principle will remain stable, but kept flexible to allow for gradual adjustments as needs and resources are changing."

Distribution of Reports

In the survey, participants were asked, "What are the titles of the executives who receive these reports and where are they located—at headquarters, regional offices abroad, or elsewhere?" A minority of participants listed only a few executives as recipients of subsidiary reports, such as

- Vice-president international division.
- Chairman of the board, president, executive vice-president.
- Chairman of the corporation, vice-president international operations, vice-president financial planning.
- Corporate president and executive vice-president.

It can be assumed that the assistants or personal staffs of these key executives read the reports and prepare excerpts for their superiors or simply point out the most important sections and items to them, and that most of the reports are then passed on to lower echelons. This seems to be indicated by the wording of one reply: "Marketing units send their reports *initially* to the marketing division's management; manufacturing companies send most of the same kinds of reports to the responsible vice-president, but in some cases less often."

The majority of respondents indicated that reports were sent to quite a number of top executives at the home office and abroad. These were among the responses:

- All group executives.
- President and staff vice-presidents, area vice-president.
- Key men both in U.S. and overseas.

- VP and director international operations, VP manufacturing, controller, three area vice-presidents.
- President, financial VP, two senior VPs, and various other officers and executives at corporate headquarters; also executive VP and general manager, senior VP operations and key staff in international corporation and regional directors.
- Managing director, chief executive officer, international controller, managing director Western Hemisphere, managing director Europe in London.
- The executive, the senior vice-presidents, the coordinators, and the heads of advisory and services departments.
- President, vice-president operations, financial VP, treasurer, international VP, international controller, international manager.

It will be noted that in most cases not only the executives of the international division but the president of the corporation and other corporate top executives receive reports from overseas subsidiaries. Some top executives such as the corporate president and the VP–International probably receive all reports, which would mean an enormous quantity; other corporate or international executives, such as the controller, usually receive only the reports with which they are principally concerned.

Channeling of Reports

Further information on distribution and channeling of reports was supplied by executives interviewed in Europe. The channeling is done in three different ways.

1. The subsidiary mails the reports directly to the various key executives and staff departments at the home office. If a regional office exists in Europe, it usually receives copies of all or most reports; sometimes it does not receive reports on matters where it has no jurisdiction—for example, financial reports. Also, in a few corporations, each of several departmentalized regional offices receives the reports on its separate area of activity. The decisions the reports may require are made at the home office, and appropriate actions, if any, are taken by headquarters executives or delegated by them to the regional office in Europe. One example, as mentioned by a local manager in Madrid: "I send all my monthly reports directly to our international division in St. Paul, with copies to the VP–Southern Europe in Paris."

2. The subsidiary sends its reports to the home office addressed to one junior executive charged with their distribution. Again, copies go to regional or area offices in Europe—if any. The advantage of this method is

that the subsidiary does not have to keep track of the many changes in headquarters personnel, which may otherwise result in having reports lying around in the wrong department, being misfiled, or reaching the proper executive only after considerable delay. It also provides a central point for registering reports and checking their prompt arrival date. This method makes it impossible for subsidiaries to delay their reports or not send them at all. The disadvantage is that the subsidiary manager and his staff often have only a vague notion who gets and is supposed to read their reports. "An enormous amount of monthly reports has to be sent to New York," said an Italian manager, "where they are circulated among heaven knows how many people, of whom only a few, I am sure, read them."

3. In those corporations that have a strong, well-staffed regional office in Europe with decision-making authority, reports from subsidiaries may be sent to this regional office with copies to the home office. This is more than a mere reversal of technicalities. It means that the first reaction, in many cases the only one, comes from the regional office—perhaps in the form of a short telephone call requesting clarification of some detail. It is part and parcel of the close and fruitful contact that exists in these organizations between local and regional managements.

A variant of this method is for the subsidiaries to send copies of reports, together with the originals, to the regional office. It will then forward them to the various executives at the home office, usually attaching its own comments. It can interpret or explain certain facts and figures to headquarters that it feels need "translation" into headquarters language. The regional office is normally better qualified to spot such areas than is the subsidiary manager, who may have no or little home office experience.

In some companies a powerful regional office does not forward copies of subsidiary reports, only summaries. This saves the home office the almost impossible task of reading and digesting all reports. Instead, it gets them in easier-to-grasp, concentrated form. In the process, however, some of the local manager's original thoughts may be diluted or replaced by somewhat different, if more objective, regional viewpoints.

A unique procedure was observed in one American corporation, where every executive who sends a communication (report, information, memo) to his line superior or to a staff executive is required to send a carbon copy to the superior of the recipient. Thus higher echelons are automatically informed of everything that is going on at lower levels. Yet it must surely increase their already burdensome reading material.

The director of marketing of a European regional office told the author that while his office has an ample staff, the subsidiaries' personnel ranges from only 4 to 25 persons each. Therefore, most of the paperwork is done by the regional staff. Reporting by the subsidiaries has been reduced to a point where it takes less than half a day per month. All local reports are consolidated at the Brussels regional headquarters, enlarged by comments, and then forwarded to the international division in New York. Brussels helps the subsidiaries prepare their reports, as it helps them in many other activities. The same is done by the Frankfurt regional office of a large tire manufacturer, which merits a closer look.

CASE BRIEF

The company had been operating in Europe for only a few years and, until recently, had only marketing subsidiaries—manufacturing was done under license by European factories. All these subsidiaries, like the ones in Latin America, Australia, the Middle East, and the Far East, reported directly to the president–international in the United States. A short time ago a very large plant was built in Germany and at the same time the first regional office was established nearby. The new European regional manager, an American, realized that he would encounter a certain opposition from the various local managers, all nationals and all used to communicating directly with the parent company. Knowing they might feel shut off from U.S. headquarters and might be afraid to lose some of their responsibilities to the new regional office, the European manager tried to convince them that he was there to help them rather than to impose either company directives or his own instructions.

One opportunity to get this idea across was in the area of reporting. The company had not achieved uniform reporting procedures and the subsidiary managers were a bit lax in performing this duty, which to them, as to many Europeans, seemed of secondary importance. For smaller subsidiaries the regional office all but took over most of the reporting. All they have to do is to send the raw information to Frankfurt, where it is put into the right form for transmittal to the home office. With the larger local units, the regional office collaborates in turning out the required reports, including sales reports and forecasts. Future plans call for computerized reporting. The data will be computerized locally wherever feasible, but programming and processing will be handled in a European computer center. From there the reports will flow to Frankfurt and simultaneously to America, as well as back to the subsidiaries for their own use.

Computerization of Reports

For many large American corporations, computerization of reports is making progress all over Europe, particularly in Germany, France, and Britain. As one subsidiary manager in Spain pointed out, computerization makes statistical and financial reports much more detailed without increasing the workload of the local staff, and sometimes it actually reduces it. The preparation of computerized reports is also very much faster, even though punch cards and magnetic tape often have to be sent by mail or courier to the computer center, which may be situated in London or a German city.

Feedback of data to the subsidiary is of great importance. It helps a reluctant subsidiary appreciate the usefulness of reports and makes local managers more willing to do their part. They soon realize the benefits they derive for their own marketing, sales, and distribution policies, product selection, promotional campaigns, budget proposals, forecasting, investment planning, pricing, and cost control. It is then not too difficult to understand the importance of adequate reporting for similar aims in the corporate or strategic plan. The local manager of one small subsidiary said that reporting in his company is very detailed and uniform throughout—whether the subsidiaries are large or small. Yet in contrast to so many other local managers, he did not seem to mind. The reason that he did not was that he put the results of his reports to good use in his own operations.

Reports as Control Measures

Reporting requirements and control patterns clearly involve a two-way relationship: The stronger the management control, the more detailed and frequent the reporting must be to enable management to exercise that control. Incidentally, it makes little difference whether control is concentrated at the home office or at regional headquarters; it only shifts the direction of reporting from one place to the other. On the other hand, the more reports arrive at regional or corporate headquarters, the more control is needed to take the necessary actions. A third connection is that the strict rules on reporting, whether or not they are always followed by appropriate action, whether or not all reports are read and appreciated by the recipients, in themselves constitute strong control measures.

To a limited extent similar control purposes should be achieved by carefully checking the reports from affiliates and joint ventures, but it is very difficult to obtain uniform reporting from majority-controlled firms and next to impossible to get them from companies with American minority participation. Since each firm may have a different accounting method and probably does have varying reporting systems, comparisons at corporate headquarters are extremely difficult. The home office will often have to ask for clarification or additional data, which may annoy local managers and local partners who consider this an unnecessary complication or an outright nuisance and waste of time.

Reporting by Licensees and Agents

The same attitude can be observed when American companies try to persuade their agents, distributors, licensees, and dealers to submit reports. Though the companies ask less in this matter than they require of their own subsidiaries, they nearly always meet with open or passive resistance.

Independent agents are particularly reluctant to report anything they consider to be within their private domain and protected by customary European secrecy, and most financial reports fall into this category. Moreover, they have to be educated, slowly and diplomatically, to understand the usefulness of sending reports to their principals. The author still remembers from his own business experience that many years ago one distributor told him: "When you appointed me, I thought you wanted me to sell your products. Now I realize you want me to report whether I sell or not."

Many U.S. corporations that deal with agents, distributors, or licensed manufacturers and wholesalers have their own district representatives to assist and supervise these independent firms. In such cases they require both their representatives and the licensees to send in reports. They are difficult to obtain from the independent agents, whom the company cannot force into reporting. Often, it does not want to lose these agents because they may otherwise be very good and almost irreplaceable. A large machinery manufacturer's European marketing manager said that while the French licensee, a large firm, now reports fairly well, this cannot be said of the dealer in a small country such as Gabon in Africa who just cannot be expected to send in regular complete reports. A regional director of operations in another corporation voiced similar opinions on reports by licensees:

> More or less exact reports depend on the individual distributor and on the business climate of the country. In France, Italy, Spain, and especially Turkey, there is an atmosphere of secrecy, even where you would not expect it, which makes full reporting practically impossible. But no European country is completely free of it. The best reports come from Germany, the United Kingdom, Holland, and Switzerland, but uniformity still cannot be accomplished with our different licensees.

The managing director of a food company in Brussels said that reporting is unified in his corporation, but that in those countries under his jurisdiction where the business is handled through agents, "reporting starts with me." This is possible because these markets are close by and he can easily visit them. In other companies local agents submit their reports to the country or area representative, who forwards them with his own comments to the home office.

VISITS AND CONFERENCES

While standardized reports are always an impersonal and often a rigidly bureaucratic means of control and coordination, personal visits and meetings are flexible, conducive to better understanding, faster, and perhaps more effective. They can hardly ever replace reporting, ad hoc information, and steady contacts via letters, cables, Telex, and telephone, but they can fill the gaps that these other means of communication nearly always leave open. They are therefore a widely used tool of the management relationship between headquarters and overseas offices.

If the corporation has no regional office in Europe, traveling is done from the home office to the foreign subsidiaries and vice versa. The visitors to Europe may come from the international division, from corporate headquarters, from various product groups and staff departments, or from all of these offices, which may be located in different American cities.

Visitors from European subsidiaries travel to international or corporate headquarters in the United States, but when the home office is a division or subsidiary of a larger corporation, they may seldom, if ever, go to the parent company's headquarters. One European subsidiary manager related that he visits his own divisional home office regularly once a year, but he has never been at the parent company's main office, nor has he any occasion to go there. By contrast, he *receives* frequent visits from executives of both, simply because his subsidiary is situated at one of the principal gateways to continental Europe.

If the corporation maintains one or several regional offices in Europe, visits follow this pattern: from American headquarters to regional office and subsidiaries, from regional office to headquarters and subsidiaries, and from subsidiaries to headquarters and regional office. But if the regional office is important in the corporate organization, it will probably send more visitors more often to the subsidiary than to the U.S. home office, and certainly the subsidiary manager and his executives will travel much more frequently to the regional office in Europe than to headquarters in America. In one very large and long-established multinational corporation, the larger subsidiaries send their general managers regularly to the regional office in Paris and are visited by executives from both Paris and New York, while the smaller local units are visited only by Paris, and visit there only infrequently themselves.

Do local managers prefer to receive visits from U.S. headquarters or from the European regional office? Even when personal likes and dislikes are left aside, this question is hard to answer. On the one hand, a smaller subsidiary manager naturally feels honored when a top executive from the United States comes to see him. But on the other hand, the regional manager or executive is always much better informed about local conditions and in a better position to offer assistance. Visits from the regional manager, to be sure, may well be inspection trips and control measures; visits from the parent company usually are more in the nature of personal information-gathering. The manager of a Swiss subsidiary that, for historic reasons, was still supervised by the larger German unit made no attempt to hide his displeasure at being regularly visited—and controlled—by the German subsidiary. He would much prefer to establish direct relations with American headquarters, from which, to his great regret, visitors come only occasionally.

Thus it can be stated that in the complex network of intracorporate relationships, visits often have a symbolic or status value that does not always correspond to their actual communication, control, or information value.

Who Are the Visitors?

The first and most numerous general category of traveling visitors is formed by the president, vice-presidents, and general managers of the corporation, its international division, the regional executives (whether located in the U.S. or in Europe), and those from subsidiaries or affiliates. The corporate key executives usually visit only the more important places: London, Paris, Germany, and the European regional office in Belgium, Holland, or Switzerland. They seldom, if ever, go to other parts of the world. By contrast, the international division executives normally add to their European itinerary the smaller countries, and they regularly travel to Latin America, where they may well visit Mexico, Puerto Rico, and Venezuela, and perhaps two or three other countries. The Middle East, Far East, and Pacific areas, with the possible exception of Japan, are normally left to the regional manager, whether he resides there or in the United States. This is also the rule with Africa and the less important markets in the Caribbean and in Central and South America.

Subsidiary managers in Europe will seldom visit American headquarters if they report to a strong regional office, particularly if it is only two hours or less by air and if it is from there that they obtain most of their technical and managerial support. Subsidiary managers in other areas of the world often do not have a resident regional manager and therefore *must* travel to the United States. But since the flight is long and costly there may be only one a year, and the visit will then last a considerable time. Also, if they are Americans, it is usually combined with vacation or home leave.

The general manager of an important European subsidiary not located near the regional office may visit there quite often. In addition he will receive so many visitors from American headquarters and the regional office that a great part of his time will be spent in traveling and in talking to traveling executives. Furthermore, he attends many out-of-town meetings, has to prepare or at least approve his subsidiary's reports, and spends several hours every week on the telephone and Telex. The end result is that he is able to devote less and less time to the actual business, which he must leave to a great extent to his staff. He becomes a kind of representative rather than operating chief executive. Moreover, his corporation may wish him to take an active part in local civic affairs, such as American chambers of commerce, associations, and clubs—just as at home. All this adds up to great psychological pressure, too little time left for thorough studies of local conditions, not enough familiarity with the business at hand, reliance on advice from subordinates and outsiders, rash decisions or suggestions based on superficial knowledge—and not enough time for relaxation and adjustment to the environment.

The local manager must establish his own system of priorities, which may or may not be in the company's best interest, or he will suffer failure and frustration. Some subsidiary managers try to solve this grave problem by restricting time-consuming visits, but the problem transcends reports, visits, meetings, and other commitments. It can be solved only by finding the best way to divide available time, even if it is twelve hours per day and more.

Production and Marketing Managers, the VP–International

Another important group of visitors from headquarters consists of production and marketing managers. A subsidiary manager in Italy reported that in routine production matters his two local plant managers and some of their subordinates have sufficient personal contacts with their counterparts and experts in the United States by direct correspondence and mutual visits. No problems there, because the Italian and American production men have by now been educated to mutual understanding and appreciation. At first, this was rather difficult, but gradually the Italian technicians adopted American production know-how and the American experts began to acknowledge the excellent Italian workmanship, which sometimes led to improvements in techniques.

On the managerial side, the VP–International comes to Europe almost every month, which the local manager considers much too often. At the same time, he feels his marketing manager and other staff members visit European subsidiaries much too seldom. Such monthly visits are exceptional—the usual frequency is one to four times per year—but many heads of international divisions do all the European traveling themselves. At best, they leave to their staff executives the other continents. This is understandable, especially if the former are men of European origin or experience and the latter are not, but it will hardly enable those staff members to acquire greater familiarity with European markets.

Product-Group Executives

Another group of visitors are the general managers or vice-presidents of product-group divisions. In those corporations where the international business has been reorganized along product lines, these visits are extremely important for the growth, indeed for the very survival, of the foreign operations. It is frequently asserted that one of the primary reasons for such reorganizations is the need to educate the product divisions to global thinking. One way to achieve this is to encourage regular visits by product-group managers to European subsidiaries.

But it is an illusion to believe that exposing key executives to what can be seen on a short visit abroad can accomplish much. It is certainly true that foreign travel *can* open eyes and minds—if it includes advance studies of the markets to be visited, and if presumptions and prejudices are discarded. Those travelers who unconsciously are determined to see their preconceived opinions confirmed are not likely to derive much benefit for themselves and for the company from a short visit abroad. In any case, their education during such a visit is a formidable task for the local manager, particularly if the American group vice-president is an engineer and the subsidiary executive is a marketing specialist.

The difficulties are compounded when there is only one local subsidiary for several product divisions and the visits by the different group managers are not coordinated. An executive with the title of vice-president and regional director for Europe said that in his corporation, presidents and vice-presidents of product divisions are encouraged to visit Europe—and that many do. Thus visitors from America arrive every week, some scheduled, others unannounced. He said that one week in May (a good travel month) the corporate president, the president and vice-president of the international division, and three product-group presidents "came all at the same time—much too much for our small office of seven men."

Staff Department Heads

A less numerous group of visitors is made up of corporate or international staff and service department heads. While they usually have no line authority, some of them can make suggestions in their particular field that are tantamount to orders. This is especially true of the controller in financial matters. But he normally comes only once a year for a few days of budget review. In fact, the directors of staff departments come better prepared to answer questions, to help solve problems, and to recommend solutions than do higher ranking executives. Also, their trips are scheduled and therefore the local manager and his staff are better prepared and the visits more useful.

A busy local manager stated that his subsidiary is often visited by personnel from headquarters in St. Louis. He encourages direct contact between the visitors—other than top executives—and their counterparts at the local level. But he is not present at these meetings because he "cannot be an expert in every field" and wants to save his precious time. Language, however, is a problem. None of the American visitors speaks the local language and some of the national staff members are not yet fluent in English. When necessary, the subsidiary manager supplies an interpreter, flatly refusing to serve in this capacity himself.

A similar position was taken by another subsidiary manager who is not opposed to the frequent visits from regional staff executives for finance, sales, service, installation, and production, because he realizes the benefits his subsidiary derives from them. He has made it a practice, however, to only shake hands with the visitors, unless they are top men, and to let them discuss their subjects directly with local staff members. Also, if the subsidiary manager thinks that their suggestions are not suitable for the local market, he does not let them impose any "recommendations" on the corresponding local executives. In cases of disagreement, the matter is referred to conversations between subsidiary and regional general managers.

The two executives mentioned earlier are strong personalities, have served long and successfully with their companies, and are highly regarded at corporate headquarters. A young local manager, or even a regional one, will of course be more cautious than these highly experienced men in dealing with visitors. He must avoid giving the impression that he objects to these visits or wants to remain in isolation, even if he may not always see eye to eye with the travelers on the usefulness of their trips. The former European regional manager of a large corporation was known among his colleagues for not tolerating any interference from New York, and everybody except the president and executive vice-president had to obtain what was commonly called a "visa" before he could plan a trip to Europe. Often he would tell prospective travelers that their trip was not needed. His successor has had to be much more pliable, and it is doubtful whether he will ever be allowed to occupy so domineering a position. This was an exceptional case, but by and large the degree of control over visits from lower ranking executives can be considered a yardstick of the authority exerted by local and regional managers.

Technicians

In addition to top and middle management, many experts and technicians are sent from corporate or regional headquarters to subsidiaries, sometimes when needed, wanted, and requested by local management, sometimes when their presence is deemed necessary by the higher level.

They must not only know their field thoroughly and answer all questions, they must also know how to listen; they must be able to impart their expertise without condescension and remain on an equal footing with the local people. All this is very difficult because these traveling experts are often young and are usually trained only in their technical specialties, not in psychology or European ways. In very large corporations traveling specialists form a special group, sometimes divided according to geographic or linguistic regions. But even then they do not always know how to avoid giving offense in matters involving national sensitivities.

It was probably significant that several subsidiary managers reported that specialists from headquarters—in marketing, production, advertising, accounting—travel to Europe frequently to discuss these matters with their counterparts, but that the local manager is under no obligation to follow their ideas if he finds they are not applicable to local conditions with which these specialists are not familiar. The specialists will then report to their own superiors, and sometimes a higher ranking staff member may come over to smooth ruffled feathers and to arrive at a compromise solution that introduces suggested improvements without hurting local feelings.

If a regional office exists where a seasoned department head is available in the field of activity concerned, a mutually acceptable solution can always be found; otherwise bad feelings may smolder for a long time and damage successful operations. To prevent this is one of the important functions of regional management; to give regional management the necessary authority is one of the wise moves of top management. In old established multinational corporations the machinery is set up and usually functions satisfactorily; in younger companies several trips by local, regional, and corporate executives may be necessary to solve such problems—if they grow to serious proportions.

Purposes of Visits

The purposes of visits from the United States to Europe and vice versa are as varied as are the visitors and are mostly, but not always, intimately connected with their functions, titles, and personalities. The principal aims of visits are:

- Control and supervision.
- Coordination and unification.
- Management and technical information exchange.
- Strengthening of teamwork.
- Assistance and troubleshooting.
- Training of local staff.

As an effective control measure, visits to subsidiaries and affiliates can be either a substitute for other means of communication or a supplement to them. Owing to the invaluable personal contact, visits can be more effective than instructions given in writing or by telephone and Telex, provided that the visitor has carefully determined the main subjects to be discussed. He must be thoroughly familiar with them because he usually travels alone and cannot call in an assistant to fill in the details for him. And to deal by himself with the subsidiary manager and his entire staff it is not enough that he be armed with authority, he must be reinforced by complete knowledge and competence. Therefore, visits to the subsidiary for control purposes can best be effected by the subsidiary's immediate line superior or the area or regional manager or one of his staff department heads—in any case, not by the president of the corporation.

In former times, when Telex did not exist, when telephone calls were uncertain and unclear, and when mail was slow, personal visits were almost the only effective means of control and supervision. This is no longer the case, but in some companies where subsidiary managers are vested with great autonomy, visits are still more important than impersonal means of control. One such local manager said that in his company there is little interference from corporate headquarters and that no regional office exists in Europe. "However," he said, "the vice-president international comes once a year to visit all subsidiaries and his European regional manager [both reside in California] much more often." The implication was clear: During these visits most questions are discussed, problems clarified, policies explained, and directives given.

Such visits by international division or regional executives are also useful tools with which to achieve or improve unification of subsidiary activities and to coordinate them within the region. This is particularly important for new acquisitions. If what is intended is not merely routine supervision, but the institution of new policies or stricter control, or a basic change in production, products, marketing, or promotion, it may be more effective to invite the subsidiary manager and one or two of his subordinates to regional or corporate headquarters for briefing by several international or functional executives. There is the danger, however, that the local manager, especially if he has no headquarters experience, will feel overwhelmed by corporate might. Corporations therefore usually sugarcoat headquarters visits by such amenities as personal invitations, entertainment, and sightseeing trips—which is exactly what the subsidiary manager tries to do when the president comes to see him.

Exchange of Information

The main purpose of many visits to and from foreign countries is not, or not exclusively, management control, but rather management information—that is, the amplification or verification of regular reports and other communications received during the preceding period from the subsidiary (or from the regional office). This does not necessarily mean that headquarters questions the accuracy of local reporting and information. It means, rather, that the higher ranking executive wants to see with his own eyes. The corporate president may very well not be sufficiently familiar with the local market and the subsidiary operations to be able to form his own opinions on the local situation. He will be satisfied to get the feel of the country and its business climate and to meet local management, employees, officials, customers, and dealers. If the high-ranking visitor is conscious of his limitations in language, knowledge, and communication, his limited purposes will be achieved. But if, without thorough familiarity with all permanent and variable circumstances, he attempts to base important decisions on a short visit or to override decisions made by his experts, then the visit is worse than useless; it is harmful.

It may be a good idea to give the local manager and his staff members a pat on the back, if he bears in mind that Europeans are much more restrained in personal expressions. But it would be dangerous to overestimate the actual information gathered during the visit or to take everything seen and heard at face value.

Again, the immediate superiors of the local manager in the regional office or international division are better equipped to compare their traveling impressions with other sources of information and to confirm or modify what they have previously learned from reports and various direct or indirect communications.

Yet, with all possible shortcomings and limitations in mind, many subsidiary managers welcome visits from headquarters as a means of injecting some international spirit into a sometimes rather parochial atmosphere at home and also to renew and maintain old acquaintances within the company. An American manager in Spain said that he would of course prefer that all key people of the international division had foreign working experience. Since this cannot be hoped for in the near future, the next best thing is to have them visit the European subsidiaries frequently, even though this puts a considerable burden on the local manager and his staff. Of course, he sees to it that the visitors get as much factual information as possible during their trips.

The American controller and liaison executive of a joint venture in Austria emphasized that the affiliate company enjoyed great autonomy and that therefore the quarterly visits by the divisional vice-president are mainly for information purposes. But often the American visitor both gathers information from local managers and supplies valuable information to them on the latest developments in the corporation or the industry. Visits contribute to the mutual education of local and corporate management, and this is especially necessary for newly established subsidiaries or newly appointed local managers. Several regional executives related that during their first years in Europe they traveled almost constantly over their territory, instructing subsidiaries in matters pertaining to production, marketing, accounting, reporting, and many other activities. This is just as important for independent licensees, distributors, and agents, whose knowledge of American techniques is normally rather fragmentary. But this goal can better be achieved by letting foreign agents or managers visit the home office with a carefully prepared schedule of interviews, lectures, and conferences in various company departments.

Training, Assistance, and Troubleshooting

This suggests another purpose of two-way visits: training young Americans abroad and young Europeans or other foreigners in America. Such visits can last several weeks or months, or even a year or more. Large corporations have elaborate programs for training prospective staff members and junior executives for positions at the international division, regional offices, and subsidiaries. In addition, they set up training programs for technicians, service personnel, instructors, and many categories of specialists.

Assistance and troubleshooting are the duties of specially qualified men sent from the home office or from regional headquarters, often on short notice. The two terms are not used synonymously. While both refer to the solving of urgent problems, "assistance" is used here when the subsidiary itself calls for help, "troubleshooting" when a specialist is dispatched to investigate and solve difficulties that have come to the attention of the higher level without a request for assistance from local management. Perhaps the latter does not think that help is needed and is trying to solve the problem with its own resources.

One subsidiary manager pointed out that his firm's London office maintains a staff of advisers and coordinators for certain activities who have special training and are fluent in one or more languages in addition to their own; yet they come only when invited. By contrast, another local manager said that in his corporation three coordinators for technical, marketing, and computer matters visit subsidiaries either at the latter's request or on direct orders from the Chicago office. The general manager of a third subsidiary was highly critical of his company's procedures. He stated that he receives very few visits from corporate or international or even European regional headquarters, because his operations run smoothly and his balance sheet looks favorable. Therefore, key executives believe that it is not necessary to call on him frequently. But his counterpart in a neighboring country, a man he refers to as "my hapless colleague," is constantly questioned by people from all three offices because his profit and market-share figures are not satisfactory. Whenever he suggests measures to improve the situation, his recommendations are investigated to death or emasculated by contradictory amendments and counterproposals. What one visitor suggests, the next higher ranking one changes—until nothing worthwhile remains. Ultimately, as the easiest way out, the local manager is blamed for all failures, even though they are beyond his personal control. Meanwhile, the steady stream of troubleshooters prevents him from doing his regular job, let alone a better job. The end result will almost certainly be that he will either resign or be forced out and that his successor will be plagued by the same unhappy circumstances—the direct consequence of faulty policies.

Some experts believe that visits often reveal a paradoxical pattern: When problems arise in production, the plant manager and the local general manager consider them of major importance because they may result in lower quality or higher costs and thus have an unfavorable effect on sales and profits. Therefore, they usually immediately call for help. The higher echelons, however, are frequently slow in sending assistance. This is particularly the case where no regional office exists or where it has no specialists available and help has to come from America. Not only does this mean higher costs, which may be considered unwarranted for a single subsidiary, but the international division very likely has difficulties obtaining the needed qualified technicians from domestic production. (Supposedly this is easier where the product groups have final responsibility.) Moreover, the home office most probably assigns priorities according to the size and volume of the subsidiary, affiliate, or licensee that asks for assistance, and therefore the smaller and younger ones, which need it most, are likely to get it last, unless, of course, the problem is extremely critical. But otherwise the plant manager may get instructions over the telephone or by mail telling him how to do it himself.

By contrast, when the monthly sales report or financial statement shows a slight decline or lower figures than were predicted in the last forecast, the higher echelons usually react with alarm. And this will happen even though local management may have given plausible explanations, such as local strikes or labor unrest, or even though the subsidiary manager may have pointed out an unfavorable buying reaction to new or changed products, or the pressures of growing competition. His information was perhaps neglected, his warnings underestimated, his suggestions disregarded, but soon troubleshooters arrive. Usually, they look for causes other than those given by the local experts. Sometimes they really find the reasons for shortcomings in deficient production, marketing, distribution, administration, or personal failures; sometimes they create scapegoats; seldom do they confirm and support the opinions of local management. Again, such unhappy events occur mostly in younger subsidiaries. They rarely happen where the local manager is a trusted company executive with long years of experience and success.

In order to avoid shortchanging small subsidiaries that ask for assistance, and at the same time to reduce traveling costs, well-organized multinational organizations sometimes make arrangements whereby they send specialists from an established, large, and successful subsidiary to a neighboring smaller and younger unit. This also solves the language problem. French technicians may visit Belgium or Switzerland, Germans may go to Switzerland and Austria, Spanish experts to Latin America, or vice versa. If such visits last longer than a few weeks, they cause problems in compensation, Social Security, insurance, cost-of-living differentials, and so forth.

A Format for Visits

All visits begin with, and indeed some consist exclusively of, personal interviews and conferences. This personal approach is usually preferred by visiting top executives and has the great advantage that specific problems can be discussed and personal and confidential questions answered. Frequently the local general manager will later be joined by some of his executives—when production, marketing, promotion, personnel, service, and other activities come up for debate and review. An inspection of the factory, the warehouse, and other facilities will be made at this time, and outside auditors, consultants, and advertising and market research agents may be invited to attend. However, all this may take more time than is usually available, especially if the visitor is the president or executive vice-president of the corporation and has no intention of getting involved in details. If, however, the visiting top executive wants to discuss the international or European problems of his corporation more fully with local executives, he may omit or curtail local visits and summon subsidiary managers and their department heads to an area or regional conference. There will be less time and opportunity to talk about local problems, but many more possibilities to take up the important common objectives and procedures of the corporation's European organization.

Visits of local executives to regional or corporate headquarters can be organized exactly the same way: individual visits, which offer each European executive an opportunity to air his individual problems and to ask for specific considerations and solutions, or group visits, which save time and make it possible to spend longer hours with more higher ranking executives and to exchange views and discuss problems that may not be so unique after all.

A visiting corporate or international expert, but rarely a top man, may also arrange a course or series of lectures in his field of expertise for a group of European executives. Visits of European staff members to America very often include such courses.

Finally, certain visitors, such as auditors, customarily travel in groups of three or so, as do some other inspection teams. Whatever the purpose of the visit, its format, and the persons involved on both sides, careful preparation and prearranged agenda are essential. The visiting and visited executives may not always agree on the agenda and the lower ranking of the two will have to compromise, but an unstructured trip accomplishes little. The following story again provides a sharply critical, but not uncommon example.

CASE BRIEF

An American subsidiary manager said he was glad that his company does not request local managers to come regularly to Chicago headquarters, because the few times he did, he found it a frustrating experience and a waste of time. Whenever he was supposed to see an executive in one of the many corporate departments, the man was in a conference or in a meeting or otherwise unavailable. He could not see even the assistant. If and when he finally got the appointment, the home office executive was too busy to devote enough time to him and was clearly not interested in the visitor from Europe. Those not belonging to the international division evidently considered the visit an unwanted burden which was not part of their regular duties. After a stay of two weeks the European visitor, who, to be sure, heads a smaller local unit, found that he had barely managed to do nine hours of work, or the equivalent of about one full working day out of ten or twelve.

This brings us to the time element involved in visits. The travels of top executives are more often than not unscheduled, undertaken on short notice, or undertaken as a surprise visit, combined with a vacation or pleasure trip. The abuse is widespread, and little, if anything, is accomplished on such trips. By contrast, combining home leave with visits to headquarters by the American executive stationed in Europe has the advantage of saving time and expense—but only if the trip is well prepared and scheduled well in advance, and not considered merely an extension of home leave. Visits by the VP or general manager–international and by the regional manager are usually made according to a regular schedule, and while the local manager and his staff may or may not look forward to these visits, the timetable and customary agenda provide a certain feeling of security. Thus several times a year there is an opportunity to exchange questions and answers, complaints and promises, and inquiries and instructions that, if conducted in an atmosphere of mutual confidence and cooperation, create a healthy operational climate.

The ad hoc visits of staff department executives from the United States to Europe and vice versa require preparations on both sides if they are to be successful. It is frustrating for one to find that the other is either unprepared or unable to discuss matters that the first considers important. In such cases visits not only do not expedite, they delay, local operations. Some strong regional offices, therefore, coordinate all travels by subsidiary executives. As a result, these executives must either have approval of their travel plans or must advise the European office ahead of time and wait for acceptance of their suggested timetable. In the first instance they have to prove that the trip is really necessary; in the second, they must adjust it to the time available.

A few powerful regional and local managers have attained a status that allows them to question the usefulness of visits by corporate executives, other than the top men. In such cases a corporate staff member will have to ask the regional or local manager for approval of his proposed trip. In exchange for this courtesy he can then expect full cooperation. The questions involved here are not only those of intracompany status and protocol, but also those concerning the borderlines between line, dotted-line, and staff relationships, and those involving the practical necessity of restricting excessive and unessential travels. The American secretary of an American chamber of commerce in one of the larger European countries stated flatly that there are far too many visits from U.S. headquarters to local subsidiaries, with the result that subsidiary executives waste valuable time showing the visitors around. Some subsidiary managers were more specific and said that there are too many useless and too few fruitful visits.

A few executives believed that visits at regular intervals are not required and should be undertaken only when absolutely necessary. "My area manager has not been here for 18 months," said one of them, "because we have at present no problems that would require his presence." This of course means a lack of strict supervision and control and a tendency toward considerable local autonomy, either as a general company policy or as an outgrowth of personal trust in an experienced subsidiary manager of proven ability. As with so many other subjects discussed in this report, the question of how many visits should be undertaken boils down to the general question of how much management control is to be exercised and where, when, and how. Another point to be taken into account is that of traveling costs and to whom they will be charged. Obviously, they must be measured and justified by the results. Many experts believe that fewer but longer visits are preferable. It is an often-heard complaint by local managers that visitors from America schedule visits that are much too short to achieve the desired results. The following is a typical schedule and a moderate one:

- The corporate president or executive VP—once a year, but only to the regional office and a few selected subsidiaries.
- The president–international—once or twice a year, alternating between the places to be visited.
- The international VP–marketing—regularly twice a year.
- The European regional manager—twice a year to New York and at least once a year to every subsidiary.

Companies new to Europe sometimes visit their new subsidiaries too little, leaving them without proper guidance and information. On the other hand, sometimes their visits are too frequent—and then they are nearly always too short and inadequately prepared. Exploratory visits to conduct preliminary market research, investigations for acquisitions, or the establishment of subsidiaries are not undertakings for hurried chief executives. An American corporation president may not be as gullible as the Russian empress Catherine II, for whom her chancellor, Prince Gregor Potemkin, built beautiful-looking pasteboard villages on both banks of the Volga River for her edification when she traveled downstream to inspect her realm. Yet such "Potemkin villages," as they have been known in Europe ever since, have frequently been erected along the paths traveled by visiting American top executives.

To avoid such incidents, the Spanish associate of an American law firm suggests that at the time of acquisition, and afterward, when legal disputes arise or important tax matters have to be ironed out, key men from the corporate legal and financial departments, accompanied by other experts, come to Europe for conferences with local counsel. Such visits may be rather expensive, but they will prevent costly surprises and save money in the long run.

LANGUAGE—OVERCOMING A FUNDAMENTAL OBSTACLE

Most U.S. companies come to realize sooner or later that there is only one way to solve language difficulties, and that is to learn the other man's language. The use of interpreters and translators is a poor substitute, and therefore, the solution is to teach the Americans the relevant foreign language and the foreigners English.

In the Netherlands, the northern part of Belgium, Denmark, Norway, and Sweden, almost every businessman and professional knows English well, and most younger people with a high school degree speak it fairly well. Therefore, only someone who deals with non-English-speaking personnel, such as an American plant manager or factory executive, would have to learn the national language. In Germany, Switzerland, and Austria, well-educated younger men usually speak or at least understand English, but this does not extend to the age group over 40. In France, Italy, and Spain, knowledge of the national language is essential for any American. The same applies to most Latin American countries, but to a varying extent.

Most companies with long experience in Europe require from all their subsidiary personnel above the level of lower middle management a good knowledge of both English and the national language. How far down the ladder English is required of subsidiary staff members varies greatly. It normally depends on three conditions.

1. The more centralized a corporation is, and the tighter its control over subsidiaries abroad, the more communications by mail, cable, telephone, and Telex will flow in both directions and consequently the more important fluency in English will be on all local levels.

2. If control of foreign subsidiaries is exercised mainly by the office of the VP–International, who may be multilingual himself or have a couple of multilingual secretaries, knowledge of English at the subsidiaries need not be too broad; but if the international manager delegates duties in part to his staff or shares them with corporate staff departments, then direct, straight, or dotted-line relationships exist between corresponding staff members on the home office and local levels, involving many more people on both sides in mutual communications. The result is that all these men in the subsidiaries must be able to read, write, and speak English, because few, if any, of their counterparts in America are able to understand the national languages. This is even more accentuated when dotted-line relationships exist with product groups, particularly when they exercise part or full control over foreign operations.

3. When a strong decision-making regional office exists in Europe through which most communications flow, it will probably be able to communicate at least in the four principal languages of Western, Central, and Southern Europe. It may even translate some reports in abridged form for the home office, and therefore the knowledge of English in the local units can be confined to the managerial level. Letters and telephone conversations between local staff members and their regional colleagues can for the most part be in the national languages.

Communication problems between U.S. headquarters and European subsidiaries are diminished considerably if some of their international executives are multilingual and multicultural. Such men—whom several experts referred to as "the new breed"—have lived, studied, and worked from an early age in several countries. They are not only thoroughly familiar with various languages and national customs, but also feel at home in a number of countries. Since these executives have an intensive knowledge of European business conditions, they are able to contribute greatly to the establishment of sound relations on all levels of the multinational corporation.

4. Tight Versus Loose Control Relationships

Dᴜʀɪɴɢ the nineteenth century, when a mill owner in Massachusetts decided to establish his own sales office in New York and appointed his first salesman as its manager, he had two choices: He could instruct the new branch manager to report regularly to him as before, and to follow his orders in all matters, or he could let him run his own show. If the mill owner was daring enough to later open a second branch in say, Pittsburgh, he probably had to give the Pittsburgh branch manager substantial latitude, because the latter could not be expected to travel the long distance from branch to factory more than once or twice a year. In some respects the international situation today is comparable, but in many other respects the problems are so much more complex that it is difficult to compare the branch operation problems of the nineteenth century with those of the twentieth.

Today's mill owner is the president of a large multinational corporation, and he no longer has only two choices in his relationship with foreign branches; he has many. Between the extremes of complete local autonomy and strict centralized control, there is a wide gray area of intermediate possibilities. It has been pointed out that control relationships are changing rapidly and that they are subject to a great many external and internal pressures. Moreover, control relationships no longer exist between one man at the top and another man farther down the ladder, but between several higher and lower levels and many people on those levels. Loose or tight control are relative terms and refer to various activities within regular business operations.

Vᴀʀɪᴀʙʟᴇꜱ ɪɴ Cᴏɴᴛʀᴏʟ Rᴇʟᴀᴛɪᴏɴꜱʜɪᴘꜱ

Which are the variables that decisively affect control relationships between American corporations and their foreign subsidiaries, in what direction do they influence or modify controls, and how are these differences put into practice? Some of these variables are inherent in the corporation, such as type of industry and personalities of top management. They may change the intensity of control over foreign subsidiaries from time to time. Other variables refer to particular characteristics of one subsidiary as compared to another and cause unequal control situations in the same corporation.

Size of Subsidiary and Market

The most significant factor influencing the degree of autonomy normally granted to local management is the size and importance of the subsidiary and its market. Usually, but not always, they correspond. However, strange as it may seem at first glance, the larger or smaller size of the local unit can have exactly the opposite effect depending on corporate policies and practices.

In many companies, the smaller subsidiary with limited business volume and fewer activities will be less strictly controlled by headquarters, especially by the international division or product group in the United States.

A local manager in Portugal explained that while company manuals provide for tight control of most of his activities, in practice Chicago does not bother him too much, simply because it must devote most of its time to the larger units where the big business is, and where the risks are therefore greater. It just is not worthwhile for the staff of the international division to exercise strict control, which requires a lot of work that can better be applied elsewhere. For reasons unknown to the author, the executive, who was formerly the manager of his company's British subsidiary, had been transferred to Lisbon and now has more freedom of action than he had in London.

By contrast, other corporations—as a rule the older and more sophisticated ones—give more authority to larger, fully organized subsidiaries that have adequate staff and facilities, particularly where controls are in the hands of a regional office in Europe. The dollar ceiling under which local management can make expenditures (within the approved budget) without special authorization usually varies according to the subsidiary's size and business volume. It is hardly ever the same in Britain, France, and Germany on the one hand, as in Denmark, Austria, and Portugal on the other. The larger subsidiary is normally also the older one, and it has already proved its ability to produce a profit. It has also developed the necessary staff for handling several major functions that therefore no longer have to be provided or guided by higher echelons, such as accounting, credit policy, and many aspects of marketing and market research.

A local executive in Switzerland described the different treatment of subsidiaries by headquarters very simply and clearly: "Theoretically all are equal, but in practice the large subsidiary in an important market carries more weight." And a regional marketing manager explained:

> In all our local units the same objectives must be attained *commensurate* with their possibilities. The larger subsidiaries are naturally better staffed and can therefore take over more responsibilities without help from Zurich. Also, they will usually have stronger executives with more experience who can exercise or supervise such extended functions and who can also make themselves more listened to at headquarters. Our approach to management control is therefore flexible.

The size and importance of a subsidiary cannot be judged as an isolated factor in the control relationship. They are closely linked with other variables, such as the age of the subsidiary, geographic location, economic and political environment, legal structure, and management.

In those corporations that have reorganized their international business according to product groups, other considerations play an important role. A big subsidiary in a large market often handles only the products of one group and therefore reports to only one product division instead of several, or it reports directly to this division and not to the regional office or international division. In both cases it will have wider autonomy, because the product group is normally interested chiefly in production or in production and marketing, but much less in all other spheres of activity with which the local unit is concerned. Even if regional headquarters retains jurisdiction over some of these operations, such as finance, auditing, or key personnel, its supervisory power is somewhat diminished.

The greater authority vested in the large subsidiary with an elaborate organization, extended functions, and numerous staff personnel, is a consequence of growth and will be attained only gradually. Like all growth it will not always be painless and smooth. Local executives often believe that their unit has already achieved a degree of importance that entitles them to more authority, indeed makes greater autonomy necessary. Regional and corporate executives may think otherwise. It might take a change of management on these levels to grant more autonomy—or to let the subsidiary exercise it without objection.

Age of Subsidiary

The older subsidiary is usually also a large one, but even if for historical reasons the older subsidiaries were established in smaller markets or if a later unit grew faster than its older colleagues, there is a natural tendency to give the senior subsidiaries special privileges or to allow them an autonomy not granted to newer units. The first subsidiary manager has by now most probably been replaced by a younger and less experienced man, but the privileged status of the local firm is still justified because of long established local contacts with government agencies, customers, dealers, and consumers, a certain tradition reflected by the personnel, greater efficiency caused by elimination of unworkable practices over the years, and adjustment to local conditions. There is a tendency at headquarters, particularly where no European office exists or where the old subsidiary is not under its jurisdiction, to assume that all problems have been solved long ago and that the old firm can take care of itself. Besides, its middle management, which is the stable element amid constant change, is well known to the home office, and many people at the subsidiary wear the corporation's ten- or twenty-five-year pin.

Distance and the Environment

The trend toward stricter control is often attributed to shrinking distances—that is, to better transportation and communication. It stands to reason that subsidiaries far away and hard to reach still enjoy greater autonomy within many corporations than those close to the home office or to regional headquarters. For the same reason regional managers stationed in Europe normally have more autonomy than those stationed at the home office. The subsidiary manager in a distant country must often make decisions that cannot wait for the visit of a higher ranking executive from headquarters, and there are questions that cannot be decided by Telex, telephone, or cable.

Furthermore, the international general manager or VP is reluctant to take a trip to some faraway place that takes too much of his time, where no other subsidiaries are nearby, and where the business volume does not warrant the time and expense. By contrast, should the subsidiary be only a few hours flying time from the home office—and perhaps located in Mexico City, Paris, or London—the local manager must expect frequent scheduled and unscheduled visits from the chairman of the board down to junior corporate and international staff members—and all of them will want to justify their trip by making observations and suggestions.

Distance, however, is not only a geographic or aeronautical fact, measurable in miles or hours; it is in many cases psychological. In companies with headquarters in the Middle West or in California, even Lisbon or Rome may seem very far. Home offices located in or near big international trade centers like New York, Chicago, or New Orleans are likely to consider their Western European or Central American subsidiaries reasonably near, while many of the companies located in small midwestern or southern towns look upon such markets as being very far away indeed.

In fact, it is often not so much distance that counts most, but rather the political, economical, and cultural environment of the market and its business climate.

In an unfamiliar market area, where local conditions for marketing, production, personnel policy, and most other activities are entirely different from conditions in the United States, headquarters executives normally feel somewhat unsure of themselves. They therefore think that they have to grant considerable leeway to local management. In Northern Europe, on the other hand, life does not appear basically too different from life in America, and visiting corporate executives are inclined to underestimate differences and difficulties, and therefore to insist that centralized instructions be followed to the letter. Mexico, Venezuela, South Africa, Australia, and New Zealand all fall into this category, as do the United Kingdom, Scandinavia, Germany, Switzerland, and the Low Countries. By contrast, an American subsidiary manager in Spain reported he enjoys much greater autonomy than the managers of larger and older company units in other parts of Europe.

Political, social, and economic stability form the ideal background for the development of American business abroad. When this stability exists, foreign operations can be as closely directed as domestic ones. But financial and personnel restrictions in Switzerland, political and social unrest in France, devaluation in Britain, all of which occurred in recent years, caused at least temporary difficulties for American business interests. But while important decisions had to be made at the highest corporate level, they nevertheless did not require immediate, forceful, and far-reaching action by local management.

By contrast, in countries where political upheavals, sudden currency fluctuations and restrictions, and changes in import regulations—to name but a few—can and do happen overnight, local management must be prepared for instant action. Many American companies learned this lesson to their regret in Cuba and in the Middle East. A lack of stability therefore requires strengthened local responsibility, which efficient subsidiary management in such countries must be willing and able to assume, and which farseeing top management must be equally ready to grant. And it must do this as a matter of policy, rather than granting too little authority too late. The rapidity of basic changes in certain less industrialized countries must be matched by an equal rapidity in company decisions. Experience has shown that only local management, provided it is adequately led and staffed, is able to make decisions fast enough.

Legal Conditions

The legal form under which the foreign affiliate operates is particularly important for control relationships between it and the U.S. corporation. Even where majority participation or a management contract assures the U.S. company of major influence in joint ventures, the local firm's general manager nearly always has greater autonomy than a subsidiary or branch manager. His legal responsibilities, his duty to report to a local board, cannot be overlooked. He may or may not at times overstress his dependence on several partners, which is tantamount to a good deal of independence from all of them, but in any case he can hardly ever be as strictly directed as his colleagues in wholly owned subsidiaries or branches. He is perhaps subject to considerable pressures as a former and future executive of the American company, but such influences are outside the joint venture. The local manager has more room for maneuvering if he chooses, and he has a stronger position in intracompany politics if he uses it skillfully.

Moreover, it is sometimes difficult for the American corporation to determine just which suggestions and initiatives and which objections to corporate decisions stem from local partners and which from the local manager himself, who must officially represent all interests and still maintain harmony.

While the legal form of the local firm's incorporation and the laws and regulations governing its operations have a marked influence on control relationships with the American corporation, so do many other legal requirements of the host country. Foremost among them is the tax structure. Where company taxes are based on individual interpretations or on explanations furnished to the national internal revenue administration—and this sometimes practically amounts to negotiating or bargaining with the government—it is best to grant local management the necessary authority to supply explanations and conduct negotiations. It will do this with the assistance of local counsel and competent subsidiary executives who are nationals or longtime residents.

Any subsidiary that, owing to the host country's laws and to special industry situations, needs regular government permits and licenses because of import quotas, exchange regulations, expansion of facilities or manpower, and numerous other regulated operations, must have the authority to negotiate for these permits. It is bad practice, though this is not always realized, to refer government officials to authorizations expected from the home office or to telephone conversations that the subsidiary manager will have with headquarters.

Another important consideration should be brought into focus here. As is well known, there was a time when complaints from some governments and many newspapers were directed against the American practice of staffing foreign subsidiaries with U.S. citizens; later, the clamor was for appointing nationals not only to middle management, but also to leading managerial positions; now, criticism is leveled at the practice of assigning so little authority to these national subsidiary managers. It is sometimes asserted that they are managers in name only, that they have no real decision-making power, and that American subsidiaries abroad are managed by remote control from the home office. It is said that local boards of directors, whether or not European executives have seats and voices on them, exercise purely formal legal functions, that the local manager reports to them only technically, and that the really important actions often deeply affecting the national economy of a smaller nation follow instructions from American headquarters. Only a few American corporations have so far reacted effectively to these accusations.

Qualifications of a Subsidiary Manager

By far the most important influence on differential control relationships within a corporation is that of the local (or regional) manager. His experience, years of service, background, character, diplomatic skill, friendly relations with key men and staff members at headquarters, the trust and esteem in which he is held at home—all these can make a world of difference in his authority.

"Not much authority is granted to local managers in our company," said one deputy managing director in Geneva, "and most decision making is concentrated in London. But this is only theory and what the directives say officially. In practice, a forceful, experienced manager like my immediate superior has much greater autonomy than on paper. He may even be consulted—unofficially, of course—in matters outside his jurisdiction due to his knowledge and the respect he has earned over many years among regional and corporate top people. Thus company policies are consistent from country to country but their interpretation and implementation vary greatly in accordance with size and other characteristics of the subsidiary, and above all with the personality of its manager."

The general manager of a pharmaceutical corporation's Belgian subsidiary stated the identical facts in a slightly different way: "All local managers are required to submit the same reports to regional headquarters, but it can be said that a man with a strong personality and wide experience files many of his reports for information only, not for approval."

Experience should of course be measured both as to length of service with the corporation, particularly at the international level, and length of service as an executive in the subsidiary or in a neighboring and somewhat similar market. Actually, however, even domestic service with the corporation will add stature and thus enable the executive to exercise more authority.

It is often claimed that corporations just do not want to give their foreign subsidiary managers enough power to run the local business efficiently. That is certainly true in some cases, but it must also be pointed out that sometimes corporate or international top management, and the European office as well, do not feel that a local executive can handle his functions without constant guidance and supervision from higher echelons. He may have been selected because of an excellent technical background, financial expertise, proven salesmanship, or an ability "to get things done" or to get along with people and to direct subordinates, and he may still not have what it takes to handle a business with authority and independence.

It can therefore be understood why a staff member of an important subsidiary told the author that his company "was glad to give a new manager much more responsibility than his predecessor ever enjoyed," because the company soon saw that the new man, who had sufficient previous experience, could exercise authority and take responsibility in a way the former manager could not. In fact, at the top of the list of criteria for vesting more authority in a local manager, many of those interviewed put this: successful management and complete confidence on the part of top executives.

Some regional managers consider it one of their most important duties to educate those local managers who need it to the use of greater authority and the exercise of more responsibilities. For that purpose they may at first supervise them rather strictly and only gradually reduce control measures. Not every regional or international manager, however, is magnanimous enough to grant more independence and thereby diminish his own authority. Where this *is* being practiced, it is done on a strictly individual basis for those who deserve it.

The great advantage of this individually tailored system of managerial responsibility is its flexibility—that is, the acknowledgment that no two subsidiaries and no two subsidiary managers are completely alike. The great disadvantage of increasing—or reducing—authority in relation to the personality is that while objective yardsticks can be used, such as profit and loss statements over a given period or the market share, these are often influenced by outside factors over which the manager has little control. Highly subjective evaluations of the local manager's performance often carry greater weight. Under these circumstances personal friendships, likes and dislikes, preferences for superficial character traits, and nepotism can easily work to the detriment of company morale—but then, all this is hardly confined to international operations.

The situation becomes serious when subsidiary executives who are

Europeans contend that those of their colleagues who are Americans usually enjoy greater autonomy because the company trusts them more. In some cases such statements are tempered by conciliatory explanations, as: "Our manager in Paris is more independent because he is an American *and* has worked for the company in the States. He therefore knows company procedures better than our manager here in Holland." Yet sometimes a respondent clearly felt that he and his superior were discriminated against because they were Europeans. These personal impressions, whether justified or not, easily spread beyond company limits and find their way into the local press, public opinion, and into political circles. They can be extremely damaging.

Operational Differences

Finally, the operations in which the subsidiary is engaged to some extent shape control relationships. All other factors being equal, a manufacturing unit is usually more strictly controlled than a marketing subsidiary because production is more amenable to centralized direction, and engineers and technicians adhere more firmly to standards and regulations. The degree of control varies with the degree of product uniformity achieved or intended in a corporation or in a product division. In newly acquired plants that continue under their former management and manufacture their old product lines, the trend is reversed and their production is quite independent—as long as no new products or processes are being introduced by the parent company.

The characteristics distinguishing one subsidiary (or its manager) from another rarely, if ever, can be found alone. Rather they are usually linked, as has been already mentioned. A large and important subsidiary is often also an old one and headed by a strong, experienced manager. A distant subsidiary is frequently at the same time situated in an unfamiliar market which may lack stability and be governed by a number of import and currency restrictions. In these cases the cumulative effect of several variables pointing in the same direction strengthens the trend toward greater local autonomy.

By contrast, a big and well-organized subsidiary may be situated in a country close to headquarters (Mexico, for example) while many small and neglected units are located far away but are young. A new and inexperienced manager is sometimes sent to a distant and unfamiliar country, simply because the position is not very desirable. In these cases the various factors act in opposite directions and may cancel each other out.

Moreover, all market, subsidiary, and personal characteristics are subject to constant change. Small subsidiaries grow; distances shrink; previously stable countries suffer revolutions and economic crises; previously unstable ones straighten out both their form of government and their economy; and finally, old and experienced local managers are promoted or retire and young executives move up. Also, the de facto exceptions granted to some subsidiaries and some managers under one top executive may be radically curtailed under a new one.

Incidentally, some of the variables discussed in the preceding paragraphs, particularly those connected with the personality of the executive, refer not only to subsidiaries, but also to area and regional managers. However, in their case the wider or narrower authority given to them by the home office is usually spelled out in job descriptions, directives, or letters accompanying their appointment. Local managers, on the other hand, enjoy greater autonomy or suffer stricter controls than some of their colleagues as a matter of practice, not because of anything specified in writing. This leads some critics to underestimate or even to deny the existence of differing controls.

A partner in an American-international accounting firm declared that flexibility in directing and supervising local units is sorely needed, but that it is usually missing in U.S. multinational corporations, "where all subsidiaries are treated in the same standardized way." He added that local conditions, the size and age of the subsidiary, and primarily the manager's efficiency, should determine how much more or less authority should be officially delegated. He said that for a capable and experienced local executive it is frustrating (and at the same time damaging to the best interests of the company) to have to refer every decision back to headquarters for approval, however urgent it may be. On the other hand, it may be equally bad for a new and untried manager to have powers that he cannot yet exercise with adequate self-assurance.

Obviously, the gentleman did not know that the flexibility he thinks so desirable already exists to a large extent in many corporations, although very seldom *de jure*. A French advertising executive with an American education put the matter clearly when he said: "The corporation manual is the bible and every local manager has to stick to it, but the bible can be interpreted in different ways, can it not?"

The View from Headquarters

The questionnaire sent out to many American corporations with foreign subsidiaries at the beginning of this research project asked a question about the determination of policies. Then it asked:

> Are these policies relatively consistent from country to country or do they vary in accordance with:
> Size of subsidiary

Function of subsidiary
Type (legal form) of subsidiary
Executive in charge of subsidiaries
Length of time within corporation
Laws of country in which located
Taxes of country in which located
Political characteristics of country
Socioeconomic characteristics of country
Other criteria (specify)

The overwhelming majority of participants indicated that their policies in control matters were consistent and did not change from one subsidiary to another. This confirms what the author subsequently found out during his interviews in Europe: The "policies" as officially recognized by corporate management are not modified in theory. However, the interpretation or application of such policies varies greatly and shows a good deal of flexibility, which official manuals and directives do not. This was only revealed during conversations in the field.

Only an insignificant number of respondents listed several variables and acknowledged their influence. The international treasurer of one large corporation added this: "Some [policies] are consistent—such as those related but not limited to finance, accounting, and acquisitions—some are not. It depends on the nature of the area covered by the policies, and the factors [variables] noted here."

To the questions "Which of these policies have changed during the past decade? How and why have they changed?" most participants replied affirmatively, acknowledging that control policies are not constant in time. The answers reflect the trend toward stricter control, the establishment of a European regional office or a shift of controls from the home office to the regional level, faster travel and communication facilities, adjustment to environmental changes, reorganization along product group lines, and several other developments in international management. Perhaps the best and most comprehensive reply was: "No policies are rigidly fixed; they are kept adapted to the changing times and the evolution of both the parent company and the international organization."

CONTROL VERSUS AUTONOMY

The treasurer and assistant to the general manager of an automotive corporation's subsidiary had a concise answer when asked what would happen should there be a disagreement between local management and New York headquarters in a matter where New York had been consulted. "Our people at the overseas corporation know local conditions well, and they have their policy directives. Therefore, there is no use arguing with them. You explain your point of view and then you just follow instructions."

This remark illustrates a trend in the control relationship between headquarters and subsidiary, especially where no resident regional manager operates in Europe. As long as a market is not well known at the home office, control is likely to be loose and hesitant, because headquarters does not have the basis for making correct decisions. Once headquarters acquires this knowledge through frequent personal contacts, through an adequate flow of information, and by employing home office executives with working experience in foreign markets, it can and often will exercise stronger control. "Educating the home office people and constantly explaining to them local market conditions is one of the main tasks of the subsidiary manager," said one such manager, "even if by so doing he helps them to exercise more decision-making power—if this is or becomes company policy. At least, such decisions will be more acceptable to local management."

There are many other reasons for the trend toward stricter control seen by a number of experts, particularly in the field. Others, mostly at headquarters and in schools of business administration, see a trend in the opposite direction—to more autonomy at the local level. The author leans toward the former opinion and believes that sometimes what may be desirable is confused with what is actually happening; and that what seems to be the right thing to say is substituted for what the unbiased observer really sees or could see if he were to look closely enough.

One thing seems to be almost universally accepted: the lack of a common approach. As one experienced American expert put it:

> There is no general pattern even among corporations of the same industry and size, regarding strict control or certain degrees and areas of autonomy. Control relationships depend on too many variables, such as corporate history and tradition, structure and development, personalities and their backgrounds. Each company develops its own way of conducting its international business and even the same methods result in quite diverging procedural forms due to basically different attitudes prevailing at a given time, while identical ideas and intentions lead to dissimilar patterns because of differences in business environment. It is therefore very wrong for a corporation to imitate what another is doing in intracompany relationships, because the essential circumstances can never be the same. Many have found out to their regret that systems that have worked well for some have failed for others.

This executive also had a word of advice for companies that intend to modify their international organization—namely, caution. "A corporation which is not satisfied with its foreign subsidiaries," he said, "should lift a particular problem area out of the multitude of doubtful activities, patterns, or operations and study the way others have solved this special question, without adopting immediately the entire structure of the other corporation. For a second or third unsatisfactory area the example of still another company can be followed or modified." This means that stricter subsidiary control could be instituted in one or two specific fields of local activity, while others can be left unchanged. Some controls could even be relaxed. This, however, rarely happens.

Shrinking Space and Time

The reason most often mentioned for moving to closer control of subsidiaries and regional offices by American headquarters is the development of jet transportation, air mail, transatlantic telephone, and Telex. When travel took at least two weeks and air mail still longer, and when telephone connections were unreliable, local managers had to have considerable freedom of action and independence, because in many instances they could not wait for approval or advice from the home office. They had to have strong personalities with the will and the ability to make decisions. An advertising executive in Germany compared these men of the early days, few of whom are now still around, with Roman consuls in faraway provinces of the empire, or British governors in the Far East and Africa, who acted like independent princes. They had their manuals, to be sure, but actually they did not need them, because through a long tradition they were imbued with the "right" way of thinking and acting. Moreover, they did not have to make their decisions amid the complexities of the present day. They stayed for many years at their posts and often built up their own small empires. As long as they were successful, nobody at home cared.

Then came the time of fast transportation and communications, and basic conditions changed. However, many international trade experts believe that American business overestimated the depth and consequences of these changes—that is, the immediate effects of shrinking time and space. They did not realize that the internationality of the human mind is very much behind the international development of technology. With the advent of faster transportation and communications, the pendulum naturally swung from complete decentralization and lack of control to the opposite extreme. But it has since swung back again in some cases to a somewhat intermediate position.

The metaphor of the pendulum was used by several participants, but its position on the scale was described in various ways. Some executives asserted that in their companies the pendulum had swung back and forth several times during the past 50, or 30, or even 10 years. A few also stated it had finally come to an almost stable position somewhere in the middle, which they believe to be a sign of growing knowledge, understanding, and maturity.

A similar view was expressed by an American bank manager and by other experts. They expressed the thought that every company, in its international development, has to pass through a period of trial and error until it finds the balance between control and autonomy that is just right for it—and in some cases it must do so several times, because its environment changes. One bank officer said that even complete failures and subsequent withdrawals from the international scene have to be expected as natural byproducts of a complex, diversified, and difficult series of experiments that by and large have been highly successful. An executive in one of the oldest American corporations operating in Europe phrased the same thought this way: "Every company must learn through its own mistakes and make the coat fit the person."

Growth

Another factor that has strongly contributed to tighter control is the constant growth and development of subsidiaries. Before World War II, they were mostly small or medium-size and rather isolated from the parent company and from each other, whether they were acquisitions of existing European firms or newly established. They were like the ranchers in the old West who had plenty of elbow room and a good deal of independence. Gradually, however, the number of local units within the corporation grew and their activities expanded until it became necessary to protect them from mutual intrusions, and to coordinate and regulate their export business, their supplies and purchases, the movement of their key personnel, and above all their share in the corporation's overall resources. This naturally meant considerable restrictions in local autonomy.

And it is an undeniable fact that control is contagious. It increases automatically and spreads easily from one sphere to another. On the other hand, steadily growing business volume increases the responsibilities of the local manager. Even when his decision-making power is taken away in certain areas, the remaining activities offer numerous opportunities to exercise his authority. In other words, he may now have less independence, but the number and importance of his decisions may be greater because the business has expanded. The degree of his autonomy is lessened, but the volume of his authority is increased. He can no longer make any financial or legal decisions on his own, but he directs a vastly enlarged staff and serves many more customers with more products, greater facilities, and better service.

While the preceding considerations may explain the trend toward stricter control, there is always a possibility that such control will be introduced before it is necessary or advisable. An American executive in Belgium described management relationships in his company: "Everything is now completely centralized, but I wonder whether this is the right approach at the right time, because we have not yet enough men with international experience at headquarters, which is a precondition for strict centralization."

The Common Market

The development of the Common Market is also a strong factor favoring centralization and strict control. It is generally agreed that American corporations were ahead of European industry in seeing the advantages of the European Economic Community (EEC) for business expansion. In fact, it is frequently alleged that they overestimated these opportunities or in any case, the speed of their development. The actual or anticipated creation of one single large unified market instead of four or five smaller markets separated by tariff barriers and many other restrictions made it necessary to rearrange production and distribution according to new principles. These principles involve the location of manufacturing where it can be done most economically regardless of national boundaries. Such considerations may eventually also bring about a reorganization of marketing along regional rather than country lines. All this leads to a restriction of local autonomy and to a shift of decision making to headquarters, preferably to regional headquarters in Europe.

Levels of Performance

And then there is, of course, a very old and common reason for diminishing the local manager's authority and putting him under tighter control: unsatisfactory performance or failure to conform with company policies. There is, naturally, another alternative: to replace him, and this has been done and is still being done quite frequently. Chances are, however, that the successor may not perform substantially better, and it is becoming increasingly difficult to find the right man, fully qualified, whether American, national, or third-country citizen. One answer is to change the control pattern for the subsidiary that has evidenced shortcomings, but, as already mentioned, stricter controls are contagious. The higher echelon that got the green light from top management to exercise tighter controls will sooner or later expand them to all subsidiaries, except perhaps those where a high-ranking, very successful, strongly entrenched manager has enough power to resist them. Incidentally, many experts argue that ever stricter controls stifle local initiative and are therefore counterproductive, and that a really capable man will not accept a managerial position where he is prevented from using the full range of his abilities. As an outstanding and veteran American executive in London put it:

> A good manager wants responsibility. He also wants to make a success of his unit. He does not cherish the idea of having to ask permission for every important step from people who often know less than he does, especially regarding the local situation, and who can give him orders only because they are at the power center. The subsidiary manager does not like the requirement of having to explain several times, often to two or three levels, the reasons for suggesting certain actions.

> Therefore, American companies which centralize all authority at headquarters or at the regional office and leave no decision making to subsidiary management, will have to be content with second-best people on the local level—that is with bureaucrats, rather than with aggressive, imaginative executives. A good administrator or marketing man or production specialist or financial expert with experience and proven ability will not accept a job where he has to get approval for every step, or if he does, he will quit as soon as he can get a more suitable position elsewhere.

Some companies may indeed put strong, capable men in charge of one or two major subsidiaries and give them adequate autonomy. These important subsidiaries may also directly report to the international division or to product groups or even to the chief executive in the United States. For the other, less important, units, the company is perhaps satisfied to have local managers who belong to middle management rather than to the ranks of executives and who actually work as employees of the regional office where the decision-making power is concentrated. Because this includes day-to-day operations, the regional manager is thus the only real executive. This system is predicated on the assumption that the operations in certain European markets can effectively be directed from Brussels or Frankfurt and do not need a full-fledged independent organization in every country.

Several local managers favored vesting strong authority in the regional office even if it meant it would then exercise stricter control over local units. They frequently expressed the view that a large American corporation with extended operations in all European markets needs a powerful regional manager, particularly in a highly competitive business with quick market changes. They realize that under such circumstances they will hardly be granted important decision-making authority in any case, and therefore prefer that it be given to the European office rather than retained by U.S. headquarters.

In fact, from the standpoint of the local manager it is often more important how control is exercised, than how much. For the subsidiary manager, autonomy is a desirable status symbol that enhances his standing within the corporation and thereby also furthers his chances for advancement, but it is almost equally important for his standing in the local American or British-American community and thereby may increase his possibilities to obtain a better position elsewhere. Psychological and practical considerations go hand in hand. Therefore, if the local executive cannot have the degree of autonomy to which he aspires, he wants at least the appearance of such a powerful position. That is why in dealings with local lawyers, banks, advertising and market research agencies, personnel consultants, and others, some executives try to overstate their authority.

Some corporations are well aware of this situation and help the local manager to appear in a more powerful and glamorous position than they actually allow him to enjoy. Europeans are particularly sensitive in this respect and those in middle management or junior executive positions like the American system tremendously because it means they do not have to obtain permission for every routine matter from their immediate superior, can sign their own letters, can often directly contact regional or even corporate executives, and are consulted by them. These privileges simply do not exist in the average European company.

This greater independence on lower levels is mistaken by some European writers for actual decision-making power and is falsely called "American decentralization." A European subsidiary manager who does not have thorough American training hardly ever gives to his subordinates these outward tokens of independence. On the other hand, he is also not used to the American system of decision making—or at least decision preparing— by committees. Moreover, he is not on intimate terms with many people at headquarters. For these reasons he is willing to take more decisions upon himself, provided he is capable and self-confident. His company may get along with him or "let him get away with it" as long as everything goes well. But when shortcomings become evident or profits decline—not necessarily through the fault of the local manager—someone at the home office will investigate (superficially) and the subsidiary manager will be sternly told that he exceeded his authority or violated rules and regulations according to the manual or job description that the European executive never fully understood anyway. These views were given to the author in a large American advertising and consulting firm in London. They may have to be taken with a grain of salt, but there are probably many elements of truth in them.

Advantages of Reasonable Controls

An advertising executive in Switzerland pointed out that the autonomy of subsidiaries in large corporations, especially where several units exist side by side in the same country, can reach the point where nobody knows —or cares—what either his superiors or his colleagues are doing. In discussing the effects of this laissez faire policy, the executive mentioned the case of a large American corporation whose subsidiary the author had just visited.

> It may seem surprising that the result has not yet been a complete catastrophe, as many theoreticians would expect. But the company is still in business with all its defects. They work like the fish market in Amsterdam, where nothing is organized and the situation appears chaotic. Yet, based on tradition and personal relationships, they still perform their primary function and continue to sell fish.

The question is, however: Can a modern large corporation operate like the Amsterdam fish market without sooner or later losing the competitive race?

During the same interview another executive of the firm discussed the question of new products and new marketing methods:

> The local manager will very likely side with his salesmen, who are frequently against new experiments unless they have been successfully tried somewhere else or a competitor has introduced them before. Salesmen do not want to "waste their time" and managers to impair their profit picture by trying something new when the old can still be sold well enough. Like most European companies, they are prone to take the short-range view. In fact, new products must be test-marketed first, and even this is no guarantee for real success. New production or distribution methods may or may not work out as expected by those who have designed them.

If the parent company wants to go ahead with long-range plans for product development or revised operational methods, it will often have to impose them on reluctant local managers and their staff, and this means strict control. By contrast, if a competitor has been able to increase his market share by introducing better products or improved service, it is local management that will try to shake higher corporate echelons out of their complacency. Centralized control of production and marketing, often without regard to market conditions, may further or hamper progress—and so may local resistance against actions or nonactions handed down from above that are not satisfactorily explained or "sold" to local management.

The "Collegiate System"

Subsidiaries should be treated as members of the family and often have to be educated, but a father-knows-best attitude is not the best educational method. Lower levels will usually admit that the high command has a better overall knowledge of the resources available, but they also know that an understanding of local conditions—that is, an understanding of how to use the resources—can only be gathered from the field.

The authoritarian approach, however, has been abandoned by forward-looking and modern-thinking corporations. They substitute consensus, arrived at through mutual discussion. In a conversation with the author the vice-chairman of the European organization of a giant American corporation referred to this approach as the "collegiate system" and he commented that the best American practices are never imposed by his company.

This most certainly does not mean that every subsidiary manager can do as he pleases, which in fact was pretty much the case with many long-established American corporations in Europe in the years before World War II. It does mean that the corporation takes the time and effort to explain its objectives and to convince the local managers of the soundness of proposed changes. Far from relinquishing centralized control, it is an approach that has signified the exercise of management control in a way that makes use of modern techniques and up-to-date sociology and psychology.

An entirely different story was related by the British member of an American international law firm. Some 20 years ago, a U.S. corporation sent one of its best men to Europe to start operations there. This executive received a contract that included a profit-sharing clause. Due in part to his personal efforts, in part to the favorable conditions after the war, the business developed beyond expectations and he eventually was earning more than the president. He closely supervised all European operations, established subsidiaries, hired their managers and executives, and conducted the business as if it were his own. There was no control or guidance from headquarters and he barely reported at all to the company's chief executive. His responsibilities had never been clearly defined because at the beginning top management was only mildly interested in what it then considered a minor experiment, and only wanted favorable profit and loss statements at year's end—which it got.

Ultimately, however, the company discovered that the executive had been disregarding the few fundamental instructions it had given him. Obviously, these instructions may sometimes have been wrong, because nobody at the home office was familiar with the situation in Europe. On the other hand, the European manager was completely out of touch with developments at home and could never understand certain general corporate policies and objectives, or did not care to understand them. An ultimate showdown became unavoidable, and as a result of it, the executive left. Corporate policy was then completely reversed and today the company is one of the most tightly controlled companies around.

Although an expert was previously quoted as saying that every company in Europe must learn through its own mistakes, this trial and error period can be shortened and its effects eased by obtaining competent advice prior to establishing subsidiaries. The author asked the Italian manager of an American consulting firm what he suggests to such a newcomer. His answer was rather detailed and explicit:

First of all, the company should conduct thorough market research through a competent agency to find out whether and in what form its products can be sold on the local market. Can the products be shipped from the United States or from another European country, or must they be assembled, semimanufactured, or fully produced locally? What is the best location for plant and office? What facilities are necessary?

Then the company through international or local lawyers and tax experts should determine the best legal form for the subsidiary's incorporation in Italy. Now it must hire the local manager, an American with Italian experience, or an Italian. He does not have to come from the ranks of company executives and he does not need a special background in the same industry. (If he has it, so much the better.) He must, however, be able to manage the company's new business, and good men are hard to find. If they are presently employed in a comparable position, they cannot easily be persuaded to change jobs, or only at exorbitant costs. However, a No. 2 man from a larger firm may be willing to become No. 1 in a smaller and younger subsidiary. After careful selection, the man who has been chosen should go to headquarters for training and to become familiar with company policy, products, and procedures.

Now comes the big question: How much authority should the new subsidiary manager be given? A well-qualified man expects and deserves authority. Past experience and company policy in other countries are not necessarily valid yardsticks, because market, job, and personal conditions may be entirely different. The newly appointed local manager should not be granted a free hand, at least not at the beginning; but he ought to receive enough decision-making power to make him use his best efforts and abilities and not to hide behind company directives or the instructions of superiors. He should, however, not be left alone. If he is a national, he should have an American controller or treasurer at his side, not as a supervisor, but as a helper and adviser, also to protect him from undue local influences.

Several American bankers, who often act as consultants for their clients in new ventures, were far more cautious. They hesitate to give a yes or no answer when they are asked whether strict or lenient control is preferable. They point out the many factors to be considered, such as type of industry and corporation, principal markets, personalities on various levels, and quite a few more. In fact, a rigidly uniform policy in management control is neither desirable, nor indeed possible, because too many variables are involved.

STRICT CONTROL OF SUBSIDIARIES

In conducting European interviews, the author never asked a local manager whether he was strictly or loosely controlled by headquarters or whether his authority was limited or extensive. The answers would have been too subjective to be of any great value. Instead, the subsidiary manager was asked several concrete questions about various areas and methods of decision making in his corporation and how they affected his managerial responsibilities. On the basis of this information, admittedly still incomplete and subject to individual interpretations, the author classified the subsidiaries and regional offices visited according to their control relationships. It appears that roughly 40 percent of all units (omitting a few independent organizations) can be considered strictly controlled, about the same percentage under rather loose control, and the remaining 20 percent intermediate, undeterminable, very flexible, or in the midst of change.

Without being specifically asked, some executives disclosed their own assessment of their relationship with headquarters—an assessment not always confirmed by their answers to detailed and precise questions. Replies are often understandably colored by individual feelings of status and prestige or adversely affected by grievances and hostilities.

A Swiss banker remarked that he has American subsidiaries as clients where local management has a great deal of latitude, and others where the subsidiary manager "calls the home office twice daily on the telephone or Telex to get his instructions and approval." Even in the second case there is still a considerable difference between the local executive who takes the initiative, suggests actions, and only asks that they be approved, and the local executive who presents the problem and asks what action he is supposed to take to please his superiors.

In many instances, it is difficult to judge which subsidiary manager has, or feels that he has, less authority: the one who needs approval for most of his decisions but usually gets it without too much delay and too many demands for further clarification, or the one who has to submit fewer matters for authorization but rarely sees his recommendations accepted. The manager of a large pharmaceutical laboratory admitted that a good many questions have to be presented to headquarters for final approval, but he did not seem to mind this restriction of his decision-making power, because normally his suggestions are quickly accepted. He therefore considers this control measure more or less a formality. Yet he pointed out that he would never dare to decide these matters unilaterally.

If, however, all unfavorable factors coincide—a small subsidiary with a limited amount of business activity, a young executive who hesitates to take any initiative and is not encouraged to do so, the obligation to obtain approval for practically all decisions, and a headquarters habit of withholding approval in most cases—then indeed a gloomy atmosphere will pervade the local office. The author came across only a few such offices, however, and in some instances the local manager had hopes that his unhappy situation would improve. It is not surprising that most of these subsidiary managers were second-rate, because no really qualified executive would accept such humiliating conditions. Moreover, because of the low standards, such positions offer only limited compensation, benefits, and possibilities for promotion.

Extreme Cases

In the subsidiary of one important textile company practically every decision on the local level has to be personally approved by the president himself. Even press releases prepared by a local agency need top authorization. While the European business of this corporation is limited, the extremely strict control seems to be the direct result of the chief executive's inability or unwillingness to delegate authority.

Another similar example was that of a large producer of alcoholic beverages whose local manager (in a different country) is nothing but a sales supervisor who visits distributors, has extremely narrow responsibilities, and has neither any decision-making power nor any chance of advancement. He has only a dingy one-room office with one secretary. Equally depressing was the appearance of the tiny storefront office of a third company's local unit. Here too a proud American corporation with coast-to-coast television and magazine advertising is miserably represented by a powerless sales manager who in all respects has to toe the line prescribed by the home office.

Because such American corporations obviously care little about their European business, it is amazing that headquarters takes the time and effort to control all local activities. By contrast, in a medium-size company with a relatively large European business, all decisions, except in a few major subsidiaries, are left to the regional office. But its control is just as stringent. Subsidiary managers are chosen by the regional manager and only confirmed by the home office, and if regional management disapproves of any local suggestions, the subsidiary manager has no redress to the parent company. The present subsidiary manager in one smaller European country nevertheless hopes that within several years he will gain some authority based on his own development and the growth of the local business. Yet if the regional manager remains in his position, a fierce resistance to any real delegation of power to local management seems likely. It could only be broken or softened by a new chief executive of the parent company.

Certain industries are known to lean heavily toward strict centralized control. Cosmetics and pharmaceuticals corporations, for example, often have extremely strict control relationships. However, the impact of rigid control is mitigated by the frequently large business volume and the resulting wide scope of local operations. It is also reduced by chances of promotion for efficient executives who do not stray from the clearly marked path of corporate policy rules. In one of these worldwide toilet goods corporations, the European financial director stated bluntly that what little decision-making power has been relinquished by New York has been delegated to the regional office in London. Practically none has been delegated to local management. The reason given: ". . . to maintain an identical company image and uniform product quality and appearance, as well as rigid conformity to corporate policies in marketing and promotion." The financial director further explained that this strict centralization is both possible and advisable because, at least in this industry, differences between markets are not significant and are being minimized by consumer education. He admitted that in the past there had been a good deal of discussion and dissension among local executives about the usefulness of strict centralized control, but ultimately it seems that they all saw the light—or were fired if they did not.

The truth is that in the cosmetics and pharmaceuticals industries, as well as in a few others—such as oil, photographic products, and electrical appliances—local market variables are nonexistent or very light. Thus arguments against strict control are less frequent. Rigid control in these companies frequently extends to levels below subsidiary management. One local manager admitted frankly that even in lower-level personnel policy his power is extremely limited. But he added: "On the other hand, if I make a personnel decision with prior higher approval, the regional office and headquarters back me up, even if they later find out that I made a mistake. The company is always right on all levels."

Local managers also accept strict control without too much grumbling in those multinational corporations whose headquarters have a lot of international knowledge and whose top executives are familiar with European conditions. In one well-known corporation the Dutch subsidiary manager described very tight control relationships with the parent company, but added that the home office knows market conditions all over Europe well, because the VP–International has lived, worked, and traveled for many years on the Continent. Decisions imposed by the home office are much easier to bear if they are the right ones, made by a superior who is respected for his knowledge and ability.

Similarly, strict uniformity and the resulting equalization of the decision-making process, which eliminates the need for many individual decisions by subsidiary managers, are easier to accept if they are not just forced upon them despite local differences, but are achieved by intelligent planning and hard work. The lack of autonomy is compensated for by the prestige of belonging to a world-famous corporation.

In some industries, small and medium-size companies do not exist or have disappeared—as in the oil industry. Subsidiaries in such industries are usually also strictly controlled by headquarters. This was explained by a local manager as being in the very nature of the business, which is worldwide, needs overall coordination in exploration, production, shipping, and storage, and is extremely sensitive to political and economic disturbances anywhere. Local management must, for example, constantly coordinate its sales and deliveries, its shipping schedules and storage activities with the parent company and through it with numerous other corporate units in order to assure smooth operations. This is particularly important in a highly competitive market like Europe, where oil and natural gas are not only produced but exported and imported, and shipped by tanker, rail, and pipeline. If a strike is expected anywhere, immediate rescheduling of shipments and production is required, as are diversions from one region to another—and this can be handled only on an international basis. Final decision making cannot be left to local managers, but they must have the ability to make split-second suggestions and to exercise strong initiative. It is not an industry in which men can solve their own problems independently, nor is it a business in which people can rely on standing directives. Initiative is not always incompatible with centralized control.

Three Relevant Opinions

The opinions of three outstanding experts conclude—fittingly, it is hoped—this discussion of strict controls. The first expert is a British regional manager of a large American corporation in the recording industry; he has ample authority himself, but keeps a tight rein on the European subsidiaries. He feels that this is necessary to see that local managers understand and follow company policies, to iron out personal and national differences among them, and to guide them in all their activities until they are able to assume greater responsibilities. He acts as a sort of father confessor to impatient junior executives who feel that their immediate superiors do not let them use their own brains and thereby bar their advancement. In such cases the regional manager has a man-to-man talk with the young executive in which he may try to convince him that he is not yet ready for a higher and more independent role. Then again, he may transfer the young man to another country, even against the will of the subsidiary manager, to give the frustrated young staff member a better chance to prove himself.

The regional manager also tries to teach local managers the advantages of strictly adhering to company policies. He "introduces" them, as he put it, to the necessities of more uniformity, more harmony, and consequently more control. He stressed his belief that if possible, a good subsidiary manager should never be forced to do anything against his better judgment, but that he can and should be shown where his judgment needs improvement. In one large manufacturing subsidiary, for example, the European manager overcame great local resistance in getting a three-shift policy adopted rather than the uneconomical alternative: expanding the plant and buying more machinery. "Cannot be done in our country" was the first reaction of the entire subsidiary staff, but the staff was proved wrong. This successful regional manager sees his task as twofold: to coordinate and harmonize the various subsidiaries so that they gradually become equal members of the corporate family—and to educate them to up-to-date methods and modern thinking. While his attitude may be described as somewhat paternalistic, he stands by his subordinates and defends them where necessary against arbitrary actions by the home office.

The second opinion was voiced by two younger executives of an American bank in Paris, one a Frenchman, the other an American. They commented that strict centralized control works well in corporations where decisions made by the parent company are understood and readily accepted by lower levels because they are based on a thorough knowledge of world and local conditions. Furthermore, they emphasized that differences between American and European business methods are gradually diminishing—in some countries and industries faster than in others—and that the younger generations of both continents who are active in international trade are much closer than were the older ones several years ago. There is a greater willingness and a greater ability to understand each other. While these men believed in a trend toward tighter centralized control, they also thought that such control meets with less resistance and resentment than it did in former years.

The trend toward increased centralization was also stressed by the third expert, a Dutch subsidiary manager, who until recently had enjoyed considerable autonomy. However, he predicted that tighter controls are inevitable—either by the parent company directly, or by a regional office that is a part or extension of the home office. Since he is close to retirement, he looks at these developments calmly and objectively, but he admits that some of his colleagues have serious forebodings. "I can understand," he said, "that they are less than enthusiastic about these aspects. But if I were younger, I would look toward the future with confidence. I do not believe that we have any choice in the matter anyway."

LOOSE CONTROL OF SUBSIDIARIES

Many factors determine the direction and the degree of the control relationship in a particular corporation and at a given time. Some of these factors are there for every attentive observer to see; others, perhaps more important ones, are less obvious and go much deeper. These are related to a state of mind that consciously or unconsciously is influenced by theories and systems dominant at some period of time or in some particular country or society. It is characteristic of our time that these philosophies are in constant flux, follow one another in short intervals, and often exist side by side despite an ostensible preference for the one presently in vogue.

If centralized control versus decentralized autonomy is analyzed under these aspects, certain correlations between them and the underlying philosophies become apparent.

1. Tight control seems to be connected with a preponderance of economic theory, especially the studies of needs and resources, of growth and planning. Loose control, on the other hand, has a certain connection with the behavioral sciences, particularly motivation research.

2. Centralization is directly related to material uniformity and to personal conformism. They grow together and strengthen each other. Decentralization, in contrast to these trends, is the consequence of variety and the fulfillment of individualism.

3. Strict direction from above is an outgrowth of standardization; together they promote efficiency and savings. Lenient guidance, on the other hand, is the counterpart of specialization and facilitates imaginative thinking and the development of a creative spirit.

4. Autocratic leadership tends to rigidity and formalism. Pragmatic leadership, by contrast, considers every viewpoint regardless of the hierarchical level where it originates and accepts ideas on their merit, not according to their source.

These and other causative relationships of **economic, psychological,** and sociological theories to international business principles and practices should be studied further, but this would far exceed the limits and scope of the present research project. Suffice it to say that the mutual influences are contradictory and can therefore be interpreted differently. Unsubstantiated statements as to certain trends are often made on the basis of purely personal impressions or to conform to the fashionable opinion.

The following pages deal with several examples of loose control relationships and their causes. Many respondents stated that lenient control relationships in their companies are due to a general policy that top management believes will bring the best results—and, it may be added, at lowest costs. It should not be forgotten that the close supervision of many foreign activities, excessive exchange of telephone calls and Telex, the requirement of numerous approvals—all mean overextended and costly communications, loss of time, and ultimately, a greatly increased staff. Most of the control measures are in practice only nominally taken by key executives, but actually suggested and prepared by staff members who are often younger and less experienced than the subsidiary managers whom they control or help to control. The fact that they are nearer the power center is no guarantee that the decisions they recommend to their superiors will be any more intelligent or valuable than those made by the men in the field. The general policy of loose subsidiary control means in effect greater confidence in local management. The more decisions are assigned to headquarters, the more they will be ultimately made by home office staff personnel, and if this policy continues for many years, the quality of foreign management will deteriorate.

Conditional and Limited Autonomy

The autonomy vested in subsidiaries is frequently conditional. All subsidiaries, large or small, may enjoy the same degree of independence as long as they are successful. However, if and when a local unit has troubles, the international division or the regional office will mobilize its available brainpower to investigate, to "help," and to advise, which, of course, cannot be done without interference.

A large electronics corporation that maintains only a small regional office in London has a somewhat different approach. It holds regular meetings of a "European council," meetings attended by all subsidiary managers, the general product division manager for Europe, the two sales managers from London, and several staff members of the international division. While the main purpose of these meetings is an exchange of information and a discussion of problems and European coordination, the council also acts as a restraining force on its members. It reminds them that local freedom of action must be limited by common objectives and the interests of the neighboring units.

Further brakes against excessive autonomy are usually provided by the requirement of regular reports, by the budget, and by the necessity of obtaining approval in really important matters. Another large electronics corporation that grants its subsidiaries considerable independence still requires special authorization for such activities as plant enlargements and the purchasing of real estate. Approval is normally given by the European office in Geneva or, in specified cases, by the product division in the United States. In less important matters, local management is on its own. It is essential that the subsidiary manager know exactly which matters need approval from higher levels and which are completely or up to certain limits within his power.

Some rather conservative corporations are among those that are lenient in their relationships with subsidiaries because they do not believe quick changes, fast decisions, and untried experiments should be imposed on reluctant local management. However, some of the most dynamic and aggressive companies also give their subsidiaries great latitude. The author found instances where a local manager was more aggressive and forward-looking than the conservative home office. In fact, he complained that practically the only real restriction of his autonomy is a restraint of his ambitious reform plans. He would like to reinvest a much larger portion of profits in advertising, even work a year or two without profits to become the leader in his market. He also wants greater product diversification and is afraid that sticking to the old product lines will result in losing ground to the competition. He adds this, however: "At headquarters they have to take into account many questions with which I am not familiar." And he has autonomy in most other matters. He says he "would hate to work for a company where I had to call the home office for every decision I have to make."

His autonomy includes product selection. He can refuse to market new products if he finds them unfit for his market. On the other hand, he can order different products from the company plant in a neighboring country. His colleagues enjoy similar leeway. When the Italian manager, for example, heard that a competitor planned to come out with a greatly improved product, he was able to beat him to the punch by obtaining a similar item from the company factory ahead of time. He did not have to go through the time-consuming procedure of asking for authorization.

Local managers of this company also do their own advertising—and therefore it is tailored to local needs and conditions. The participant was firmly convinced that for a company that makes highly competitive items, the best policy is to leave wide decision-making power in the hands of local management; such a policy assures flexibility and quick adjustments when and where necessary. He acknowledged that exercising this power involves great risks at times for the local manager but that he must be willing to take them. He will then be judged by accomplishments that are truly his own.

Complete freedom in advertising matters, on the other hand, may not be fully appreciated by the subsidiary's advertising manager. In one such case, the advertising manager complained that he did not get enough guidance and support from headquarters to conduct a campaign as efficiently as he would like. Also, he felt that his colleagues in other local units were not striving to maintain a common corporate image. He felt this hurt the interests of both the corporation and the subsidiaries. It could be argued that the home office can never please the local people: They complain when they do not get enough responsibility and they complain when they get too much. The author does not share this evaluation. Rather he thinks that an interest in home-office support is a healthy sign of a real sense of responsibility on the part of a local executive. He wants to exercise his responsibility within the framework of corporate objectives, wants to coordinate his activities with similar ones in nearby subsidiaries, and wants support from headquarters.

Exaggerated Autonomy

However, local autonomy *can* be exaggerated. This was the case in the Paris subsidiary of one of the chemicals divisions of a large oil company. Since the division has only resident or traveling representatives in other European countries, its subsidiary operates as a limited regional office; in other words, it covers the whole continent. Its general manager has an almost incredible independence. For example, he does not submit a yearly budget, only profit forecasts. He exchanges very few letters with the division manager in the United States and has practically no telephone or Telex communications with him. He had not seen him for over a year at the time of the interview. The division manager seldom visits Europe, and the European manager has not taken his home leave for three years. He does not even use American accounting methods, and his reporting is extremely limited. The divisional business is small compared to the volume of the oil business, and the European business is only a part of the divisional total.

There is only one cloud on the horizon: The newly formed European headquarters of the parent oil company may one day wish to incorporate, or at least coordinate, the various divisional subsidiaries. The oil operations are quite different from the chemicals business; they are performed by wholly owned local units in most countries, while the chemicals groups have only sales engineers without adequate offices or staffs. The anomaly of a completely independent European chemicals subsidiary may therefore end some time in the future in the interest of better coverage and deeper market penetration.

Well-Balanced Autonomy

Several older corporations, which were among the first to establish subsidiaries in Europe, are also among those that have a policy of broad local autonomy. Their process of careful personnel selection, their tradition of assigning responsibility, the absence of sudden or unexpected decisions, the wealth of knowledge and experience on all managerial levels, the confidence of headquarters in local management and vice versa—all of these enable such companies to work successfully. That is, they make it possible for these companies to give their subsidiaries all the authority required for taking the initiative and making fast decisions—decisions basically the same as would be made at the regional, international, or corporate level.

There may have been differences in the past, but they have long since been settled, and none of the animosities are apparent that so often arise in younger organizations. Where personal rivalries appear, they are not allowed to damage the spirit of intracompany cooperation. No local executive has to fear that his responsibilities will be suddenly curtailed by a new superior or by radical organizational changes. Yet some of these same corporations are among the most modern in product development and in advanced management techniques.

A VP–Europe said that his company's overall policy is the same as set forth in the American Constitution: Everything not specifically reserved for the federal government belongs to the jurisdiction of the states. Similarly, about 20 basic policies are specifically retained by the parent company. These include basic higher personnel policy and benefits and worldwide R&D. All international activities not specified are within the authority of the international corporation. Several additional items are reserved for the New York headquarters; the others are delegated to regional offices—for example, the European office in Paris—and the remaining operations are handled directly by the various subsidiaries. Dual or overlapping responsibilities are thereby reduced to a minimum and every executive knows exactly where he stands in discharging his duties, as does his staff.

Not only a corporation's general policy, but also special conditions in its international trade may bring about loose control relationships. Some companies are more sensitive to such specific situations and better able to recognize them than are other firms, particularly where an open mind and a pragmatic approach prevail in top management. "We are a practical company," said a local manager in Milan, "and adjust our controls to local conditions." In this corporation, controls are therefore usually lenient and always flexible. Some time ago, an attempt was made to unify basic personnel policy for all levels, but it did not work and so was quickly abandoned (except for key staff members). This area of activity reverted to the jurisdiction of the subsidiaries with the result that compensation and benefits vary considerably from one country to the other.

This company produces electronics and telecommunications equipment. In Europe it works mostly with government-owned and government-operated telephone and telegraph systems. Bids usually have to be submitted within 90 days. This requires fast planning and calculation, based on full knowledge of the local situation. Consequently, subsidiaries have the power to make important decisions and need regional or home-office clearance only where exceptionally large sums of money are involved, or long-range financing is needed, or several subsidiaries have to work jointly on the project.

This considerable autonomy in several fields was quite naturally extended to others. For example, larger subsidiaries do their own R&D and need no approval for putting product improvements into effect. While practically no advertising is done, publicity connected with important public projects is handled locally. But it is communicated to other subsidiaries in Europe through the regional office and to units in other parts of the world through the home office.

The importance of consumer preferences and differences for decentralization was emphasized by the managing director of an automotive subsidiary. He pointed out that in the automobile business unifying trends are strong all over Europe, but that certain differences, based on climate, terrain, road conditions, and consumer habits, will not disappear. Detroit is quite familiar with such differences in many parts of the world—including the United States. There are several ways to meet them organizationally. The managing director described his organization as halfway between centralized and decentralized, with considerable autonomy granted to various units, whether manufacturing or assembling, but with strong decision-making power vested in its European headquarters. Relatively little supervisory authority is retained in Detroit.

If a subsidiary makes different products or employs different marketing methods from those of the parent company, it thereby has a powerful stimulus to local autonomy. This often includes independent R&D on a subsidiary, area, or regional basis. It does not exclude the exchange of technical information and mutual visits of specialists with the corporate

R&D department, of course, provided the products are in the same general category. However, these factors alone are usually not sufficient to insure loose control relationships; they must be combined with other equally strong influences.

One particularly strong but nowadays rare factor is the existence of only one or two European subsidiaries. Where this situation prevails, the subsidiaries have a naturally strong position. There is of course no regional office; reports go directly to the international division or even to corporate top management. Such a subsidiary is usually headed by a strong local manager with exceptionally lengthy experience in the market, and there is usually nobody at the home office who knows much about his particular business. The author visited such a subsidiary. It has sales functions only, and for the most part sells products supplied by independent sources in the same country or other parts of Europe. These products are freely chosen by the local manager. In addition, he can establish his own branch stores in other cities of his country without higher approval. Practically the only thing he cannot do is open branches or sub-subsidiaries in other countries. Even this privilege was once sometimes given to such men, on the premise that they were pioneers and explorers in international trade.

Lengthy experience in one market is another contributor to wide local autonomy, especially when the subsidiary is one of long standing. This does not necessarily mean that a new manager in a newly established subsidiary may not also enjoy strong decision-making power. In one local office the new executive, though he had no foreign experience, was allowed to make capital expenditures of up to $5,000 without regional or home office approval. While this was probably allowed partly because such expenses are needed in the first year of operations, the main reason for his being granted so much latitude was apparently a complete lack of international knowledge on the corporate level and the obvious weakness of the understaffed regional office in Brussels.

How to Exercise Autonomy

This company relies chiefly on the subsidiary manager. His experience was in the domestic sales department and he does not appear to have all the necessary qualifications to warrant such confidence. By contrast, many companies are extremely reluctant to put much faith in their local managers. In some companies, trust can be gained only by a continuous record of complying with orders and instructions without too much questioning. But such executives will remain yes-men even when they have finally attained the level of confidence that might enable them to make their own decisions. In fact, many top executives have no use for strong personalities among their subordinates. The presence of strong personalities among local managers is therefore usually a sign of self-assurance on the part of higher ranking executives. While it must be granted that not every strong subsidiary manager is an outstanding one, a weak man is rarely able to perform as well as he should. As the managing director of a tire and rubber company's subsidiary remarked: "I was formerly with another corporation in the same industry, but there local management is so strictly controlled that we were nothing but puppets dancing on the strings pulled by headquarters. I could not stand it any longer and quit."

In a Swiss subsidiary that also serves as the European office for supervising many local agents and distributors, the influence of a strong managerial personality was evident. This manager's predecessor, by contrast, had lacked not only strength but also an understanding of market conditions. He had been dismissed because the company, a medium-size corporation, wanted a man to whom they could entrust the widest possible responsibilities. Thus it was not so much the strong personality of the local manager that brought about his autonomy, but rather that the general policy of the company made it necessary to find a man with a personality sufficiently strong to meet the company's requirements—for it was unwilling to give him more than general directives. In fact, the second manager completely overhauled the organization, changed its entire local staff, and introduced modern marketing techniques. Corporate management relies on him in all respects and his recommendations are always accepted. The corporate president has visited him only once in five years and he himself returns to the United States only for vacations.

Joint ventures, even when majority-controlled, usually have considerable local autonomy. This autonomy is naturally greater if:

- U.S. participation is 50 percent or less.
- Other partners are few and powerful.
- These partners are particularly strong in local production, marketing, finance, or government contacts.
- Local participation is protected, demanded, and supported by laws and administrative practices (as in Japan, Spain, Mexico).

If the manager is an American, he must be a strong personality if he is to preserve his independence against local influences; he will then be equally resistant to attempts by American headquarters to exercise too much control over him. In fact, under the circumstances just mentioned, he can succeed only if he protects his autonomy from all interference and reports only to his own board of directors.

The influence of the size and growth of a corporation in general, and its European business in particular, on the direction of its control relationships with subsidiaries and regional offices is not clearly able to be determined. Most corporations modify their controls as business expands and diversifies. They may do this as part of a general reorganization or in their relations with local management only; they may accomplish the desired adjustments either gradually or in a radical and complete change. But in some cases the end result will be a tightening of controls and in others a loosening. In many companies, as a consequence of such changes, controls have been made stricter in some areas of activity and more lenient in others. It may take time to ascertain what the net result will be.

In one very large and diversified corporation the trend toward ever increasing local autonomy was explained by the size of operations (over 100,000 people are employed) and by the many different and rather independent product groups, each with its own international organization. Still, all European units are branches (not subsidiaries) of a Delaware corporation with a board of directors and regional headquarters in London. Stricter controls could therefore easily be put into effect without organizational changes.

Local Decision Making

How is loose control expressed in actual decision-making power? With all due allowances for subjective impressions and limited opportunities for comparison with situations in other corporations, the following cases can be cited as fair examples.

In the tire and rubber company mentioned earlier, the yearly budget is approved by the local board of the joint venture and submitted to the American corporation for information only. Its international division may ask questions regarding specific items, but it neither authorizes nor rejects them. In production, marketing, advertising, and personnel policy, local management is entirely autonomous. Except for some key personnel, the local manager can raise salaries and wages, increase the number of workers and employees, and create new jobs. He selects his own advertising media and can change advertising methods and policy.

However, unrestricted autonomy in personnel policy is rare. Usually it is limited. Blanket salary increases for whole groups of employees, for example, or exceptionally large individual increases require home office approval in one electronics corporation. Otherwise, the subsidiary managers have the widest possible latitude.

A specialized machinery production company also gives its local managers great authority in personnel, marketing, market research, and advertising. It seldom questions budgets submitted by experienced subsidiary managers, except when marked overall increases or exceptional changes in specific items are not sufficiently explained—for example, general shifts of advertising media or a change in the employee benefit program.

The local manager of a business machine company summed up his independence in these words: "As long as we show a profit according to our forecasts and adhere to general rules and directives, we can pretty much do as we think best." The general rules refer to such customary items as the layout of the trade name (but copy can be freely chosen) or total amount of salaries (but hiring and firing is a local responsibility). Also, leasing of machines must be strictly observed (no selling is permitted), but the terms can be adjusted locally. Larger subsidiaries are encouraged to help their smaller neighbors (Sweden helps the other Scandinavian units, Germany gives support to Switzerland and Austria), but all details are worked out directly between these local managements. Theoretically, budget proposals can be rejected by regional headquarters. But in practice they are being discussed before final figures are submitted, and they are therefore always accepted. While the corporation's general policy on control cannot be described as extremely loose and is not so regarded by its own subsidiaries, a stable balance has been reached. This precludes frequent changes and makes reorganization unnecessary and improbable.

Local managers in marketing subsidiaries that import their requirements from America or from European manufacturing subsidiaries frequently pointed out that they can reject products or models they do not regard as suitable or as competitive for their market. They emphasized differences in consumer or customer preferences, which the home office, often after a lengthy period of persuasion and "education," has come to recognize as valid. In most cases, however, a simple rejection of new products is not admitted. Various explanations and comments are required, ranging from a plain statement of facts as local experts see them to elaborate market surveys and test marketing.

Another yardstick of local autonomy for marketing subsidiaries is their freedom in selecting their source of supply from among the corporation's various European subsidiaries and American plants. Here, too, explanations are sometimes required, especially if the source of supply is suddenly changed. Many companies find it necessary to coordinate these activities through the regional office or the product group, but others leave local managements free to correspond directly with each other. These examples were provided by a nonferrous-metal corporation and one in the chemical industry.

A company manufacturing pleasure boats has one manufacturing subsidiary and a general European marketing office under joint management. An annual budget and monthly reports are presented to the home office in Florida, but it receives no other reports except for occasional voluntary market information in case of significant changes. In marketing, advertising, personnel policy, the selection of sales agents, and in European production, local management has almost complete freedom of action within rather general policy directives. The only important exception concerns sales to Eastern Europe, which would be contrary to corporate policy. However, a subsidiary executive believes that the president of the two European units could obtain the authorization to fill orders from an Eastern country if he thought it worthwhile.

The transfer of employees from one subsidiary to another or to regional and corporate headquarters is normally within the jurisdiction of the European or home office, but in some companies this too is delegated to local managements. They settle such matters among themselves, whether the employee himself wishes to move or a local unit needs the services of a staff member of another subsidiary or wants to send one of its own members for training elsewhere.

This section and the preceding one contain one example each of exceedingly strict and very loose control relationships within two product groups of the same American corporation. It may therefore be interesting to analyze the differences between the two cases in the light of what has been said previously about the reasons for different control patterns.

First of all, there is no important product difference, nor are there apparently divergent general policies, even though one product division is headquartered in upstate New York and the other in one of the northeastern states. But there are several other differences.

Product group A (with strict control) has a powerful European office with an autocratic regional manager; product division B (with lenient control) has no European headquarters, but only a coordinating liaison officer who believes in gentle persuasion rather than imposing his ideas.

The two subsidiaries visited by the author are both situated in small European countries, but this is their only resemblance. Subsidiary A is a marketing unit that imports its supplies from America or from two other European subsidiaries. This and all other activities are strictly controlled by the regional office. Subsidiary B is a formerly independent local plant acquired by the American corporation with 20 percent of the shares still owned by the former proprietor. Its operations, including export of its products, continue under the efficient old management, tactfully guided in financial and a few other key areas by the American coordinator. By contrast, the manager of subsidiary A is young, new, and inexperienced. His business volume is very small compared to other European subsidiaries, while the operations of subsidiary B are among the most important foreign ventures of its product division. Subsidiary B definitely constitutes a separate self-sustaining profit center; subsidiary A, on the other hand, can really only be considered part of a larger profit area that comprises several smaller markets.

TIGHT VERSUS LOOSE CONTROLS

Describing controls as tight or loose is in reality only a convenient simplification. There is hardly ever a control relationship that can be evaluated without considering a variety of factors. Each type of operation is subject to a multitude of separate controls, and whether the overall control situation is tight or loose depends on various forces exercising their power in different directions and with various degrees of strength.

The control relationship within a modern corporation is not like the constant, equal, predictable pull of gravity emanating from the larger, more powerful body and directed toward the smaller, dependent one. It could perhaps better be compared to a beam of light, which, whether bright or dim, is the combination of the spectral colors that can be separated by refraction through a prism. In this analogy the different spectral colors represent the various subsidiary activities—production, marketing, administration, finance, personnel policy, advertising, legal matters, accounting, and others.

The percentage of loose, medium, and strict controls for these different activities will determine the final evaluation, but if it is to be a truly accurate one, the importance or weight of each control should be taken into account. Because financial controls are usually strict, a lenient control relationship in financial matters should count more than a lenient control relationship in almost any other activity. Because most subsidiaries are more or less autonomous in personnel policy concerning lower-ranking employees, tighter control in this area should weigh heavily in the total classification. Moreover, newly established control or increased control in an area where local management formerly enjoyed a certain latitude counts for more psychologically than an already existing control, however strict.

Yet a tire and rubber company's local manager recognized that a newly introduced regional centralization of procurement will mean lower prices and faster deliveries. He therefore did not mind this limitation of one of his former responsibilities. The manager of a marketing subsidiary in Spain, however, proudly pointed out that he can purchase merchandise anywhere he wants and that 80 percent of his goods are supplied by Spanish manufacturers.

Divided Responsibilities

Such exclusive assignment of a special activity to a regional office is rare; even in financial matters, where most important decisions are made at headquarters, and in sales and lower personnel policy, where normally the local unit enjoys wider responsibility, decision making is usually divided among two or three company levels. To a varying degree, the subsidiary shares with regional or corporate management in the process of conducting ordinary business operations. Stricter controls or greater autonomy are therefore in most cases not a question of who makes the decision, but rather a question of how much and which part of the decision-making procedure is performed by higher or lower management. The difference between loose and tight centralized control thus becomes a quantitative problem.

When introducing new products that have already been launched by domestic production in the United States, the subsidiary may or may not have the right to reject them if it believes them unsuitable for its market. In both cases, however, such actions will be the result of long discussions. The home office or product division will try to convince local management that a new product is likely to succeed or at least should be tried out. Local management will point out the reasons for objecting and the risks involved. Only if the two opinions cannot be reconciled will the final decision have to be made by one level or the other, but even where the subsidiary manager has the right to refuse, he will be careful how he uses this right and how often, because his future may ultimately depend on it. The regional manager and even the home office will normally be equally prudent in exercising their rights to enforce their viewpoint, because neither can they afford to be wrong and to antagonize lower echelons too frequently.

Rejecting a new product or forcing it on the subsidiary is normally, therefore, a last resort. A skillful local manager does not need to be stubborn, for he can have his way more often than not by gently and persuasively suggesting solutions that can be a compromise between his original point of view and the first recommendations by headquarters. A skillful regional or international manager, on the other hand, does not need to be domineering; he can also use gentle persuasion and avoid dictating decisions and imposing his will. He too can make the final outcome look like a .compromise. Sometimes, of course, executives lack diplomatic skill and clashes of personalities are then the inevitable result.

The foregoing remarks should not be construed as suggesting that wider or narrower autonomy is not an important issue for subsidiaries, nor that differences in control are nonexistent. All they are aimed at is creating a proper perspective and bringing the discussion from a theoretical plane down to living realities.

In the area of local production greater autonomy often leads to the practice of manufacturing exclusively for the home market—and possibly for export to some neighboring countries—products that are entirely different from the company's usual lines. At the same time, such special home production brings about greater autonomy because headquarters has little interest in controlling purely local manufacture. Whether such independent production is feasible and desirable depends on a great many factors: size of the market, competition, local facilities, history of the subsidiary, available engineering talent, research and development, and, most important, the degree of flexibility or rigidity in top management philosophy. However, in most corporations even autonomous local production is subject to certain checks and balances instituted by higher management. While the subsidiary may often continue to manufacture current items, new products need higher-level approval, and this is sometimes given only after painstaking inspection, testing, and market studies.

Determining the proper time for introducing new products to local markets is a matter for joint decision on the part of subsidiary, regional, and corporate management. Many subsidiaries want this date to coincide with the launching of the product on a national basis in the United States because of American advertising, which reaches important customers and dealers in Europe. Other local managers prefer to wait until the new product has proved successful or has been improved, should that be necessary. The view of headquarters may be at odds with that of local management. In some companies, new items are always introduced simultaneously in the United States and in Europe, or at least in Europe shortly after being launched in America. Discussions between local and regional managements and between the latter and the home office are held prior to deciding on dates—to iron out differences of opinion and to correlate needs and resources.

The role of the regional office in these matters is often that of an intermediary. It speaks for the subsidiaries to the home office and vice versa. It may not have a voice in fixing the dates under consideration, but it is asked for help by the subsidiaries if they feel strongly about the introduction of new products, marketing methods, or advertising campaigns. Regional management is also asked for its recommendations in these matters by the international division, product groups, or top management.

In marketing, corporate and international headquarters usually confine themselves to general policy directives and leave operational decisions to the subsidiaries and regions as long as the two levels (strategic and tactical) can clearly be separated. The regional office, however, frequently exercises great influence over subsidiaries in marketing. Many regional managers consider this one of their main tasks, since they often possess considerable knowledge and experience in local market conditions.

If marketing operations are closely directed by the home office in the United States, as happens occasionally, this is regarded as an anomaly and efforts are made to correct the situation.

Whether certain marketing methods conform to general corporate policies or strategy or must be considered exceptions is a matter of interpretation and therefore reverts to higher jurisdiction. An Italian subsidiary manager explained the prevailing control situation, perhaps somewhat euphemistically, by saying that he has autonomy in marketing and distribution methods and channels, but that New York from time to time "makes suggestions." Milan then has to explain why some of them cannot be carried out. He does his own market research, however, without "interference" from the home office. He communicates only the results to New York, which it may or may not check by hiring an independent agency to do additional research. But New York does not necessarily inform the local manager of the results of its follow-up research. As a result, this joint endeavor in an important phase of marketing is a bit one-sided.

A Swiss banker summed up the situation when he said that within the average American subsidiary the marketing manager or the general manager in his marketing function usually has much more authority than does the local treasurer or the subsidiary manager in the financial area. This, he maintains, is not entirely rational, because in both fields errors or deviations from corporate policy can have equally bad consequences. Yet traditionally the financial sphere has been jealously guarded by the corporate controller and his department.

Sometimes anomalies also exist when there is much greater autonomy than usual. The manager of a subsidiary in Spain enjoys a degree of independence that in most other companies would be considered excessive. Corporate policy in general is to give local units as much decision-making power as possible—and what seems possible here includes many things that other companies might consider quite impossible. It was explained that the isolated position of Spain, still protected by tariff walls and quotas, and not belonging to either of the two trading areas of Europe, facilitates this policy of broad independence. Only those local practices that could hurt the best interests of other European subsidiaries are stopped on instructions from the home office.

Surprisingly, in this company even certain legal matters are delegated to local management and handled in cooperation with local counsel without the normal advice or guidance of the corporate legal department. Patent and trademark matters, however, are unified and centralized, but before a new trademark is universally adopted and registered, all local units are given a chance to comment or object.

Responsibility in Personnel Policy

Many of the respondents who talked about their various activities in relation to autonomy or control stressed their authority in personnel policy, either because they felt it was of major importance, or because it was one of the few areas where they enjoy real independence. However, only in a few instances was the local manager's authority virtually unrestricted. Very few can select their own assistants, staff members, and trainees, or refuse to accept them when they are assigned to them by the home office or "recommended" by top management. In matters of compensation, home leave, transfer, and promotion, key personnel in subsidiaries usually remain under the jurisdiction of regional or corporate headquarters.

In personnel policy affecting the lower ranks, however, local management normally has wider autonomy. Yet while it usually does the hiring and firing, the number of employees is often limited and cannot be increased without special authorization. Nor is the subsidiary manager usually free to increase salaries without approval. While some older, higher ranking local managers with strong personalities and a mind of their own have succeeded in wresting greater latitude than this from the home office, the fact remains that personnel management is also a joint effort of lower and higher levels, though the decision making is weighed in favor of local managers in varying degrees. Not many corporations have uniform benefit programs for middle and lower employees or other unifying general personnel policies, except in training such personnel as repair and service employees, instructors, and demonstrators. As in other activities, uniform programs (worldwide or throughout Europe) diminish local autonomy, and such training programs are on the increase, particularly in technical matters.

Another variable is the separation line between higher ranking personnel usually paid, moved, and to some extent directed by the home office, and lower ranking employees and workers directed by local management. Middle and junior executives belong sometimes to the first, in other cases, to the second, category. Middle management may include local sales or production managers, and their appointments often are made by or need the approval of regional management.

An example of great independence in personnel matters was provided by a German subsidiary manager to whom New York headquarters had recommended a young American for training. He flatly replied, so he said, that to his regret he could not for the time being find a suitable job for the young man. By contrast, a British manager of a very old and important subsidiary reported that he certainly has complete authority to hire and fire people up to the rank of local executive. But he added that as a matter of courtesy he will inform the home office of personnel changes in higher brackets. Also, in this corporation, the transfer of a man who wants to move from one subsidiary to another is handled by the two managers involved. They will then jointly inform headquarters, but will not have had to ask for prior approval.

Where the home office does not keep an accurate file on every foreign executive and staff member with up-to-date information and regular performance reports from their superiors, it may ask a local manager whether he has a man he could recommend for promotion as assistant manager or even as manager of a small subsidiary elsewhere. One subsidiary manager related that when he receives such an inquiry he first asks a candidate of his own choice whether he would like to be transferred; he then sends to the home office a complete description of the candidate's qualifications, including his and his wife's adaptability. What the local manager did not reveal was whether he might be tempted in a special case to thus get rid of a man for whom he has no use or, conversely, whether he might not overlook the abilities of another man whom he wants to keep. Sometimes, in personnel matters, as in other fields, great authority vested in local management can have its drawbacks.

Some rather strict controls of subsidiary activities by corporate headquarters are caused by U.S. government regulations in such areas as antitrust laws, export control, and tax legislation. In some countries, including France and Canada, the government, news media, and a certain sector of the public regard the insistence of American government agencies to extend their jurisdiction over U.S. subsidiaries abroad, which are incorporated under the laws of these countries, as encroachment on their sovereignty. While no French or Canadian company would ever be forced to do business with Cuba or Red China, French and Canadian circles resent the fact that American subsidiaries in their countries are prohibited from doing so on instructions from their parent companies.

HEADQUARTERS' VIEWS ON RESPONSIBILITIES

To determine the direction and extent of control relationships for various local activities, companies participating in the questionnaire survey were asked which executives determine the policies of the foreign subsidiaries and branches regarding types of products sold, types of products manufactured, changes of products, changes in production, quality control, patents and trademarks, technical research and development, promotion and advertising, design and packaging changes, marketing and merchandising, exporting to third countries, pricing, credit, distribution, marketing research, inventories, purchasing, investments of funds, expansions of facilities, acquisitions, legal and tax matters, financing, budgeting, accounting and auditing, selection and training of key personnel, executive compensation, employee benefits, and other important policies.

While many participants in the survey did not respond to some of the other questions, all of them filled in the lines of this question. The answers can be broadly classified in three main categories.

1. A minority of respondents listed for all activities various executives or departments at headquarters. While these participants may have been misled by the word "policies" at the beginning of the question and therefore did not consider purely operational activities, it still seems certain that these corporations leave little autonomy, if any, to their local managers abroad. In some medium-size companies or those with a young and still somewhat limited international division, the VP or general manager–international makes most important decisions himself. In larger, more developed corporations, various executives of the international division and of the corporation have final responsibility—for example, the general manager of operating division for types and changes of products, the director of manufacturing for production and quality control, the director of research and development, the advertising, marketing, and credit managers for their areas, the corporate treasurer for investments and financing, the international controller for budgeting and accounting, the directors of law and the patent department for these fields, and the international personnel director for selection and training of key personnel and for handling their benefits. The corporate executive committee will decide on acquisitions.

Still other corporations divide responsibility between the president of the international division or corporation and several vice-presidents (manufacturing, engineering, marketing, finance, administration, treasurer, legal, and controller). The president reserves for himself decisions in such matters as types and changes of products, expansion of facilities and acquisitions, and selection of key personnel.

In a large pharmaceuticals corporation, on the other hand, 16 of the 28 activities listed are under the jurisdiction of corporate management, with the president himself deciding major questions; 8 more are jointly handled by corporate and international vice-presidents, and only 4 are within the exclusive authority of the executive VP–International (export to third countries, distribution changes, market research, and training).

The foregoing participants do not list regional or local managements at all as deciding any policy, except in some cases one or two major subsidiaries such as Canada and Britain.

2. Many respondents, however, indicate either headquarters or subsidiaries as having responsibility for various activities. Some of these participants make clear distinctions as to where the authority lies—at the home

office or in the field. They sometimes list vice-presidents or general managers and corporate or international staff executives together—for example, the VP–International together with the international marketing manager, manufacturing manager, or assistant treasurer, all at the home office. Or the managing directors of subsidiaries are listed either alone or with their controllers. The board of directors or certain committees are occasionally mentioned instead of individuals.

Naturally the number of activities assigned to local management varies greatly—from very few to a maximum of 18 out of the 28 listed in the questionnaire.

3. The greatest number of respondents indicated headquarters and subsidiaries as being *jointly* responsible for many spheres of operation. One company went so far as to state that "all policies are determined by managing directors of subsidiaries in conjunction with corporate headquarters." Others specified those areas where local, regional, and international managers have separate and exclusive jurisdiction and those where two of them have joint responsibility. For example: Credit practices are handled by the subsidiaries autonomously; patents and trademarks as well as R&D are handled by the home office; export to third countries, legal and financial questions, and matters regarding key personnel are in one way or another decided by common action of the international division and the regional office; the remaining matters are under the joint authority of regional and local managements. No decision-making power is shared by the home office directly with subsidiaries where a European office exists.

Again, some corporations list presidents or executive vice-presidents and staff department heads at the international division "in coordination" with subsidiary managers or with regional managers. Those corporations that indicated joint, common, dual, or coordinated responsibility for several areas and separate or single authority for others seem to have made a real effort to avoid forcing a complex situation into an easy scheme and thereby come closest to reality.

The survey also confirmed that all important financial matters are decided by the higher executives of the corporation or international division (president, executive or senior vice-president, controller), sometimes jointly by corporate and international or regional top executives. However, this does not always include accounting, except for determining principal methods, nor does it include all phases of acquisitions and financing, except for final approval.

The wide variety of assignment of decision-making power in other activities, such as production, marketing, and key personnel, reflects the difference between certain degrees of local autonomy and tighter subsidiary control.

5. Control of Key Areas in Subsidiaries

INTERNATIONAL executives, when discussing their control relationships, often distinguish between major and minor problems, or between questions of substance and questions of routine, or between general policies and operational matters, or finally between strategic and tactical decisions —the former being reserved for corporate management while the latter are made in the field by local executives. Those European headquarters that are considered a part of or a substitute for the international division can be assumed to exercise delegated strategic decision-making power, while the less powerful regional offices take over some important tactical problems from the subsidiaries.

STRATEGIC AND TACTICAL DECISIONS

This clear-cut division of decision-making authority makes plausible reading at first, but closer scrutiny creates some doubts. The reason is that in practice this question immediately arises: Which of the many decisions that a local manager has to face can safely be included among tactical, routine, operational, or minor matters, where he may assume independent responsibility, and which other decisions can with certainty be classified as major policy matters or strategic areas where the local manager can at best submit suggestions for approval? If in doubt, a younger or newer subsidiary manager will play it safe and consult higher levels, and in many companies he will frequently be in doubt.

In some spheres of activity, manuals and job descriptions clearly draw the line between the two categories of decision, as in financial matters; but in other areas the local manager can only rely on company practice or tradition. And often he will have to ask. But a question as to whether a problem may be solved independently by local management will frequently elicit not a yes or no answer, but rather a recommendation as to how the decision should be made. Therefore, a local manager's asking if a given matter falls within his jurisdiction is often tantamount to relinquishing responsibility.

The arbitrary limits imposed by top management to determine which expenditures (capital or operational) are major range from $100 to $1 million, depending on the size of the corporation and subsidiary and the nature of the expenditure. Moreover, there are normally different levels of expenditures for various management levels: local, regional, international, and corporate. One automotive company, for example, has the rule that a new project costing more than $1 million or involving more than one subsidiary or more than one product division must be submitted to the parent company. Corporate staffs then prepare comments and recommendations, which are put in final form by the administrative committee, approved or modified by the finance committee, and ultimately signed by top management.

In another, smaller corporation, all capital expenditures, new acquisitions, and organizational changes are considered strategy and referred to the parent company, but of the remaining decisions many are still classified as major and need approval by the regional office. Thus this company distinguishes not two but three classes of problems—strategic, major tactical, and minor tactical—and assigns them, respectively, to the home office, European headquarters, and local units. The manager of the important Paris subsidiary admitted frankly: "I often do not know where my authority ends and therefore prefer to discuss many questions with London and they with the home office."

In personnel policy the transfer and appointment of key executives to local units can hardly be called strategic. Yet in most corporations this matter is under the jurisdiction of the home office. By contrast, while rules for compensation and benefits for lower ranking personnel are certainly general policy questions, because of local laws and customs they are normally left to subsidiary managements.

The important question as to whether new products developed by the parent company should be introduced in all subsidiaries obviously belongs to the sphere of strategy. But in quite a few companies this is decided by local units. By contrast, while the further question of when and how these products should be launched in a particular subsidiary is clearly a tactical decision, other corporations reserve such decisions for the highest corporate levels.

Whether and to what degree promotion and advertising matters are operational or a part of general policy is decided differently in accordance with the industry involved, marketing methods, and personal preferences.

No overall distinction between major and routine problems can be observed that would apply generally.

In one computer company, the regional office (instead of the subsidiaries) has wide authority in operational matters; yet even in these purely tactical questions it must sometimes refer to the parent company—for example, to get approval for special discounts. By contrast, the local unit can decide to sell rather than lease equipment if a special customer so wishes, and only if total sales versus lease revenue should be off balance would the regional manager intervene. What little advertising is being done in this company is also a strictly local matter.

Activities regarding pricing, credit policy, and distribution are border areas in which the demarcation lines between general policy as laid down by the home office and implementation as carried out or suggested by the subsidiaries are often blurred. This is because the parent company, while reluctant to abandon directing these operations from headquarters, recognizes the need for local exceptions and adjustments.

By contrast, accounting, which certainly is an operational matter, is mostly uniform and strictly controlled by the parent company, as are statistics and reporting. Here, general policy rules are—and must be, according to the very nature of these activities—so far-reaching and detailed that there is practically no room left for tactical decisions on lower levels.

It must be added that simply speaking of decisions to be made at various levels is a somewhat misleading way to describe the actual relationship between subsidiaries, regional offices, and parent company. In many cases, decisions represent a period of investigations, inquiries, preparations, negotiations, contractual arrangements, and final implementation. Several steps are involved and each may or may not require separate authorizations from various corporate or regional executives. During the preparatory phase of, say, negotiating a long-term contract with a new customer, a general authorization to continue exploratory talks may be the rule. But as the talks progress, new authorizations will be necessary, as will assistance by staff departments in such areas as law, patents and trademarks, supplies, credit terms, financing, shipping, and quality and specifications. In some corporations, depending on the magnitude of the proposed new contract or its specific purpose (for example, dealership) or particular conditions (for example, cooperative advertising, warehousing, or service clauses), corporate or regional specialists may enter the negotiations as advisers or take over certain parts of the discussions. The legal department and local counsel will be called for preparing the formal agreement and final approval by higher management levels will normally be necessary before signing the agreement. The implementation, however, may again be in the hands of local management with or without regional support.

FINANCIAL CONTROL

The one area that in the overwhelming majority of multinational corporations is centrally controlled is finance, which may be subdivided into three principal categories: (1) budget and forecasting, (2) capital and operational expenditures, and (3) short- and long-term local financing. In certain industries, especially banking, construction, and engineering, a fourth group of related activities assumes major importance: credit.

While these activities are practically always centrally controlled, there still remains a wide variety in the degree and direction of such controls, the modifications or deviations made possible, and the corporate groups or entities that exercise or share in these responsibilities.

While in other fields of activity control is often decentralized and sometimes relaxed, so that no definite trend can be established, the tendency in financial matters is definitely toward strengthening and deepening the parent company's control. This is because ever increasing amounts of money are involved and the manner of planning, financing investments and operations, and wisely spending the amount of cash or credit available so that it will do the most good is becoming more and more complex. Multinational corporations have financial limitations while the opportunities for investments and spending are—at least for the time being—greatly expanding. Obviously, judicious choices must be made on the corporate level —choices that will not always be fully understood on the local level. Yet modern-thinking corporate and divisional management will not exclude subsidiary managers from participating in this process. A regional manager in Frankfurt put it this way: "We receive the necessary facts and figures from all subsidiaries and then work out in cooperation with them their forecasts and budgets for the coming year. These we send unabridged with our comments to the home office."

The Budget

Where a regional office exists, local budget proposals are usually channeled through it, but the manner and degree of regional participation in this most important company activity varies considerably. In some corporations, the European regional office only forwards the various subsidiary budgets to the home office with its recommendations, not making any changes itself; in others, it forwards them to the parent company after reviewing and revising them; in still others, it approves the local budgets, and mails them to corporate headquarters only as a formality. Normally, the regional manager sends all subsidiary budgets to America in toto, adding only his own explanations and suggestions. But in a few corporations, the regional office consolidates all local budgets into one single European budget, which is then modified, approved, or rejected by the parent company. Naturally, this gives the regional manager enormous power, or, more correctly, it happens where he has already acquired such far-reaching authority. In one big American corporation, regional headquarters in Rome submits such a consolidated European budget to the parent company without breakdowns by national units. It is the European manager's responsibility to split the amounts finally approved by the home office among the various local subsidiaries.

In most cases, budget requests are submitted (either directly or through the regional office) to the international division at the home office, which usually refers them to top management after reviewing them with the controller's office or the financial department. The very large independent international corporations of multinational companies have their own financial staff departments, and so do some of the bigger regional offices. In this case, there is a lower-level dotted-line relationship between the subsidiary's financial officer (treasurer or controller) and his counterpart at regional headquarters, and a second, similar relationship between the latter and the financial staff at the international division or corporate office. In a few cases, the financial functions on the regional level are separate from and independent of the administrative or marketing regional office, and sometimes are even in a different location. Thus, in one large diversified corporation, regional headquarters is in London, but the European financial office is in Geneva. Budgets and forecasts in this organization are submitted to London with copies to Geneva, then discussed in personal meetings of the subsidiary manager and his staff with the London office. Because the controller in Geneva has supervisory responsibilities once the budget is approved, he is present at these meetings.

Such preliminary discussions between local subsidiaries and regional office, often with the concurrence of delegates from the home office, were observed in a good many cases. They can be an excellent way of providing local participation—just so the "discussion" is a true meeting of minds and not window dressing. In any case, these meetings offer the subsidiary manager the opportunity to explain or defend his forecasts and budget requests.

At one major corporation, every large subsidiary works out its own "operation plan" (forecast and budget) for a two-year period and sends it to regional headquarters. It is then discussed with the regional staff in Paris by the subsidiary manager, his production, marketing, and personnel managers, and his controller. Smaller subsidiaries are visited by representatives of the Paris office for the same purpose. The reviewed and revised plans are forwarded to New York for final approval. The procedure is repeated the next year, again for a two-year period, so that the plans overlap and can be changed every year. However, amendments can also be proposed during the year.

In most large companies, the budgets submitted for approval by the subsidiaries are very detailed and form a thick book of figures and explanations. They are subdivided into several sections, such as production, sales, technical, and marketing research, advertising, and personnel. Each section is separately analyzed by and discussed with the appropriate regional staff and the various experts of the international office or corporate headquarters. The advertising budget is often treated separately in consumer goods companies, where special attention is brought to it and where it is subdivided by media and product groups. The personnel budget also may be handled apart from the other items and subdivided into various personnel categories, such as high-ranking executives (Americans or nationals), middle management, and employees and workers.

The personnel budget may have to include the exact number of people in each category, in addition to the total salaries and wages; higher-category salaries are often specified for each job. Where a subsidiary produces and sells different products—products that in the United States are handled by diverse product groups—not only the advertising budget, but other items as well, may have to be split up according to these product lines as far as possible. All this makes the budget more complex and requires closer consultation between subsidiary and regional managements.

In one recently established regional office in Paris, local budgets are first discussed with subsidiary managers and their staffs, then revised and consolidated, and then personally taken by the general manager–Europe to New York, where he in turn discusses them with the VP–International and the corporate president. In another company, the budgets are first submitted to European regional headquarters in Basel by mail, then discussed there with financial delegates from the American home office. The general manager–Europe is present, of course—a local subsidiary manager explained that he often needs his support to "sell" the local budget to the parent company.

In one very large and diversified corporation where the regional office was abolished some time ago, budget proposals are now sent by the various subsidiaries directly to New York, where the treasurer and several specialists examine them carefully. Then the VP in charge of the international division goes to Europe to discuss the budgets with local managers. Of course, he has the comments of the treasurer and the other staff members as a basis for discussion. The final approval will come later—from New York. In another company, a unique method of working out the budget was found: All European subsidiary managers discuss the local proposals among themselves and then submit them jointly to regional headquarters in Switzerland.

Contrary to the usual pattern, a pharmaceuticals company requires that its subsidiary managers first send a general preliminary budget request to the international division and, after it has been approved or modified, that they then submit a second, much more detailed, final budget proposal. Incidentally, one of the local managers said that while he should receive ultimate approval of this final budget by December 1, the beginning of his fiscal year, it has never arrived on time. He therefore simply notifies the parent company that he assumes he may proceed according to the budget as submitted.

Several subsidiary managers told the author that their budget requests are usually accepted, perhaps with minor modifications, so that they consider the whole thing more or less a technicality. Others said that, regardless of whether or not the budget is ultimately accepted, some items are always questioned just to demonstrate that the home office is watching. The manager of a majority-controlled joint venture in Spain maintained that "they just want to show that they have the power to make changes" in the budget as proposed. How many major changes will be made by the parent company or by the regional office depends on many things: the general policy and philosophy of the company, the pattern of the control relationship, the mutual understanding between headquarters and subsidiary, the quality of the budget proposals, and the skill and experience of the local manager and his staff.

Overexpenditures and Budget Revisions

Once the budget has been finally determined and approved, it becomes in some corporations a rigid set of rules that must be strictly adhered to come what may; in others, overexpenditures may be made by local management up to a limit that ranges from 3 percent to 10 percent. Still other companies have more or less flexible methods for allowing exceptions, although they have to be thoroughly explained before being authorized. Finally, a few corporations have built-in methods of revision that assure greater adaptability to changing conditions. Such budget revisions are usually connected with revised forecasts.

"The budget is the bible and must be strictly followed," said a subsidiary manager in Frankfurt. "However, a 3 percent margin is always permitted. Otherwise detailed explanations have to be furnished to obtain approval of a larger discrepancy."

Increases in the operational budget are normally treated more leniently than those in the capital budget, and operational budget changes are often allowed within a wider margin than capital budget changes, and may be authorized by a lower level in the corporation (for example, by the regional manager instead of the head of the international division or top management). By contrast, in one giant chemicals and pharmaceuticals corporation, exceptions from the operational budget must be authorized by New York, while capital budget increases under a certain limit can be approved by the regional office in London.

Normally, monthly reports include a comparison of actual expenditures with budgeted outlays. Such comparisons are of limited value in the first months of the fiscal year because many budget items cannot be pinned down accurately to a certain month, nor can they be projected monthly on a pro rata basis. But after several months, when the cumulative effect becomes more evident, the picture begins to clear up. In one company visited, each monthly budget report is accompanied by an explanatory letter giving the reasons for divergences, and by an "opinion" that projects the aggregate differences between budget and performance to its cumulative result at the end of the year. A half-year revision is also provided to translate these actual and projected differences into proposals for budget changes.

Budget Shifts

A different type of deviation from the approved subsidiary budget consists of shifts within the budget that do not increase the total amount. These shifts are handled in different ways by multinational corporations, and the greater or lesser latitude given the local subsidiary is one of the few real yardsticks for what can truly be described as tight or loose management control. The difference in treating these shifts again reflects not only distinct corporate thinking or general control patterns, but also diverse evaluations of the local manager's proven ability and past performance. The shifts in budget items either generally permitted or individually authorized and approved in each case, can be:

- From one group to another—for example, greater expenditures for personnel and smaller outlays for office equipment.
- From one subgroup to another—for example, more for travel and less for telephone calls and cables.
- From one item to another—for example, more for maintenance and less for repairs.
- Where there is no change in expenditure—for example, the same amount for two higher-paid sales engineers as for three lower-paid salesmen.

Shifts from one budget group to another are seldom allowed without approval of a special request. Particularly, switching amounts from production to marketing or from sales to general administration is normally excluded. Few companies will also consent to shifting expenses from the advertising budget to marketing. In some groups, even minor turnaround changes are unacceptable. This applies frequently to advertising and personnel and, within the personnel budget, to shifts between higher executives, middle management, office help, and workers. Sometimes the personnel budget is so specific that even minor modifications are frowned upon and the local manager can only replace one employee with a similar one at the same wage level, and this only for the lower personnel categories.

In one cosmetics company where extremely tight, if not always happy, control relationships prevail between top management and lower levels, even the smallest deviations from any budget detail must be approved previously by the home office. No shifts of expenditures from one budget item to another are ever allowed even within the same subgroup. No employee can be switched from one area of employment to another and no other personnel changes can be made without clarification, detailed request, and specific approval. In another company, one that makes soft drinks, shifts that do not represent an increase in total expenditures may be authorized in each case by the regional manager, but changes resulting in greater expenditures must be approved by the international division. A pharmaceuticals company has the rule that personnel shifts must affect neither the total amount paid in salaries nor the total number of employees. In one of the big oil companies local autonomy exists only in marketing and personnel, while everything else is centrally controlled. Yet even in these two areas shifts from one budget group to another cannot be effected without prior permission from regional headquarters.

By contrast, the regulations of an instrument-manufacturing company allow shifts within the budget, particularly for the larger subsidiaries and those headed by experienced managers. Similar latitude is given to local managers in the military and aerospace division of an electronics company and to several others who were interviewed. The underlying problem—to meet sudden changes in the conditions that formed the basis for the original budget—is solved differently in a food producer's European organization, where budget items may neither be shifted around nor increased, but every budget includes a sizable contingency fund for emergencies or unexpected situations. This can be used at the local manager's discretion up to a given ceiling, but beyond it, he will need the approval of the regional manager.

In a few companies with strong regional managements that exercise considerable control over rather powerless local units, the regional manager has, within certain limits, the right to switch budget items from one country under his jurisdiction to another, as long as the total European budget remains essentially the same. Usually, this power is confined to shifts within a budget group. Thus when the regional advertising or market research manager finds that he needs more money for programs in one country he can obtain it by suggesting a cut in another unit's projects. Obviously, such power in the hands of the regional office, unless it is used very sparingly and wisely, can lead to frustration, rivalry, and bickering among the subordinate subsidiary managers. It is much better to include in the European budget or in the separate budget of the regional management a reserve fund for unforeseen shortages.

Special Budgeting

Some industry groups cannot follow the normal budgetary rules and methods. An international stockbroker's subsidiary in Germany does not submit an annual budget, but instead what it calls an "estimate of annual expenses." Some expenditures, the author was told, cannot accurately be anticipated, others cannot be estimated at all. The local manager needs no approval if operational expenses do not run more than 10 percent above his estimates. He does need it, however, for all capital expenditures, such as additional office machines or new furniture.

In the construction and engineering industry, the nature of the business makes normal annual budgets impractical. In one such subsidiary in Germany, the general manager flatly stated that budgets and forecasts at the beginning of the year would be meaningless. He said this was because it is impossible to predict the number and sizes of construction jobs that will be obtained through accepted bids or offers and because projects may last from six months to three years. Only those already in progress by the end of one year can be projected for the next one or two years.

The manager of a competitor's British subsidiary, who also acts as European coordinator, was more specific. In his company, every project over $500 that is being negotiated must get preliminary clearance from the home office. When the offer is accepted by the customer, a detailed budget and timetable are submitted and must again be authorized by American headquarters. This budget determines, among other things, which European unit alone or in cooperation with other subsidiaries or outside firms will perform the various tasks. Engineers, construction specialists, and supervisors must be assigned to the project; often they will be transferred from one location or country to another according to need. Workers must be hired at customary local wages, and taxes and fees must be estimated in accordance with the country or countries where work is to be done. For various transalpine pipelines, work was performed by several subsidiaries of different American and European construction companies for a consortium of oil companies and public enterprises in Italy, Switzerland, Austria, and Germany—an enormously complex project, where major cost items could not possibly be estimated with accuracy even after actual work had already begun.

FORECASTING

Accurate forecasts form the basis for realistic budget proposals. In turn, forecasts are based on company objectives and on local economic conditions. Worldwide company objectives that may considerably influence local business forecasts are frequently only vaguely known to subsidiary managers. And while local economic conditions should be well known to them, often they are not because the manager may have been transferred to the country only recently and may not possess the necessary economic background. This is one reason why the appointment of national subsidiary managers is more and more preferred by many American corporations. American managers appointed to local management should stay in one country at least five years, preferably longer, which is normally not the case.

Exact forecasts should be based on continuous market observation, but only very large subsidiaries of big corporations are staffed with expert market researchers. The general managers themselves seldom have market research training and experience. They rely mostly on sales reports and company statistics, and also examine the data published by national newspapers, magazines, associations, publishing firms, and government agencies. Where well-staffed and well-organized regional or area offices exist, they effectively support local managers in their forecasts with pertinent data they are better qualified to collect. This they can do through their more powerful research resources, supplemented by consultants and research agencies.

Except for the construction business and a few other industries with special conditions, forecasts are usually submitted annually for a five-year period, which means that this period is extended and revised every year. Sometimes, revisions are made every six months or whenever specific economic or market changes so require. One of these rapid changes that cannot easily be predicted occurs in all industries connected with fashion— for example, the textile or synthetic fiber industry. There, accurate forecasts are very difficult, revisions have to be made frequently, and there is a tendency for the regional and the home office to revise original subsidiary forecasts downward—"because they are always too optimistic." Or such was the opinion of one regional marketing manager in Brussels.

In the household appliance field, forecasts are easier to make because buying trends are less subject to sudden change. Yet one general manager complained that his company requires annual "action programs" for every type of activity in such detail and with such precise dates that they can never be kept and that for a five-year term they are pure guesswork. This satisfies only the lower-level staff members at headquarters, who have never worked at the marketing end—a rather familiar criticism.

At the European headquarters of one major corporation, the author was told that the company recognizes the difficulties facing a new subsidiary manager in accurate forecasting, even though practically all of them are nationals of the country in which they work. Therefore the local manager is allowed to shift budget items within the same group, and even, with the approval of the regional office, from one group to another. But after a few years of experience he is expected to come up with more and more accurate forecasts, always under the assumption that no major changes occur that would upset these forecasts. Unforeseen events such as the long strike and crisis in France in 1968 will necessarily change earlier forecasts. Moreover, the subsidiary managers are encouraged to make changes in their estimates whenever they feel this is warranted by changed conditions. Thus this corporation has a completely flexible policy in matters of forecasting, although it also has extensive marketing and economic research facilities to provide subsidiaries with all necessary facts and figures.

It stands to reason that manufacturing subsidiaries have to provide their regional or home offices with much more detailed forecasts than marketing units, that accurate forecasts are more important in large subsidiaries than in smaller ones, and that they should be particularly reliable where two or more producing subsidiaries work together in the manufacture of component parts, or where they must rely on other plants of the corporation for their supplies. If their forecasts are way off, they may find themselves without merchandise. Conversely, the supplying units may have excessive, perhaps unsalable, inventories to dispose of.

In one of the big automobile manufacturing corporations, both production and sales forecasts must be submitted by the subsidiaries to regional headquarters four months before the end of the year. If there is a surplus, the regional office decides where these cars will be shipped or where large inventories will be kept. Legal requirements and consumer preferences, especially in auxiliary parts, vary from one country to another and must be taken into account when planning production, sales, and inventories. In a car-rental company, forecasts and budget proposals used to be made annually, with little provision for revision. Now, they are reviewed and, if necessary, modified every three months. One of the area managers said it was like being freed from a straitjacket.

Rigidity versus Flexibility

In fact, a system of rigid adherence to forecasts and budgets without the possibility of adjusting them fairly easily and quickly to unforeseen changes is self-defeating and, as with inflexibility in other important activities, stifles local initiative. A German subsidiary manager had a different viewpoint. He said a good local manager can and should be measured by his ability to make accurate forecasts and workable budget proposals and stick to them. Emergencies and unforeseen problems may sometimes occur, he admitted, but as a rule, the subsidiary manager, "if he is worth his salt," must be able to anticipate developments and should not come back after a few months asking for a revision, or for a major supplementary appropriation of funds.

Many experts consider this dangerous theory and dangerous practice. It may lead to an overcautious attitude, to a preference for limited estimates of business potential. It may cause, not only at the local, but also at the regional and international levels, an unwillingness to admit mistakes in judgment and to correct them and a blindness to changes, whether or not they were predictable. Managers will then avoid as long as possible adjustments to such changes until they must be made—usually too late and at too high a cost. Instead of planning production and marketing according to market conditions, they are forced to follow the plan no matter what. The local managers may forgo and hide new or increased potentials they did not anticipate, just so they will be 99 percent right in their estimates at the end of the year. Since it would be much worse to have overlooked unfavorable developments, they will always underestimate their sales and tailor them to these low estimates.

Another subsidiary manager with many years of experience was asked: "What happens when you feel that you could do more than anticipated in your forecasts and need more money and more people to exploit these unpredicted opportunities?" His answer was: "I can do two things. I can be a bureaucrat and say: 'This was my forecast and my budget. I must abide by them. . . .' Or I can say: 'I am not infallible and am not going to miss a business opportunity just because I did not see it five months earlier.' Luckily, my superior, the VP–Europe, thinks the same way and takes a lot of responsibilities on his own shoulders, if necessary."

Unsatisfactory forecasts are often nobody's fault, except of those who expect too much from too little. But there are also those who do not expect forecasts to be correct and who are therefore not surprised at failures. A general manager of one participating company believes that, in general, Americans put too much trust in forecasting and Europeans too little, which can be explained by different historic and economic developments on the two continents. Much of the forecasting done in Europe is still, according to this manager, guesswork rather than scientific analysis, especially where medium- and long-range forecasts are concerned. "The main value of forecasts," he says, "is not that the company can bank on them, but rather that managers on various levels are educated to think."

If this opinion is accepted, if the requirements for good forecasting and budget proposals are backed up by the necessary tools and kept flexible, then they can be a real incentive and not a straitjacket.

The question of meaningful forecasting and budgeting should be explored from a few more angles: For one thing, smaller changes in the original forecast do not usually affect the budget in any significant way. That is, a greater or smaller volume of business can be handled and is generally handled with the same personnel, overhead, sales costs, and even production costs (except for raw materials and packing elements). Nor will promotional efforts be immediately increased or decreased. Therefore, to be absolutely correct in the original forecast at the beginning of the year is more a matter of pride and prestige than of cost calculation. These problems can be almost completely eliminated by having the subsidiary make regular sales forecasts, product by product, quarterly, as is done in one large photographic corporation. Since products are uniform and little difference in consumer preferences exists throughout Europe, the changes appearing in these three-month forecasts can be compared not only from period to period with due regard to seasonal ups and downs, but also from country to country, taking their known purchasing power into account. If larger discrepancies show up, the local managers are expected to explain them. This does not hurt their initiative in any way. It rather encourages them to think and to investigate their markets, and not to do forecasting in a routine, mechanical way.

Initiative and Responsibility

Another important question is where forecasts and budget proposals really originate—that is, who takes the initiative? It does not matter so much whether or not they are finally accepted without major changes; what does matter is whether they have been worked out under pressure from and according to the wishes of higher levels (regional or corporate management) instead of in accordance with an honest and sound evaluation of the local market situation by the subsidiary manager and his experts. If the local unit is an affiliate or joint venture, if it has its own active board of directors who are more than mere figureheads, the forecasts may not always be correct, but they will at least be genuine, and so will the budget proposals. If, on the other hand, the local unit is a subsidiary without any independence whatever and with a weak, submissive manager who is a puppet of the regional or division manager, then the initiative will come from a higher level and it should also take the responsibility. Perhaps it is better qualified and equipped to make forecasts and establish budget proposals, but this should then also be made clear to everybody concerned, including top management.

Initiative and responsibility cannot be separated. Many companies consider their local subsidiaries profit centers. This means the local manager is responsible for the profit and loss picture at the end of the year; if so, he should also be responsible, at least within certain corporate interests and limits, for his forecasts and his budget. If not, the profit center should be moved to regional or international headquarters.

Finally, forecasts and budgets must be submitted in time (normally four months before the end of the fiscal year) and approved in time so that the subsidiary can function without a "gray" interim period of continuing business on a day-to-day basis. But, incredible as it may seem, this is not always the way things are done overseas.

CASE BRIEF

One Belgian subsidiary reports through a regional office to the international division, but important decisions are made by top management on the corporate level. The corporation represents a merger of two companies. The president, coming from the older company, is very cost-conscious; the executive vice-president, coming from the younger firm, is mainly interested in growth. The international manager and the European regional manager do not want to get involved in controversial decisions, and they want to avoid issues they consider dangerous.

When the local subsidiary manager submitted his budget proposals, the European regional manager forwarded them without major changes and with hardly any comments to the international division, and from there they went in the same manner to top management. Nobody on lower levels wanted to take any chances. The executive VP liked the local budget suggestions and approved them—or so it seemed. That was in November. The subsidiary manager proceeded under the assumption that his proposals had been accepted, but in March he received a cable directly from the president informing him that his budget had been rejected as excessive.

The president and the executive VP came to Brussels a few weeks later but, as happens so often, they had very little time. The subsidiary manager pleaded with them to have a long talk with him; they agreed and came to his home—but with their wives, which meant that little business could be discussed. The next day they left on a trip to other European countries. In desperation the local manager asked the European regional manager what to do and how other subsidiaries solved this problem. Apparently they did not bother and just went ahead with their budget as originally proposed, until instructed to make specific changes. It may not come as a surpise that this subsidiary has had three different managers in five years.

While this story is certainly an exception, it illustrates weaknesses that appear in milder form quite frequently. In fact, several subsidiary managers said they considered all budget items as approved unless specifically rejected or modified.

EXPENDITURES

When a budget has been approved or revised, it does not necessarily mean that all amounts included can be freely spent. Only routine operational expenditures can usually be made without further authorization. For capital expenses and for larger operational outlays there are normally two or three levels: The first is a ceiling under which the local manager can make the expenditure (for example, $5,000), the second (say, $5,000 to $10,000) requires approval from regional management where it exists, the third needs special authorization from the home office. Sometimes this means approval from the international division (or from the product group or from the controller) up to a final limit. Beyond that, consent from corporate top management is required. Capital and operational expenditures do not always have the same limits. The lowest level (for local subsidiaries) may vary according to business volume, size and importance, age and structure, the activities engaged in (manufacturing, assembling, warehousing, service, sales), distance from the home office, and whether or not the subsidiary is under the jurisdiction of a regional office. Although never spelled out in manuals or job descriptions, the local limit of expenditures without special authorization may very well be different for an experienced subsidiary manager of proven ability and higher rank and a new, younger man who still has to earn his spurs. While the limits are officially the same, a request from the experienced manager may generally be granted without too much questioning, while the other manager's request will be closely scrutinized.

Official authorizations frequently have to come from the subsidiary's board of directors, but this is mostly a legal technicality, because the members of the board (if the subsidiary is wholly owned) or a majority of the board (if it is a majority controlled affiliate) vote according to instructions after the request has been previously submitted to corporate or regional management.

Certain categories of expenditure are quite often completely excluded from the local manager's jurisdiction. In most cases this applies to real estate transactions, including the acquisition of even the smallest parcel of land adjacent to the local factory or office building. It may include rentals or moving—even from one floor to another in the same building. In one case observed by the author, such restrictions applied to any and all expenditures connected with the premises. In another case, the exception applied to donations. Obviously the company has had some bad experience in the past. Any equipment and machinery are usually also excluded from lower level decision making and often reserved to the highest levels. Requests for replacements or improvements, whether included in the budget or not, must be very specific and indicate the exact type, size, model, power, capacity, and expected performance. But in case of a breakdown, emergency provisions have to be made, and here the support of a regional manager willing and able to step in and take the responsibility is extremely valuable. As one of them expressed it: "When I get a telephone call from a plant manager anywhere in Europe, that he needs a new boiler or else would have to shut down, I have no time to call or Telex St. Louis; I authorize the replacement and get my own approval from the home office later."

Credits

Separate levels of authorization exist not only for different limits of expenditures, but also for distinct credit ceilings. If the granting of credit is part of the regular business practice—and in Europe it is frequently granted for both consumer and industrial goods—a larger subsidiary and a well-organized regional office will usually have their own credit departments, which contact each other to request and approve routine credit. At the home office, the request would be handled by the international or corporate credit department, which get the requests from the subsidiary either direct (with copy to regional headquarters, if any) or via the regional credit manager.

Naturally, this question is of particular importance to American banks with branches in Europe. In one of them the author was told that local branch managers have some latitude in granting normal credit to their customers, but this is one activity more strictly controlled than others. In some banks there are only two levels for the approval of loans: local and by the home office. In others there are three or four, but the various types of loans are not treated identically. There is also a difference depending on whether the applicant is a local business firm or a U.S. subsidiary. In the latter case the loan request may not come from the local unit but through or with the support and guarantee of regional or corporate headquarters. For loans to national business entities, this was the word: "The New York office recognizes that the branch bank manager is more familiar with local regulations and customs governing credit policy than the home office." In another country, the manager of the bank's local branch related that credits over $1 million have to be approved by New York. "But," he said, "it is often difficult to obtain such approval, because European clients are not used to revealing the type and volume of information to a bank which is quite customary in America, and therefore also required by U.S. banks in most cases abroad."

The credit ceiling varies from one bank branch to another according to the banking volume and therefore normally increases steadily. But in a very old London branch of one of the largest American banks, the credit limit also varies with the rank and expertise of the branch manager. Thus if a local manager is transferred or promoted, the new man may have to start at a considerably lower loan level than his predecessor and gradually work his way up. However, in this bank, the branch manager has a certain degree of autonomy in adjusting credit terms and methods to local conditions. Generally speaking, the branch managers must follow the bank's credit policy as closely as possible and achieve a satisfactory middle ground between American credit policy and that of the host country.

LOCAL FINANCING

Until a few years ago, the financing of a subsidiary's needs, particularly for capital investments, was in most corporations part and parcel of overall corporate financial planning. The necessary funds according to the approved budget were allocated to the local unit by the international division or by top management from the corporate funds, whether they came from surplus earnings, reserves, stock increases, or loans. The local manager had very little to do with financing. Once his capital budget proposals had been accepted and his request for the actual expenditure was approved, he could only wait until the bank advice arrived—and more often than not, subsidiary managers rightfully complained that the transaction was too much delayed in slow-moving company "channels."

The regional manager or regional controller had only an intermediary role but could sometimes expedite the matter. Tax questions played a major part, and for each larger transaction the counsel of tax experts was prudently sought with the result of further delays and sometimes missed opportunities. In the earlier postwar period—and in some countries even recently—currency fluctuations and devaluations had to be taken into account, and constituted major obstacles to quick decisions.

Owing to the balance of payment difficulties in the United States this picture has now partly changed. More and more the European subsidiaries' capital investments are being financed locally, and European banks have shown an increasing interest in such loans, despite outcries from certain nationalistic quarters. This new development has in many cases increased the status of both the local manager and the subsidiary's board of directors, who have to execute the various legal agreements involved. A loan from local banks necessitates close cooperation among a good many people; even more will be involved if the parent company's guarantee is required. These will include the subsidiary's board of directors, the local manager and his controller or chief auditor, local legal and tax counsel, the regional manager and his financial staff, the international division and its controller, the corporate controller's office, and top management.

Of course, not all of these executives will be involved in all phases of the negotiations, but it is fair to assume that the subsidiary manager will have to participate in most of them. His knowledge of local conditions can be invaluable; hence if he is an American recently transferred to the subsidiary and has no previous local experience, it will be advisable to bring in someone better qualified from the regional office.

The degree of financial experience and familiarity with the country will determine how big a part the subsidiary manager will be able to play or to capture for himself; he may be the initiator and chief negotiator or he may be a glorified errand boy. Here is an example of the former position.

CASE BRIEF

A Texas corporation's Dutch subsidiary, headed by an American manager, is engaged in the construction of pipelines for water, oil, and natural gas. The subsidiary manager enjoys wide autonomy; through mutual representation on the various boards of directors throughout Europe he is in close contact with other subsidiaries. These subsidiaries frequently provide each other with technical assistance and consultation. Mr. T., the American executive, arrived in the Netherlands five years ago. After one year he had been authorized to do his own borrowing from Dutch banks without the parent company's guarantee. This was because of the subsidiary's high local credit rating.

Very often, in fact usually, joint ventures with Dutch companies or other European firms are formed for a particular project or for a series of projects. The American corporation furnishes the technical know-how and personnel, some equipment, and overall direction; the client firm contracts for the supply of raw materials. The amounts to be laid out by the American company are therefore mostly for labor; they are relatively small and periodically reimbursed by the client. For all this, no prior approval from Texas is required, but the home office is constantly informed so as "to keep the peace." There is naturally a thick book of rules and guidelines. "As long as everything goes well and smooth, you are on your own and have full responsibility," said Mr. T. "If you have any problem, you are supposed to call the home office for technical or financial assistance and it will be forthcoming. If you don't call and something goes wrong—well, that's the end."

The main reason for vesting this great authority in a trusted local manager is that in this particular business, important, quick, on-the-spot decisions must often be made and the construction work cannot stop. Therefore, the subsidiary manager must in turn delegate considerable power to his construction supervisors on location and assume the responsibility for *their* decisions. "In my experience," said Mr. T., "companies which refuse to give their local people this independence will not be very successful, at least not in *our* business. Of course, you must have the right man, carefully selected, in the right place."

Nevertheless, the author found other construction companies that delegate considerably less authority—and they too seem to be doing well.

Developing Local Responsibility

While it is certainly true that wide authority, especially in financial matters, should only be given to the right man, it is also true that a subsidiary manager will never become the "right man" if he is not gradually given more autonomy. Not every detail can be controlled from headquarters. This thought was expressed in challenging form by the vice-president of international operations of a well-known company that manufactures razors and blades. He said that the limitation on American investments abroad was a blessing in disguise. Too many U.S. companies have spent too much and too freely without really investigating or being properly informed by their subsidiaries whether the expenditures were necessary and worthwhile. Many a local manager has acted like a spoiled son used to getting and spending all the money he thinks he needs. Therefore he never became tough and self-reliant. The executive continued:

I will send my two sons to distant relatives who still own a farm in Illinois. There, my boys will work and earn their keep. A corporation should do the same with its subsidiaries once they can stand on their own feet. They must not always come to the parent company for money to spend on investments or to get them out of trouble. Otherwise they will never grow up.

Another question is: To what degree will the "sons" be allowed to spend the money they have earned? This is the reverse side of the coin.

It is the natural inclination of every subsidiary manager to try to keep earned surpluses as a reserve or to invest them on short terms locally so that he will have them available when needed. It is a lot easier to make requests for expenditures when at least part of the money for intended investments or salary increases is at hand. The subsidiary manager understands that dividends have to be paid to the parent company, especially when there are also other, local shareholders, which is still the exception rather than the rule, though it now occurs more frequently. What the local manager may not readily understand is that his earned profits should be transferred to some other, younger subsidiary, perhaps on another continent, to be invested there in new production or assembling facilities. He may argue that local investments will bring handsome dividends, but the parent company has many worldwide considerations, such as taxes, higher financing costs in other countries, currency convertibility, and bilateral trade agreements. The surplus on hand can also be spent to buy at favorable prices and terms raw materials or auxiliary parts not necessarily within the same country, but possibly for supplying the company's subsidiaries in third countries.

An American subsidiary manager who was originally with the parent company will normally better understand such overall corporate reasoning than a national manager who has never worked for the company in the United States. But it is always hard for a local manager who wants to make a success of his subsidiary and who is responsible for its profits and growth to see beyond the borders and to make what he can only regard as a sacrifice. Corporate and regional management can, and often must, impose decisions in the interest of the entire corporation; but it is far better to take the time and effort to persuade rather than force the subsidiary manager to go along.

Accounting

One of the knottiest problems encountered by American business abroad is the difference in accounting systems. Long-established companies know and newcomers soon find out that bookkeeping methods in Europe vary considerably from those in the United States. These differences are threefold.

First of all, European accounting procedures are simpler and cheaper, but they usually do not give a complete and clear picture until the end of the year or even later when the annual balance is established. During the year, the profit situation is often only estimated by looking at the cash flow and expenditures, and comparing accounts receivable with accounts payable. This system is geared to and mostly still found in small and medium-size European companies, including those that may be purchased by American corporations or in which they acquire minority or majority interests. Needless to say, such an accounting system is unacceptable to the great majority of U.S. corporations and they will want to change it as soon as possible. This, however, creates considerable difficulties in some countries and greatly increased costs in all, because skilled accountants familiar with American methods are both hard to find and expensive. If the present trend toward ever increasing American investments in Europe continues, this situation may become even more difficult because few schools exist where American accounting is taught. American subsidiaries must either train their accounting personnel, use Americans or specialized Europeans for quite some time, or obtain assistance from the local branch of a reputable American-international accounting firm. Normally, a newcomer will use all three of these expedients.

The second difference between American and European accounting procedures has to do with the tax laws of various countries, although efforts toward equalization are being made within the Common Market. These differences involve the evaluation of inventories, the depreciation of capital assets, the deduction of expenditures, and several types of reserves. The American subsidiary in Europe must of course follow the methods prescribed by the host country, but for consolidation within the corporation and for comparison of the various subsidiaries among themselves, with other regions, and with the domestic business in the United States, a uniform system has to be used. Following the requirements of the U.S. Internal Revenue Service the details of the annual balance must be expressed in accordance with the accepted methods and procedures of the American accounting system. This dual purpose can be achieved in two ways: Either the subsidiary establishes its monthly and annual balance sheets simultaneously according to both local and American procedures, or else the accounting department of the U.S. home office or the European regional office "translates" the local figures and adapts them for use by the parent company. Older and larger subsidiaries will normally adopt the first method; newly established or small subsidiaries, the latter.

The third problem stems from the time-honored "double bookkeeping" method for tax purposes. This is still widespread, especially in France, Italy, Spain, and some other countries. An American corporation that takes majority control of a local company usually ends this doubtful practice fast, but generally has to overcome strong local resistance.

In all three cases described above the changeover from the local European accounting system to the American system involves greatly increased operation costs.

Unification

When an American corporation owns only a minority interest in a joint venture, the accounting system is usually not "Americanized." Occasionally this happens even when the American company holds controlling shares. In one such case, the Spanish affiliate of a large American corporation, the latter exercises full control, but while it requires a budget and forecast and regular reports, it permits accounting procedures to follow the Spanish pattern. The consolidation is done by the parent company.

One of the leading oil companies had installed a computerized area accounting system in Hamburg for Germany, Switzerland, and Austria, and another in Stockholm for the Scandinavian countries, but had to discontinue them due to the different legal requirements in these countries. Otherwise, the parent company exercises strong centralized control over its wholly owned subsidiaries and maintains the area computer service for statistical purposes. By contrast, the Austrian affiliate of a medium-size U.S. company continues under its old management with little interference from America. Yet the accounting system was brought up to American standards, which admittedly caused some difficulties. The balance sheets made up in accordance with Austrian tax laws are adjusted for comparison and consolidation. Even the large local subsidiary of a major American corporation in the electrical and electronics field could not go much beyond this limited accounting unification, although this subsidiary dates back to the nineteenth century.

The unification, however, includes an identical coding system that makes the necessary "translation" and adjustment easier, whether performed at the subsidiary level, the European headquarters, or in the home office. This generally accepted accounting code can seldom be achieved where the network of affiliates comprises joint ventures with majority control, with minority participation, and even licensees. In these cases, it may very well be—and the author found several such instances—that each of the European affiliates has entirely different accounting procedures, and as a consequence, diverse reporting methods. This makes the consolidation much more difficult and contributes to the tendency to convert the licensees into affiliates and the affiliates into subsidiaries.

A further difficulty lies in the fact that European managers and accountants in the American subsidiaries, whether newly established or acquired, very often are not immediately convinced that the more complex and more expensive American methods are really worth the cost and effort.

As with many other American practices, they can be imposed on the subsidiaries by the parent company—but that is rather unwise except as a means of last resort. A European general manager, an Englishman of Swiss ancestry, told the author that "at first it was difficult to make the Europeans understand the advantages of the American accounting system. Finally, they found out that it made it easier for them too—not only for headquarters. Of course, in this, as in so many other matters, we must always avoid the mistake of going too far and of underestimating legitimate national differences." Resistance against unification of accounting may even come from an American subsidiary manager, who for many years has been used to great autonomy. The author found such a case in the French subsidiary of an important U.S. chemicals corporation. Surprisingly, the parent company has so far done nothing about it.

A striking contrast was provided by a joint venture in the Netherlands. The partners are an American company and its French and German manufacturing licensees. Each controls $33\frac{1}{3}$ percent of the shares. The local manager sends his monthly financial reports to all three partners, and although the reports are based on the accounting procedure required by Dutch law, he has to attach to the original, adjustments that follow the American, German, and French practices. The Dutch affiliate is rather small and these requirements put a considerable burden on the shoulders of the manager.

In large American corporations, the auditing of the local subsidiaries' books is usually done by the local branch of one of the U.S. auditing and accounting companies. In addition, some corporations send teams of company auditors regularly to all subsidiaries to help with and to supervise the work of the local subsidiary accountants. Such teams may be composed of Americans, of citizens of the European headquarters country, of third-country nationals, or of a combination of all three. They are normally sent out by the European regional office, but may report directly to the home office in the United States.

PRICING

American industry in Europe shows a wide variety in pricing patterns, this being caused by numerous variables. Two of them, however, are outstanding in determining price policies. First of all, in local subsidiaries that *import* their goods from company plants outside their countries, whether in Europe or America, a trend toward controlled prices can be observed. There are few exceptions. The control is exercised either by the home office, or, more frequently, by a strong regional office. Sometimes this is under policy directives from or in consultation with corporate head-quarters, where in turn decision making may be concentrated principally in the international division or corporation, in a product group, or on the highest corporate level.

The second major pricing pattern involves those subsidiaries that op-erate their own *factories*. They show a trend toward various degrees of price autonomy, again under general directives or in consultation with regional offices or U.S. headquarters.

For importing and marketing units, prices must take into account dif-ferent transport costs, particularly for bulky and heavy items if the source of supply is far away; they must also take into account import duties and taxes. If both the plant and the importing subsidiary are located within the European Economic Community (EEC) or the European Free Trade Association (EFTA), duties no longer exist, but taxes levied at the time of import or at the time of sale continue, and some have even been intro-duced or raised when duties were abolished.

In setting prices for manufacturing subsidiaries, all the usual cost fac-tors have to be considered, such as labor, raw materials, component parts, and power supply—and all these elements vary greatly from country to country, even within the two European economic areas. In a company pro-ducing industrial electrical items, the manufacturing costs of the British subsidiary were in 1968 double those of the Italian plant. Labor accounts for 60 percent of total costs, and British labor is much more expensive; but more important, Italian labor productivity was about twice as high as in the United Kingdom. Under such conditions the question of who sets the prices within the company is academic. In fact, the British plant worked only for its own domestic market; all the rest of Europe, even the other EFTA countries, were supplied from Italy.

Regardless of whether goods are imported or locally produced, the sub-sidiary's proportionate overhead is an important cost and price factor, and this depends on its size and wage level. Other elements that enter into con-sideration according to the nature and quality of the products are the gen-eral local price level and living standard, and the competitive situation. Moreover, prices will be influenced and differences accentuated by addi-tional local conditions, such as distribution channels, wholesale and retail markups, credit terms, interest rates, packaging and warehousing costs, sales volume and inventory size, advertising costs, and return of merchan-dise. There is little doubt that the local executives are in a better position to judge these elements, but this does not necessarily mean they can deter-mine prices, nor does it always assure that their suggestions will be fol-lowed at higher levels where several other factors must be considered.

Importing Subsidiaries

While price control by higher levels of management is the rule, headquarters influence can vary considerably in direction and rigidity. If the products are uniform, the control is usually tight. In a corporation making consumer items that are almost identical throughout the world, corporate headquarters gives the subsidiaries only a narrow margin within which they can establish their catalog prices. The company thereby tries to unify prices as much as possible. Every price change contemplated by local management must be submitted to the parent company for approval, but if, for example, a new sales tax has been instituted or tax levels have been increased, such approval will be given quickly. In a synthetic fiber company, prices are almost identical all over Europe. This is necessary because the products are used as raw materials by many European clothing manufacturers that also have subsidiaries in several countries. Differences due to customs tariffs and transport costs are absorbed by the parent company. For some items of purely local importance the subsidiary has a small margin within which it can make allowances; for all discounts exceeding these limits or outside the restricted product group, the regional office in Brussels must be asked for permission. Prices are fluctuating rapidly and European headquarters sends only brief summaries of price changes and trends to the home office.

The marketing manager of a paper corporation's subsidiary remarked that pricing in his company must be controlled directly in New York, because neither the subsidiaries nor the rather weak regional office have on hand all the information as to cost factors. In fact, he seemed to be quite happy not to have any responsibility in the matter, which he considered onerous in this very competitive industry. He confines himself to reporting competitive trends to the parent company. He willingly leaves to them the decision as to how to cope with them.

Exactly the opposite situation was found in an oil company's Belgian subsidiary, which handles its products (specialized mineral oils, greases, waxes, and fuel oil, all imported from the United States) in several countries of the Continent. Because of the necessity of adjusting prices quickly to competitive conditions, the subsidiary manager has the power to set his prices without interference from the home office—as long as his sales are profitable. He therefore also has full knowledge of all cost elements. In fact he knows some of them, like transport and storage costs, better than the parent company. This is a notable exception from the general trend toward price control in importing and marketing units. In this connection, however, it should be mentioned that the oil subsidiary described has very little autonomy in other activities. They work with independent non-exclusive distributors who also carry competitive products. This makes it even more important that the local manager possess the necessary authority to remain flexible. Outside the sales activity such adjustments are not essential—or at least not urgent, and strict central control is exercised.

A Swiss subsidiary in the instruments industry imports all its items from several corporate plants located in other countries. The local unit negotiates freely for the delivery of these goods with the supplying subsidiaries. This is not unusual. What *is* unusual is that they also negotiate with them their resale prices without recourse to the parent company. In one case of highly specialized instruments where there is practically no competition, all prices are fixed by the supplying factory, including exact resale prices with discounts for the selling subsidiary. In this rather unique case, prices are determined not by the local marketing unit, or the regional office, or the parent company, but by the manufacturing supply unit.

Manufacturing Subsidiaries

Frequently, manufacturing subsidiaries do their own pricing; they may, however, have to submit their price lists to regional or corporate management for checking and final approval. Also, higher management levels may set upper and lower limits, which leave enough leeway for competitive pricing, but must not be exceeded without special prior authorization. Comparing these companies with the importing subsidiaries, the reader will find that the difference between price control and price autonomy is more often than not quantitative rather than qualitative. There are few cases where one or the other is complete and unconditional. Moreover, there are exceptions in both types of subsidiaries. Thus a large corporation in the telecommunications field with many manufacturing subsidiaries does not allow them to determine their own price levels; neither does it force them into any uniformity. But it takes production variables and competitive conditions into careful consideration. Furthermore, price schedules are discussed between top management, the regional office, and the subsidiaries in common meetings. Mutual agreement, not unilateral control, is the aim. This consensus is necessary because the company has embarked on division of production within the Common Market, with certain items made only in one or two countries and others elsewhere. Thus each manufacturing subsidiary at the same time imports other products from neighboring company units.

A regional manager in a corporation with uniform products told the author that some of his local executives lack the ability to find the correct price level that would best serve both corporate objectives, and the subsidiary's interests. When a local manager wants to raise his prices without regard to the price level of other subsidiaries, the regional manager points out to him that this would only lead to greater unauthorized imports by dealers from neighboring countries. If, on the other hand, he wishes to reduce his prices unilaterally, the result may be that retailers would not pass the reduction on to the customers, but pocket the difference. Moreover, lower prices in that particular industry normally do not increase sales, which depend primarily on quality and brand name. An experienced regional manager who knows the various European markets and the nature of the company's business thoroughly, can distinguish between the various aspects of competition and correctly judge the influence of price changes on sales volume, corporate image and prestige, and intersubsidiary relations. He knows how to educate local managers, especially those who come from the outside, to understand such marketing complexities.

Pricing and General Control Policy

In general, corporations with tight control, whether exercised by corporate or regional headquarters, include pricing in these controlled activities. But, as has been shown before, even subsidiaries that enjoy a great deal of autonomy in other matters are often controlled by higher management in pricing. This is perhaps done in a more conciliatory form, with an opportunity to make price suggestions. And this can make a big difference in stimulating initiative and independent thinking, and in obtaining the necessary information and evaluations on all levels.

An executive in a chemicals corporation who exercises an extraordinary degree of autonomy in his territory told the author that pricing is one of the very few areas where he has to consult his superior, the head of the product division. For certain reasons, the European manager must agree on prices with his colleagues, the manager of the Latin American, Near East, and Far East regions, and if an agreement cannot be reached, the matter of uniform pricing is referred to the product division manager.

By contrast, in a household appliance company, pricing is one of the few activities where a degree of autonomy has survived from former times. Now the trend is clearly toward increasing control. As much as a local manager regretted this general trend he agreed that it is necessary in pricing—so that the enormous price differences among country units can be gradually eliminated. Guarantee terms also vary (replacement parts to be paid for or to be supplied free of charge, duration of guarantee, and so forth), which is considered bad policy for an internationally known brand name.

A special pricing situation exists in the pharmaceuticals industry. If the drugs have been accepted by the various social security systems (semiofficial sickness and hospitalization insurance funds), prices are controlled by the national governments. In the case of new products they must first be submitted to the national health authorities for analysis and approval; then cost calculations have to be presented for approval of the price suggested. Moreover, there has been a tendency lately among the Common Market nations to equalize drug prices throughout the area. In some pharmaceuticals corporations, prices in Europe are, wherever possible, matched against American prices to avoid difficulties with the American government. All these circumstances make it necessary that prices suggested to European governments for approval be determined by top management while the actual negotiations and explanations may very well be conducted by local management.

ADVERTISING

Decision making in advertising does not follow a specific pattern, but usually follows the general pattern of management control. Most corporations that tightly control their subsidiaries from U.S. headquarters or from the European regional office also tightly control advertising and promotional activities. Therefore, observing the division of decision making in advertising normally makes it possible to draw valid conclusions about decision making in general.

As in some other activities, there are good arguments for and against centralization or decentralization, strict or loose control in advertising. The advocates of strong centralized control stress the necessity of using and reproducing the corporation's trade name and various trademarks in a uniform design and color throughout the world. This is of course particularly important in consumer goods. In fact, even in those companies that leave most of the advertising decisions to local subsidiaries, names and trademarks must conform to a single scheme in every respect. There are very few exceptions to this generally observed rule: One is in a country where the corporation did not secure rights to one or several of its trademarks. Another involves an American corporation in the soft drink industry. In several North African countries, the red, white, and blue colors on its bottle caps and in its literature had to be changed. These are the French national colors, and they cannot be used in some of the more sensitive independent nations that were formerly French colonies.

Another argument for uniform advertising and packaging in the consumer goods industry is the increasing number of travelers from America to all European countries. This makes it desirable to have a product whose advertising is immediately recognizable anywhere. But those who oppose uniform advertising will argue that even in countries where the same language is spoken, the same slogans or pictures or emotional appeals very often must *not* be used because consumer preferences and attitudes are different. Most U.S. companies have learned this fact, sometimes the hard way, as far as America and Britain are concerned. Not too many know that the same situation exists with regard to France and the French-speaking parts of Canada, Belgium, and Switzerland; with regard to Germany as opposed to Switzerland and Austria; or with regard to Latin America as opposed to Spain and Portugal.

A further point stressed by the proponents of unified advertising is the great saving realized in preparing pictures and texts in a central location —at U.S. headquarters or at least in a few main locations at regional offices. Centralized advertising in international magazines and through an international advertising agency will also reduce the rates considerably. Opponents of centrally controlled advertising, however, can rightly emphasize that such media as television, radio, daily newspapers, movie shorts and slides, posters, and billboards cannot be used in every country. They are excluded by law or custom in some countries, ineffective in others.

Most American corporations that conduct an effective multinational business have therefore found it necessary to work out a compromise solution between fully centralized, uniform advertising and a completely loose, diversified, and local approach to this important problem. But the compromise solutions can be very different. The author asked specific questions about advertising in 30 company interviews. Of these, 11 companies give their subsidiaries a wide range of decision-making power, and 7 others grant their local units considerable influence in cooperative efforts with the regional and home offices. It should be noted that strong objection to centralized advertising is directed by local subsidiaries mostly against the home office in the United States because few if any people there are familiar with local conditions and differences. Opposition is normally nonexistent or much less vocal concerning decisions made by the European regional office. This is because it is so much nearer both geographically and mentally, because it usually employs several Europeans, and because it understands the local problems much better.

Complaints are often voiced not only about too much interference and control by the parent company, but also about too little aid and assistance. Sometimes it is the same subsidiary manager who complains in both ways— usually against the home office rather than regional headquarters. Naturally, it is easier for the regional office to help local units because it knows what is needed and, when necessary, can send an advertising expert on short notice. All this is contingent, of course, on a sufficiently large organization of the regional office. From the home office help is often hard to get and is always slow in coming. The advertising department of the parent company is usually too busy, engaged in too many diverse activities, and has to serve subsidiaries in many areas. It will quite naturally concentrate its major efforts on the more important markets and neglect the smaller subsidiaries. If the international division does not have its own advertising department or if the international division has been disbanded in favor of "integration" of the foreign business in domestic product groups, the subsidiaries can expect even less assistance from the parent company. Oddly enough, such lack of prompt and efficient help can sometimes be found in corporations with tight centralized control. In such cases, grave discontent on the part of local managers is bound to arise. They accept tight control more readily when it is coupled with continuous, effective, and fast aid.

It is not only important who makes the final decision, but also where advertising ideas originate: in the home office, at regional headquarters, or at the subsidiary level. If they originate outside the local unit, will they be forced on the subsidiary manager against strong objections, or does he have a veto power if he feels that the decision would be harmful? Naturally, such veto power will only be given, if at all, to local managers who have successfully directed the local business for a good many years. It therefore cannot happen in companies that rotate their subsidiary managers very often or that appoint men who are unfamiliar with the intricacies of the local market. On the other hand, managers of smaller subsidiaries that do not employ a local advertising expert, may not have the necessary knowledge and experience to decide advertising questions submitted to them by the parent company's advertising department or the advertising agency. As in all other activities, the size and staff of the subsidiary, its organization, and the experience and personality of its manager play such an important role that no two subsidiaries can truly be compared.

Another decisive factor is the organization of the parent company's international division and regional office in Europe. If the international division (or the regional office) has its own advertising department and works with a truly international advertising agency, the decisions will usually be much more acceptable to the local subsidiaries than if the international division has been disbanded or reduced to staff functions, and the corporate or domestic advertising department or similar departments in various product groups take care of and direct foreign advertising. Disagreements on important questions, misunderstandings, mistakes, conflicts of jurisdiction, and personality clashes often result. It is also possible that the lack of adequate knowledge and direction at the parent company leads to complete freedom of action on the local level with equally unsatisfactory results, which can only be prevented by a strong, well-staffed regional office.

Where Decisions Are Made

An American executive in a subsidiary of a major U.S. automobile manufacturer stated flatly that advertising is the responsibility of local management with practically no interference from the international division at home. The managing director of another automotive corporation's marketing subsidiary, located in a different country, was more specific. He explained that a promotional campaign for a new model always originates with the manufacturing subsidiary that makes the model. Its suggestions are then discussed with all marketing subsidiaries throughout Europe. All local sales and advertising managers attend these meetings. The local units are usually given several advertising texts from which they can select those best suited for their country. They will have to be translated, of course, and this is problematical because certain expressions cannot be translated literally. Certain slogans may be effective in one language, but sound silly, or unappealing, or even offensive in another.

In such a case an entirely different approach may have to be used in one country. The name suggested for the new model is given to all subsidiaries many months in advance. The possibility of registering the name as a trademark in all major countries will have already been explored. If several important subsidiaries object to the name as unsuitable for their markets, it is dropped. If only one or two local units in smaller markets find the name unacceptable, an exception is made for them. In all these discussions the regional office plays an advisory role, but in advertising matters the parent company in the United States communicates only with this regional office, not directly with the subsidiaries.

Some regional offices do not cover advertising. They may control finance, production, and administration, but advertising for all or part of Europe may be concentrated in another location where the facilities are better, where most advertising is being done, where executives with special experience are available, or simply for "historic" reasons. The author found that in one large corporation with regional offices in London, advertising was handled from Milan. In another well-known company that also had its regional headquarters in London, the advertising for the Benelux countries was done in Brussels with considerable local autonomy concerning copy and media selection. These are quite different in Belgium and Holland even though half the Belgian population speaks the same language as Holland. The Belgian subsidiary of still another corporation has wide authority in many fields including advertising, but the local manager gladly accepts the help of the French and Dutch subsidiaries in preparing his French and Flemish texts, though he usually has to make some changes to adapt them for local use—a task that could hardly be done outside his country.

A company in the food industry leaves most advertising activities in the hands of the area managers. The manager covering the Benelux countries and Switzerland, for example, selects the media and prepares the copy. He also prints his own international label for all these countries. This is not easy since the label must not only be in the individual language, but it must also conform to regulations in all three countries. Another manufacturer of packaged foods follows a somewhat different pattern. The initiative and original suggestions for advertising ideas, text, and media usually come from the area managers, but are then reviewed by European regional headquarters, and finally approved by the vice-president–Europe at the U.S. home office. Although in this and similar systems of decision making, the executives concerned speak of a joint or cooperative effort, it is difficult to determine which of these various stages is the decisive one. It all depends on the strength, experience, and drive of the different personalities and how much importance they and the company in general ascribe to advertising in the corporate, regional, and local efforts to attain the objectives assigned to them.

A corporation in the soft drinks industry follows exactly the same direction for advertising suggestions: from the area to the regional office, thence to the international division in New York. But a major competitor reverses this pattern: Most advertising originates in the parent company on a worldwide basis, then goes to the international division in the United States, and from there for further discussion to European regional and area managements. Local units have to convince higher levels through the same channels of the validity of any objections or suggested changes they may have.

A limited number of American companies still work in Europe mainly through licensed distributors or agents. An even smaller number do not conduct direct company-sponsored and paid advertising, but give distributors an advertising allowance proportionate to their sales volume and with the condition that the agents spend an equal amount for advertising out of their own pockets. The selection of media is usually a cooperative effort and since the American company may not have a local manager or supervisor, the agent frequently has a major influence on media selection. He often collaborates with an advertising agency chosen by the American company and receives from it advertising material such as radio and television shorts, mats, or printed material. If the company has a local sales manager or an area executive who acts as supervisor or liaison for the agents, he will usually transmit their wishes and suggestions regarding advertising to headquarters and convey the replies to the agents. This arrangement is often very unsatisfactory for both sides and is used mostly in the initial phase of marketing. It is replaced as soon as is feasible by firmer control.

Centralized Control

The strictest centralized control in advertising can be found in companies dealing with pharmaceuticals and cosmetics. Several factors explain this situation. First, these companies usually have a strong headquarters control pattern in most activities, the reasons for which were indicated in a previous section. Second, advertising plays a major role in both businesses. Third, these products are internationally among the best known and most widely used under uniform trademarks and in almost identical packaging. There are also factors favoring local influence on advertising—such as the different health department regulations in each country and certain restrictions on advertising claims, such as the prohibition on superlatives in Germany. In spite of this, the home office in the United States usually gives out general directives for each product that have to be followed by all subsidiaries. These directives specify which claims can and cannot be made for the product under normal circumstances, based on U.S. laws and regulations. The local subsidiary must not add any claim, but it can reduce them or leave them out entirely if this should be necessary according to local regulations.

This is a typical control pattern, in pharmaceuticals and cosmetics companies, and it does not make the subsidiary manager any too happy. He feels that he has to work under a competitive disadvantage since he is forced to observe the restrictions of *two* countries—his own and the United States. Unless he has worked previously in the home office—and sometimes not even then—the local manager has little understanding of global considerations. He feels that they are frequently greatly exaggerated and often an excuse for the desire to concentrate as much power as possible at headquarters.

In one of the most tightly controlled worldwide corporations, one where practically all important decisions are made by the parent company, advertising is the one activity where some very limited authority is delegated to the European marketing manager, but not to local units. Media selection, however, is always handled in New York, and advertising copy and pictures must be as uniform as legally possible. Subsidiary managers consider this a straitjacket.

Naturally, there are exceptions to tight advertising control even in the cosmetic industry. One well-known corporation gives its subsidiaries considerable autonomy in several activities, and advertising is one of them. The initiative for advertising campaigns, media selection, and copy preparation is within the jurisdiction of the local unit, which is therefore envied by other much less independent subsidiaries.

A middle-of-the-road approach to the problem of advertising control is followed by some corporations, usually those with long experience in European business. Central and local management are well balanced with divided responsibility: Headquarters sets overall policies and provides guidance, advice, assistance, and support to all subsidiaries. Imposing decisions against the expressed and explained will and intentions of local units is avoided—except where a local unit has not yet gained, or has lost, the confidence of the parent company.

A more sophisticated method, that of joint management, was observed in a major chemicals corporation. Advertising plans usually originate with the local subsidiary, which, however, has no advertising department of its own. All suggestions are therefore submitted to the large and well-staffed European regional headquarters, which works out a detailed advertising program with an America-based international advertising agency through its local branch office. However, before the program is begun, it is again sent back to the local subsidiary manager for his comments and approval. Then the regional office begins the actual work in cooperation with the agency. It is essentially a three-way pattern with support from the American headquarters of the corporation and the agency.

A slightly different pattern was observed in another chemicals and pharmaceuticals corporation, where the European regional office is considerably smaller and has fewer employees, less experience, and less influence, while several subsidiaries have their own advertising men and work directly with local advertising agencies or branches of American agencies. The actual work is therefore done locally, and the support and supervision from regional headquarters is much less pronounced.

In a third chemicals corporation, the regional office is also rather small and not yet fully developed; it was established only a few years ago. The international division in the United States has no advertising department, a fact that the advertising manager of a local subsidiary lists as a major weakness and that he hopes will be corrected as the international business expands. For the time being he must consult the American domestic advertising department, which is supposed to act in an advisory function but has neither the knowledge required for international advertising nor sufficient interest in it. Furthermore, the local advertising manager must write to a staff member of the international division and attach his letter to the domestic advertising department. The staff member then delivers it. This man is also supposed to keep after the domestic advertising people who handle the specific problem in question to make sure that they reply without too much delay. Copies of this correspondence are mailed to the fledgling European regional office, but for information only. This is a typical case where the advertising manager of the local subsidiary would gladly give up some of his independence in exchange for more support from a more developed regional office or from a better staffed international division in the United States.

Uniformity and Diversity

A company making synthetic fibers advertises in fashion magazines. Since fashion trends move so fast from one country to another, the company tries to unify its advertisements as much as possible in pictorial content, style, general appearance, and copy—with due regard to local language and usage. Suggestions from the subsidiary are carefully studied, but advertising is centralized, because it serves a truly international industry and uses international media. This is recognized by the subsidiary managers, who do not try to go their separate ways.

By contrast, advertising for sewing machines cannot be completely unified; pictures can be prepared by American headquarters or by the European office, but copy must be rewritten locally by each subsidiary. Even copy prepared in Germany and France is not used in Switzerland, because the attitudes of the Swiss housewives are quite different. Only the texts of brochures and instruction pamphlets prepared in France and Germany are used in Switzerland (and Austria) to save costs. Thus, while local differences are generally more pronounced in the consumer goods industries, such corporations also usually try harder to unify their advertising efforts and to "educate" the private customers or end-users to more international thinking. This effort has certainly been successful in many fields, such as household appliances, radios and TV sets, cosmetics, clothing, and photographic equipment.

A few American corporations, including some very important ones, have so far only one subsidiary in Europe large enough to have its own advertising manager. In such cases, this advertising executive will lend a helping hand to other, smaller local units and will probably eventually become European advertising manager—if and when a regional office is established. He works with the home office and usually with the local branch of an American advertising agency and in the meantime gains valuable European experience.

During the course of this study the author visited several corporations that either established their European regional office only a few years ago or developed it slowly by combining various separate functional departments in Europe. Normally, finance and accounting are the first activities to be centralized in a regional office. Production and marketing usually follow, and advertising, as part of marketing, arrives soon afterward. A wise regional manager will leave a lot of initiative to the subsidiary managers, who may have a longer European experience. He will also listen to their suggestions regarding text, media, and the budget share to be given each. Some types of advertising may be left to a greater extent to local subsidiaries if they are strong enough to handle them. In such a case, routine advertising, more or less regularly repeated and approved by the regional office or the parent company within the annual budget, is the subsidiary's responsibility. Meanwhile, headquarters takes care of special campaigns, as when new or improved products are being launched, or when new distribution channels are being tried out, or when different promotional techniques are to be tested. In such special advertising campaigns the subsidiary has little to say and is simply charged a certain percentage of the total European costs whether it agrees with the campaign or not.

A major manufacturer of computers has three levels of advertising: worldwide, continental (European), and national, but following its general policy of giving the local subsidiaries as much autonomy as possible, it permits them to modify a text they consider unsuitable for their particular country. Of course, this is not a consumer goods industry, and due to its recent development and high technical level it is among the most international industries in existence today. Yet the author was told by the regional manager: "If you have a local subsidiary executive who is a good man and supposed to know his business and his country, you'd better listen to him."

Of course, a good thing can go too far. In the Dutch subsidiary of an American corporation that manufactures office machines it seems that until recently not only the texts but even the illustrations for advertisements and descriptive literature had been printed by each local unit—clearly a waste of effort and money. This is now being changed. Since the equipment produced and sold all over Europe is identical and interchangeable, all texts and pamphlets are now printed in one spot. Holland has been selected for this centralized activity because the Dutch printing establishments are equipped to handle copy in all western-European languages.

The Advertising Agency

Most American corporations which feel that the greatest possible uniformity in advertising is desirable try to work with a single American multinational advertising agency. This policy also reduces costs, secures better terms, and helps attract favored treatment on the part of the media. The large and established agencies are well aware of local differences and perform a valuable service by protecting subsidiary managers against unreasonable and damaging unifying tendencies on the part of their headquarters. But they also protect headquarters against unreasonable claims by subsidiaries, which sometimes have a tendency to magnify the differences.

All these advantages can fully be realized only if the corporation can use the same agency in all European countries, or at least in all important markets. This requires that the agency have its own subsidiaries in all major markets and at least closely connected correspondents in smaller countries. It also requires that the agency still be free to handle the corporation's account all over Europe without competitive limitations in any country.

If these conditions are met, the agency occupies a most important place within the company's advertising program, but it often has to navigate skillfully and diplomatically between parent company, regional offices, and subsidiaries. The agency's account executives must know where the decision-making power rests or how it is divided among the various levels. No wonder that the executives of European subsidiaries of large American advertising agencies are among the best informed, most enlightened experts on relationships between American corporations and their subsidiaries.

The author visited the subsidiaries of four different American agencies in Frankfurt, Geneva, Paris, and London, interviewing both American and European account executives or managers. Two of these agencies have their European regional office in London or Brussels. The third, a smaller agency that went international much later than the others, also established its European headquarters in London, but disbanded it a few years afterwards. The fourth had no European headquarters. The oldest and largest agency established itself in Europe many years ago, not because it looked for more business or had acquired capital interests in European companies, but because its biggest clients had at that time begun their first European operations and wanted the same service from their advertising agency they had had in America. Many years ago, European advertising methods were so far behind the United States that this seemed the only possible solution. This agency thus followed its clients to Europe in the first European ventures of American corporations before World War I and particularly in the second large wave after World War II. Today, however, the agency has in some countries like Germany about 50 percent local clients, and here the U.S. parent company of the advertising agency naturally plays a minor role.

In working with American corporations the advertising agency adjusts itself to the pattern of control observed by the corporation. If advertising is centralized at the corporation's home office, the agency's nearest branch office in the United States will act as coordinator; if international advertising is directed from an international division in New York, the agency's main office in New York will perform this function; if European advertising is concentrated at the corporation's regional headquarters in London, Brussels, Paris, or Zurich, the agency's subsidiary in these same cities will be the coordinating office. If responsibility for advertising is divided between the corporation's U.S. home office and the European regional office, the agency will adapt a similar pattern by making its nearest American branch the coordinator and its nearest European subsidiary the subcoordinator of advertising programs in Europe.

A major problem in the advertising relationship between headquarters and subsidiary is the budgetary question of how much money should be spent for advertising, who should spend it, and what kind of advertising it should be spent on. A conservative subsidiary manager, especially an older European, may wish to spend less than the home office thinks the subsidiary should spend. He may not be convinced of the value of certain advertising media. A more modern local manager, particularly a younger American, may very well want to spend more for advertising than the parent company deems advisable. Also he may wish to see the fruits of local advertising efforts during the two or three years of his management of the subsidiary, and such a consideration could seriously influence his outlook.

Normally, planned advertising forms part of the annual budget prepared by the local manager and is submitted by him directly or through the regional office to the international division, and finally to corporate headquarters. In some corporations, however, the advertising budget is separate from the general operational budget, and in a limited number of cases, advertising expenditures are determined as a fixed percentage of sales or in some other proportionate manner. A car-rental company sets aside a certain amount per car and mile. This is split three ways: One part is used for international advertising, another for advertising within each country, and the third for local districts. Local advertising supplements national programs, and national advertising supplements worldwide campaigns. Local and national texts are submitted to international headquarters for approval. Similarly, international advertising copy is sent to the subsidiaries for their modifications and suggestions.

Special Cases

In a subsidiary of an international brokerage firm, there is a great deal of autonomy, yet one of the few centrally controlled activities is advertising. This is because media, copy, and type of advertising have to conform to Securities and Exchange Commission regulations. In addition, such advertising must of course conform to the regulations of the host country. In some European countries any advertising in securities is excluded either by law or by private agreement.

A particular type of advertising refers not to the specific product by brand or company name, but rather to the use of the product in general, a use that may be unknown to a majority of consumers in a certain market. This educational advertising requires a thorough knowledge of the historic and cultural background and the attitudes and behavioral patterns of consumer groups, as well as psychological skill. It can therefore best be achieved by a team of experts in all these fields, some from the home office and some from the local units of both the corporation and the advertising agency. The author was told that in southern Italy advertising for shaving products must still stress the desirability of shaving more than once a week. In some African countries educational campaigns are required to tell the men how and where to shave and to advise them to put the blade into the razor instead of holding it between their fingers.

PERSONNEL MATTERS

Time and time again the author was told by subsidiary managers that one of the areas—sometimes one of the very few—in which they enjoy almost complete independence is hiring and firing local employees and determining their compensation. One local executive added: "Of course, I send regular reports about personnel movements and payments to headquarters and reply to their inquiries; but all this is rather informal." Further questioning revealed that the "almost" complete autonomy he had spoken of had to be taken with a grain of salt. First of all, subsidiaries usually have to submit an annual personnel budget indicating the total and individual size of salaries in all employee categories, and the number of personnel, more or less broken down by type of work, length of employment, and perhaps also level of education. Practically all subsidiary managers must stay within the budget, but this can mean different things. In some companies local management can exceed neither the total amount paid in wages and salaries, nor the total number of personnel, and these limits have to be maintained for each specified category. Sometimes even shifts of employees from one job to another or replacements with lower-paid personnel need the approval of the regional or the home office.

A subsidiary manager may get around such restrictions by hiring temporary factory workers, and he would only have to report this afterwards. Complete autonomy in personnel matters, bound only by the budgetary limits, has become the exception and can be found mostly in new acquisitions, for a longer or shorter transitory period, and in joint ventures. It creates differences in salary and wage levels from one subsidiary to another that can be damaging if the corporation has several acquisitions in similar product groups within one country.

Subsidiaries that operate large plants generally have more autonomy concerning factory personnel than marketing subsidiaries with regard to their salesmen and office employees. This is because it is much more difficult to enforce uniform international standards in manufacturing plants, which are subject to many legal controls and union rules. Sometimes staff members of the home office's personnel department may question one of these rules and will have to be content with the short explanation that it is the law—as, for example, certain requirements in the Netherlands for employing Spanish or Turkish workers (one-year contract, special food and living accommodations, home leave once a year) or special allotments for workers' children, or several weeks' maternity leave before and after childbirth for women employees.

Standards and Qualifications

The setting of standards and qualifications for hiring middle- and lower-level employees is normally left to the subsidiary manager and his personnel staff, because most corporations realize that this is an area the local people know far better than anybody else. The subsidiary manager will have to ask for permission and explain the necessity to hire new salesmen, but he usually is free to select the best men he can find.

Some corporations have tried to introduce some of their American educational requirements for certain categories of employees; they recommend, for example, the hiring of high school graduates. But this is difficult because there is no exact equivalent in Europe for the American high school: European schools for this age group are either much above or much below the average American high school level. Furthermore, there are far fewer graduates from the higher level schools available. Or the home office suggests that the subsidiary use more college graduates for other employee groups. Again, European university studies do not correspond to American college studies, and university graduates aspire to higher positions and pay than might be expected.

A medium-size U.S. company has established a uniform test for prospective salesmen throughout the world. The firm produces items for women and believes that there are few local customer differences in its line, and hence that selling standards should be much the same anywhere. The test was worked out by a consulting company in Chicago and was tested in Europe before being generally applied.

After the local manager has received approval to add a man to his sales force, or when he has to replace one, he selects a person he thinks is qualified. He then has to conduct the prescribed test and send it to the consultants for grading. If the applicant is rejected by Chicago the local executive must start again with another candidate. This procedure, however, would be considered by many experts a gross interference in the proper responsibilities of a local manager, and it is doubtful whether the company can get high-caliber subsidiary managers under such circumstances. In fact, it had to drop its requirement for college graduates for sales jobs, since they are just not available in Europe (or Latin America) and would never accept such a job even for high pay. On the other hand, it would be desirable to develop testing methods for higher-level and middle-level employees, both American and European, if certain differences between the domestic and the international conditions were duly considered.

In one very important corporation, the author found an index system that establishes a given ratio between local business volume and the number of employees in various categories and that takes the efficiency level of different areas into account. Deviations from the index have to be explained to headquarters.

Several corporations found that new acquisitions and even old subsidiaries that had been left free to employ as many people as was customary or had been set by tradition, were grossly overstaffed and in the words of one VP–Europe they "induced" the subsidiaries to decrease their inflated manpower. Reportedly, more is now being produced and sold with fewer people. However, in many European countries the dismissal of workers and employees is an extremely difficult matter. High severance pay must be disbursed and long notice must be given.

Finally, it may be of interest to add here the opinions of a university professor who is a member of the British Council on Exports. He first pointed out that Britain has a century-old tradition of trading with many foreign nations and of sending her young men abroad. British foreign affiliates are mostly in present or former Commonwealth countries. Relatively few are on the Continent, especially in manufacturing. British companies are therefore faced with fewer problems than American firms, particularly as regards personnel. Company loyalty is still rather strong, but moving from one firm to another is becoming more frequent than in the past. British executives are used to staying a long time in one foreign country, but they too now want to come home after several years. On the basis of research conducted for this study, the author concluded that many similarities between British and American companies exist in facing up to various problems, especially those with personnel. The differences may be a matter of size and volume rather than essence.

6. Product-Related Control Affecting Subsidiary Operations

THE SEASONED general manager of an international division, if permitted a free hand by top management, can usually distinguish between necessary uniformity and blind conformity. Conformity has been and is much criticized in Europe, especially if it extends outside the confines of the corporate structure into relationships with government offices, semi-official organizations, customers, and suppliers. Here the experienced international executive will try to arrive at some adjustment to and compromise with local customs and practices.

Most U.S. corporations in Europe have been engaged more or less successfully and in varying degrees in efforts to unify and Americanize their subsidiaries' activities, extending these efforts sometimes only to a few selected fields, sometimes to nearly all of them. It may be helpful to divide unification attempts and procedures into two main parts: those that are independent of the products sold or manufactured, and those that can only be effective where the products are uniform. The unification regardless of products is directed mainly toward these areas:

- Accounting, statistics, and financial reporting.
- Budget preparations and forecasts.
- Sales reports and other communications.
- Administrative procedures.
- Personnel policy and executive compensation.
- General systems and procedures.

In all these areas uniformity is important. Indeed in some, like accounting and budgets, it is essential. But all these efforts are directed at the difficult task of overcoming old and established practices. This takes time, and newcomers are well advised not to attempt total unification all at once. Rather, they should phase out these practices over a period of time, beginning with the really important areas and leaving unessential matters for later.

PRODUCT AND PROCESS UNIFORMITY

To get uniformity in product lines, complete equalization is frequently attempted in the following areas: identity of product, production methods, and processes; design, shape, size, color, and so on; packaging, label, name, and trademark. As far as possible, it is also attempted in literature, advertising, marketing, distribution, pricing, and service.

The attempt to maintain a single international identity for most products of the same category is motivated by the desire to reduce capital investment and operational expenditures. At the same time it is aimed at securing high quality through uniform raw materials, components, and equipment, unified or centrally directed technical research and development, and equalized manpower training. When these principles are applied to foreign operations, it means that the factories abroad share in the common savings. Thus the foreign markets share in some benefits of the single U.S. market, which is recognized to be one of the main sources of the success of American business. But product uniformity also has its drawbacks. The international operations become oriented toward the demands and resources of the U.S. market, which is usually the largest and always the best known among the corporation's markets, with the result that smaller and less researched markets may be neglected. When new products are developed, the demands and requirements of foreign countries take second place, which is one of the biggest complaints by subsidiary managers in Europe who would like to have all the benefits of the large U.S. domestic business, but do not wish to be dominated by it.

However, managers of marketing subsidiaries who can purchase their goods from various suppliers among their company's producing subsidiaries are quite happy to know that if necessary they can shift their orders from one plant to another. This interchangeability of products is even more important when different parts are manufactured in various factories. The important possibility of shifting supplies of parts and finished products all over Europe and beyond is particularly valuable in emergencies caused by national strikes or other disruptions.

Product Identity

A universally identical product can be achieved even without complete unification of production methods and procedures, but the same reasons that prompt the corporation to attempt product identity throughout its various plants will normally also lead to efforts toward similar production. However, due to numerous local obstacles, the goal of complete unity and uniformity of production can seldom be achieved. One obstacle is the necessity of using local raw materials that may have different qualities and specifications. Another is less sophisticated equipment. Then there are various legal requirements and restrictions that vary from country to country and are of particular importance in the food and pharmaceuticals industries, but also exist in everything from building materials to television sets. Some of these rules may not be of governmental origin, but are enforced by associations, unions, agreements, or simply tradition and custom. Sometimes the regulations are stricter and more onerous than in the United States, and sometimes they are more lenient. Yet because of the unavoidable adjustment to the local business environment, they always result in deviations from uniform manufacturing processes.

The toilet goods industry is usually strictly uniform even though it faces local health department regulations, regulations on alcoholic content, and others. Uniformity is necessary because these products are sold chiefly on the basis of their standardized quality and consumer appeal; uniformity is not too difficult because production processes are simple. The parent companies often try to market in Europe all products sold in America, but sometimes they reluctantly have to omit one or the other of their home market items from some or most of the overseas markets. Seldom, if ever, do they manufacture and sell abroad a product that has not first been on the domestic market. This is frequently a bone of contention between European subsidiaries and the home office, with the regional headquarters sometimes siding with local, sometimes with corporate management. All this applies to those companies that market their products under unified trademarks known to consumers at home and abroad.

Other companies in the toilet goods industry—a distinct minority— follow a different strategy. Often their subsidiaries are acquisitions with established local products and trade names that are sometimes unknown in America and even in distant European countries. In these cases, unification, if attempted, must proceed slowly. "There is some general uniformity among the various European plants," said an Italian subsidiary manager. "However, it was accomplished not by dictum from the home office, but rather through mutual discussion and agreement." In this company the local managers themselves recognized that at the very least, European uniformity is desirable. In fact, some European manufacturers are moving in the same direction. Yet many items manufactured in Europe are different from the American products and vary from country to country. Also, the ultimate decision on whether to introduce a new product that has been successfully launched in the United States—or in France, where the largest European plant is situated—rests with local management. New York seems to use some persuasion and light pressure, however, to convince the subsidiary managers of the potentials of new products and the advantages of marketing them throughout the continent.

The food industry shows a great diversity of products and production methods in large corporations with subsidiaries in many countries. To try uniformity here, without thorough market research in every market, can lead to significant failures such as have been experienced by a canned soup manufacturer in Italy and by a cereal company in Britain. Some companies are therefore extremely careful not to impose an American product on a subsidiary that believes it cannot be successful in the local market—at least not without an enormous amount of promotion and advertising. A Spanish subsidiary executive explained that 40 percent of his business is in a single product type and that his country is very conservative. His considered opinion: "Product uniformity in our business and in our market simply does not work."

Several other executives in the food industry agreed, and pointed out that European subsidiaries cannot possibly sell exactly the same products as in the United States or, for that matter, as in other European countries. Some items are made and sold in most European markets, but not in America; others are strictly local, but may constitute the main part of the business; and a few products are truly international. To know or to find out which is which requires thorough market familiarity and, frequently, consumer surveys; it places a heavy responsibility on the shoulders of the local or area manager.

By contrast, there are no consumer preferences in the photographic industry, except for price and quality. Therefore, complete product identity is the rule and improvements in cameras, films, and slides introduced in the United States—or in Germany and Japan—are eagerly accepted by customers everywhere. In the non-consumer-goods industries, office machines and computers are the classic examples of almost complete product uniformity. They do vary in electric current capacities, and so require some slightly different parts.

Design

Uniformity does not always extend to design. A Dutch executive in the office machine industry said he has the power to reject a new American model he believes unsuitable for his market. That is, he can reject it, but he cannot get it modified. The parent company, of course, would never launch a new model that was in any way unfit for the U.S. market, nor would it consider the slightest change in design. It is always a take-it-or-leave-it proposition. The executive explained that this corporate attitude creates a great disadvantage inasmuch as some European customers (German, Swedish, Italian, and others) pay a great deal of attention to the exterior design of office equipment—and the European office machine competition has therefore been emphasizing appearance. The progress this American corporation has made over the past several years in understanding European problems has so far not penetrated to the isolated halls of the industrial designers.

In color, shape, size, and material, efforts to achieve worldwide product uniformity are also not always successful. And they can be harmful to a subsidiary's profit picture. It is easy enough to convince consumers everywhere of the advantages of an unbreakable plastic bottle, but it is difficult in some countries to sell the so-called large economy size, because many consumers in Europe are price-conscious and not willing to calculate long-range savings. To explain this fact to top management at home is sometimes an impossible task and can lead to serious friction and lack of confidence between the home office and local management, especially if no regional office can act as mediator. Because great differences exist in these matters within Europe, and because similar conditions sometimes do not produce similar results in consumer purchasing patterns, the acceptability of a certain product or its presentation in one market and its rejection in another are hard to explain.

The use of plastic tubes, for example, varies widely. In Italy, where the labor costs of filling the tubes are low, even such inexpensive food items as tomato paste can be packed in tubes. In Sweden, labor costs are very high and tube-encased products are therefore expensive. Still, tubes are popular there, because the consumers are used to high food prices and can afford them. In contrast, their use in Holland is very restricted because of the extreme price-consciousness of the Dutch. Thrift and spending attitudes must therefore be balanced against costs of product and packaging.

In color and smell there are strong local dislikes and taboos. As was mentioned earlier, certain color schemes are excluded in some countries because of political associations.

Packaging

These considerations must be taken into account in the widespread corporate efforts to unify packaging and labels. Again, the pharmaceuticals and cosmetics industries, as well as several other consumer goods manufacturers, are normally strong supporters of uniformity. Identical packages convey the picture of identical high quality and create consumer confidence; they also produce a universal company or product image that is valuable for unified promotion. Contrary to the objections against product uniformity outlined previously, local managers usually accept identical packaging willingly, except in the case of local dislike of certain colors. One of the subsidiary managers most critical of other aspects of his corporation's international policies described the strict requirements for uniform packaging and labeling enforced by the home office without the resentment he expressed in most other matters.

In another pharmaceuticals company the local manager tried to impress the author with the great measure of autonomy supposedly granted him by the parent company, but he did not hesitate to mention that every box and every label must be submitted to headquarters for inspection and approval. Even in recently acquired pharmaceuticals firms, where traditional product lines are being continued, the trend toward unification of packaging is often unmistakable, though slow.

Yet pharmaceuticals and cosmetics are rigorously controlled by government agencies, and this applies especially to labels and inscriptions on boxes, cans, and containers. Unification is therefore a formidable task, because all the elements of each package must conform to the regulations of all countries where the package will be used. In one cosmetics company with subsidiaries all over the world, not the slightest deviation is permitted to local firms in production, product selection, colors, or fragrances, and a local manager may not even suggest a modification if he does not want to jeopardize his job. Nevertheless, in packaging and labels, adjustments to various national regulations must be made.

A soft drink company varies the size of its bottles according to different market conditions, but insists on strict uniformity of product and of bottle shape. Even the quality and weight of the bottles supplied by local manufacturers are strictly controlled.

Several corporations in the food industry accept or have learned to accept necessary diversification and local adjustment of their products, even though this sometimes makes it impossible to adhere to uniformity in packaging and labeling. The result is that the American visitor hardly recognizes his favorite brand except for the name and trademark. In fact, uniformity of trademark and name throughout the world is universally regarded as essential by most multinational corporations, particularly those making consumer goods. A trademark is not only a very valuable asset in marketing and promotion, it is in some industries almost more important than production or product selection. After all, products can often be duplicated and even patents may offer only limited protection, but the advantages of a properly exploited trademark are long-lasting ones. The problem is that few American corporations, before registering their trademarks, have investigated to see whether a certain word that sounds good in English could convey an adverse impression in another language.

It should be noted that a few American corporations try to create the image of a transnational corporation, one not bound in any way to a particular country. Where well-known foreign firms have been acquired, the new parent company sometimes attempts to continue the acquisition as a national firm and to conceal the passing of control into American hands. Whatever the advantages or merits of such national images may be, they cannot succeed if at the same time products, designs, packaging, and advertising are Americanized. The only possible compromise is to substitute a pan-European image for the unwanted American image. There are many experts, however, who have their doubts about such efforts and who recommend Americanization within limits and adjustment to European conditions where necessary or useful. This, they contend, creates much more goodwill for the corporation than efforts to veil its American identity.

On the other hand, unification of products and product appearance should not be based on the desire to please the American tourist in Europe. To overrate his importance as a consumer of U.S. products abroad would be a grave mistake. By contrast, the rapidly growing intra-European tourist trade is significant in some consumer industries. Here again, a unification along European lines is worthwhile.

In smaller and less industrialized European countries, the subsidiary may still encounter some difficulties in obtaining locally the quality of packaging elements required by the parent company—or the costs may be prohibitive and deliveries slow. But such difficulties are confined at present mainly to Asia and Africa and some Latin American countries. It is then a question of whether or not the higher quality materials can be imported from another country, and, if this is feasible, whether or not the small and poor local market can bear the costs. It is astonishing to find that in such matters local management is sometimes more cost-conscious than headquarters. In fact, while a subsidiary manager often fights for larger investment authorizations to enlarge and improve local production, he seldom does so to improve and unify packaging.

Packaging not only educates consumers, it also plays a great role in appealing to their preferences. Preferences are based on both objective and subjective considerations, and one kind is often as strong as the other. Photography makes a good case in point. This industry has not only complete product identity, but also uniformity in packaging. This is necessary due to the great impact of the tourist trade, which makes it essential that travelers be able to purchase the same easily identifiable items wherever they go. Yet there has long been a certain consumer preference for film made in America as opposed to the same brand produced in Europe. This was based on the assumption that products stamped "made in U.S.A." were of superior quality. Some dealers took advantage of this consumer preference and tried to sell American-made film at higher prices, while discount houses sold European products for less. One corporation made every effort to eradicate this imagined quality difference and to convince the consumers everywhere of the uniformity of product quality regardless of country of origin. Identical packaging and literature are potent weapons in this struggle.

Descriptive Literature

Instruction pamphlets and other descriptive literature are often a part of packaging, and attempts to achieve uniformity are usually extended to them. However, many legal provisos and local habits must be taken into account—more, in fact, than the home office realizes or wants to accept. A common misconception with quite a few American companies is that mere translation into the national language is sufficient. Except for some highly technical items in the production goods industries and a few that are used exclusively by professionals (doctors and engineers), pamphlets should not be translated, but rewritten according to the level of consumer knowledge of and familiarity with the type of products involved. What is self-evident to the American consumer may call for a more extensive explanation for many Latin Americans, Asians, and Africans. European men are far less technical minded and experienced than the average American homeowner, and do-it-yourself kits can hardly be sold in most foreign countries. To take anything for granted in this area, as often happens, is a widespread and costly mistake. Subsidiary managers have to battle constantly with the parent company's technical departments, which prepare excellent pamphlets for the domestic market but do not realize they are all but useless abroad.

The knowledgeable international manager will insist that uniformity in literature applies only to format and style, not to text material, which should be sent abroad for re-editing. In writing pamphlets describing drugs and cosmetics it is important to keep in mind that claims which are unlawful in America may be acceptable in other countries, and vice versa. Literature is therefore often prepared by the local units using the American, Canadian, Latin American, or neighboring European texts as a working base only. These local texts are then sent to regional or corporate headquarters for approval. It is important, however, that home-office staff members not check them against U.S. legal requirements or question how they would sound to the American consumer, but leave such considerations to local experts.

The same problems arise in efforts to unify advertising. Since they were discussed in detail in the previous chapter on advertising it is sufficient to mention here that attempts to achieve greater uniformity in this area must proceed with the utmost caution. They depend on numerous factors relating to industrial and product categories, national differences and consumer habits, advertising media and philosophy. Experts agree that few general rules can be given, except that national differences should not be underestimated, and every case should be treated according to its own merits.

Marketing

Uniformity in marketing is easier to achieve. American marketing methods are recognized as superior and are therefore eagerly imitated all over Europe. Distribution channels, however, are a different matter. The photography business was mentioned as one where uniformity is dominant. Still, in Germany, Switzerland, and Austria, equipment and film are sold in specialty stores and not in variety stores as elsewhere. And a company that manufactures plastic household articles and sells them worldwide through home demonstrations must make an exception for Austria. There, home demonstrators must not take orders and must be salaried full-time employees. A local sales manager felt that U.S. corporations should be careful not to impose their marketing methods down to the last detail, particularly in consumer-sensitive industries, but should only insist on maintaining the broad principles of their marketing policy. This remark strikes at the heart of the matter: *centralized uniformity in overall strategy, adjustment to national environmental conditions in tactical details.*

The application of this doctrine is not always easy, however, because the question is often whether a particular activity belongs to the strategic or to the tactical category. This again varies from industry to industry and from country to country. American efforts to achieve uniformity are in some cases resented as intrusions on the national way of life; in others they are willingly accepted. In the automobile industry, for example, arrangements with dealers are almost identical the world over and for all major manufacturers. But in several other industries, patterns in the wholesale and retail trade are stubbornly maintained with all their national and sometimes local differences. In some countries, such differences are protected by law and by powerful semiofficial associations that are remnants of the medieval guild system. Yet these remnants do disappear—as evidenced by the successful introduction—against enormous resistance in some countries—of supermarkets, frozen foods, soft drinks, radio and television commercials, and motels.

Whether unification or adjustment to national market conditions is preferable depends mainly on the cost and profitability factor, and this is influenced by the size and conservatism of the market and by the time element. An American executive of an accounting and consulting firm's German subsidiary phrased the problem as follows:

> The difficulty is that the U.S. company often applies to the smaller, less advanced market, methods developed in and geared to the gigantic continental American market. While these marketing and production methods may work in certain large industrialized European countries in the long run—and even that is not always certain—they are usually very expensive for small countries in the short run. Therefore, initial losses are inevitable for a transition stage that can last five years. Not every U.S. company wants to wait that long and few anticipate such a long period.

Along with uniform marketing methods, a few corporations try to attain a limited uniformity in pricing. Until some years ago such attempts would have been utterly impossible, and they are still confined to certain industries and mainly to the Common Market. There, in recent years, a clear trend toward a leveling off in prices has developed, a trend caused by the elimination of tariffs. The greatly increased traveling within Europe has also contributed to price equalization. This is because consumers and dealers can immediately take advantage of price differentials by freely taking goods over the borders within the Common Market area.

Uniformity in retail prices still poses many problems for U.S. corporations because production costs at their various European plants are different. If the parent company insists on equal prices, there will be different profit margins at several subsidiaries, with a shift in the system of profit centers. Any attempt toward price equalization is nearly always limited to Europe. Its chief purpose is to avoid shipments of similar products from one subsidiary's territory to another's.

Service

Some very large corporations have successfully unified their service, maintenance, and repair programs. In this area they encountered practically no resistance from lower levels of management or from customers and dealers. On the contrary, American methods in these activities are usually highly appreciated. Since the first technicians who performed this service were Americans, uniformity developed naturally. Later, training centers were established and there too, at least in the beginning, U.S. instructors taught a uniform program with a single training manual. Other training centers exist for salesmen, demonstrators, and certain categories of local middle management. These are organized on a uniform basis with centralized directives and thus greatly contribute to uniformity. In fact, uniformity brought about through instruction is more effective and more readily accepted than uniformity ordered or "recommended" by headquarters. Uniformity within a multinational corporation should grow almost by itself.

Uniformity versus Adjustment

If such gradual uniformity is not possible or if it develops too slowly, the question is whether a more or less forced uniformity will be worthwhile. What must be considered are the possible adverse effects in management relationships, local efficiency and initiative, customer and government goodwill, and all the other imponderables of the international trade. Similarly, adjustments to local conditions must be considered not only in terms of their favorable impact on the local business, but also in terms of their possible negative effects on global corporate objectives.

A situation involving inescapable adjustment was described by the managing director of a defense-industry subsidiary. He pointed out that the various NATO governments, particularly the German federal government, no longer accept a certain weapon simply on the strength of its approval and use by the U.S. Army or Air Force. They have established their own standards and specifications and have developed their own tests. While they may not yet be as efficient as those used by the Americans, the spirit of independence within NATO has nevertheless become so strong that one can no longer speak of uniform standards, products, or procurement practices. It is apparent not only in defense contracts, but also in dealings with civil government agencies and with public and large private enterprises.

In a large construction and engineering company dealing with public and private entities, a spokesman mentioned both kinds of experience: "In some European projects the company has been successful in persuading clients to accept American methods. In others we have had to bend over backward and adjust ourselves to their standards." Another case of client adjustment, a negative one, was related by an advertising executive. It seems that his firm lost a large American corporation's local subsidiary as a client because, under the influence of the advertising firm's own New York headquarters, the advertising subsidiary acted as though the client subsidiary were completely dependent on its parent company, which it was not. From this experience the advertising firm concluded that it had to be more flexible in its approach to local American client companies.

On the question of flexibility and adjustment versus centralized control, a British subsidiary manager in Germany pointed out that these policies are not necessarily contradictory. One of the biggest assets of large

American corporations, he said, is their ability to react quickly to technical, economic, and competitive developments and to enforce changes that thus become necessary to meet new conditions: for example, to discontinue a product that is no longer competitive and concentrate on the manufacture and marketing of other products, or to reduce prices and increase production or vice versa. It is often local management that opposes such changes, and Europeans are usually much slower to react and make needed adjustments. The American corporation is usually fast to adjust to changing market conditions, but it is often slow to adjust to existing situations in other countries.

Adjustments can also go too far. The marketing manager of a major chemical corporation's regional office made the following pertinent remarks:

> When I first came to Europe, some ten years ago, I thought that American corporations with subsidiaries here should "go European" and adjust to this environment as much as possible. I still believe that this is advisable in matters of personal contacts and behavior, in consumer and public relations, also in distribution channels, and to some extent in product design. However, the internal organization of a U.S. corporation's European operations, its method of decision making, and its management relationship should follow the successful American patterns which have been recognized in European business administration literature and are often duplicated by large European companies. The American committee method, for example, however much criticized, is still preferable to the European hierarchical system which depends on the infallibility of one man.

In fact, most European experts would agree that European governments, associations, corporations, dealers, customers, workers, schools of business administration, and writers all hope that the American companies in Europe will be understanding friends, but that they will remain Americans rather than disguise themselves as new Europeans.

Uniformity and Control

The natural assumption that uniformity is *always* connected with tight centralized control is simplistic and in many cases wrong. One reason for product and service uniformity, for example, is that some multinational corporations for the most part service and sell to other international corporations. In spite of this situation, some of these companies are to a large extent decentralized and grant considerable autonomy to their subsidiaries.

As a further case in point, the automobile industry manufactures cars in Europe that are adapted to European conditions, yet some of the big automotive corporations have a much tighter centralized control than others. Then there is the cosmetics industry (tight control and wide uniformity) and the food industry (mostly loose control and product diversity).

Certain companies produce naturally uniform goods—such as oil, tires, chemicals—and therefore need not worry about uniformity. However, whether or not they are centrally controlled depends on factors other than the nature of their business.

Some of the most tightly centralized companies, particularly those dealing in well-known consumer goods, have a centralized tradition that began with the founder, who often had invented the product on which his business was based. The top executives of such companies tend to disregard local differences and to insist on their own way of doing things—often quite successfully, through sheer stubborn drive and single-mindedness of purpose. But while these companies, which are frequently family-owned, may continue for one or two generations their policy of uniformity and strict personal control, this does not last indefinitely. Usually, by the third generation, there are changes in company structure and spirit that serve to soften the original hard line.

The president of a well-known car-rental company refused to listen to the European experts who told him that renting a car in one country and returning it in another just could not be done. He would not adjust his thinking to what he considered outmoded concepts stemming from conservative nationalism, but instead forced an adjustment of these old-fashioned ideas to *his* plans—plans that he thought were in step with the young European spirit. At first the difficulties were many and enormous, including numerous lawsuits, and they would doubtless have discouraged a less determined man. He finally succeeded, but now, many years later, the company is under more flexible ownership and management, and adjusts its operations more willingly to local conditions.

SOURCES OF SUPPLY

The problem of determining the source of supply is a natural one for marketing subsidiaries without manufacturing facilities and for manufacturing subsidiaries that produce only a limited range of products, but sell a wider range of them. The problem exists, of course, only where there is a choice of various sources of supply, not when there is only one. The problem can be approached in several different ways.

1. Sources of supply, prices, and terms are fixed in advance for each

marketing subsidiary by the parent company's international division or by its European regional office. (Exceptions are sometimes permitted, but must be authorized, or headquarters must at least be informed, depending on special reasons and on type, size, and origin of order.)

2. Sources of supply are determined for each larger order individually, including inventory orders, or for new customers only, by home office or regional headquarters. Prices and terms may be fixed in advance or determined from case to case upon receiving inquiry.

3. Supplying subsidiary can be selected by ordering subsidiary (or licensed distributor) from a list of authorized sources of supply (which may even include independent companies, especially for components or raw materials). Prices and terms can often be negotiated between supplying and ordering units with or without previous approval from headquarters, sometimes within a margin established by parent company.

4. Free selection of source of supply by marketing subsidiary and direct negotiations between them, at prices and terms established in advance or approved from time to time by parent company or negotiable.

These different approaches all have their advantages and drawbacks and their supporters and critics. Usually, a centralized company with tight controls determines sources of supply from headquarters. And usually, a strong and adequately staffed European regional office determines the European source of supply or grants exceptions. But it also happens that establishing sources of supply is a responsibility delegated to local or area management in an otherwise strictly controlled organization. Conversely, in a loosely controlled corporation, it may be one of the few activities where decision is reserved to higher levels. This depends on the nature of the business and on local conditions. Centralized determination of sources of supply does many things: prevents unsound competition between marketing subsidiaries for deliveries and between manufacturing subsidiaries for orders, reduces friction between them, avoids the possibility of preferential treatment of one subsidiary by another, and guarantees that European or worldwide objectives will carry the necessary weight regardless of parochial interests.

On the other hand, the elimination of the local manager from the decision-making process in this important field of activity may diminish his chances of making a large enough profit. He can then not be blamed for smaller profits or even losses. In fact, he may find it a welcome excuse. To cope with this, several corporations have adopted compromise solutions by which they let the subsidiary manager share responsibility to some degree or at least allow him to explain the reasons for his or his customers' preference for certain sources of supply. Where products are identical in quality and price, deliveries uniformly fast and efficient, and the receiving

subsidiary or customer compensated for any difference in duties or transport costs, local management will have few reasons for either preferences
or objections.

Competitive Reasons

Normally, these conditions will be taken into account when determining the source of supply, no matter who makes the final decision. To sum-
marize the "normal" or "competitive" reasons for allocating sources of
supply:

- Tariffs (membership of the receiving and supplying countries in the
  Common Market or European Free Trade Association), overt or
  hidden government export subsidies, governmental import restrictions against or preferences for certain supply countries (which exist
  at present in Europe only in the Eastern communist countries).
- Transport costs and speed.
- Availability of inventories for immediate delivery, or speedy deliveries due to production facilities and volume of orders at hand.
- Quality, special specifications (unless strictly uniform).
- Prices and terms, unless completely uniform. But in this case the local production costs are still a determining factor for the European
  region as a whole or for the entire international division.

The managing director of a women's wear manufacturer's Dutch and
Belgian marketing subsidiaries said that his source of supply is always determined by New York, but that he did not care one way or another because uniformity and identical quality are strictly enforced throughout the
company, and prices and models are the same regardless of where a shipment originates.

Tariffs and transport costs may balance each other. There may be no
customs duty to be paid for exports from Britain or Sweden to Switzerland
because they belong to EFTA, but in case of heavy and bulky goods the
costs of the long transport could be prohibitive. Shipments would therefore have to be made from nearby plants in France or Germany even
though they may be subject to high duties. The added advantage of much
faster delivery could very well be the deciding factor.

Company Policy

However, there often are overriding factors of company policy which
lead to decisions about sources of supply that must appear irrational to
those unfamiliar with such factors. If a company makes the mistake of not

explaining them to its local managers, particularly where the local business is unfavorably affected by the chosen source of supply, this will invariably create resentment, lower morale, and stifle initiative. The overall factors influencing the parent company's decisions in matters of sources of supply are, from the corporate viewpoint, mainly these:

- Shift of production from a plant working at full capacity or overtime to one not fully used, considering available manpower, capital investment, inventory of raw materials and components, fixed costs, and overtime pay.
- Comparative costs of overtime.
- Comparative amortization of manufacturing facilities, particularly in case of new investments.
- Desirability of lowering production costs in one manufacturing subsidiary by increasing production, thereby increasing its profits or reducing initial losses after new investments.
- Overall financial considerations, on a global, international, or European basis. However, government regulations must be taken into account. Lowering prices in intracompany business and thereby reducing local profits is usually frowned upon by the government of the host country, unless it can be proved that lower prices were necessary to switch an important order to the particular factory.

The size of the company's interests in an affiliate or joint venture may be an important but controversial factor.

The different approaches to and solutions of the problem of sources of supply lead to diverse relationships between supplying (manufacturing) and receiving (marketing) subsidiaries and are in turn influenced by them. These various lateral relationships can be described by the following types:

1. There is no direct relationship; all communications go by way of the parent company's international or regional headquarters.

2. Direct communication exists only in minor matters relating to the execution of orders such as packing, shipping methods, and delivery time. Communications are on a lower level; regional or area office may be informed.

3. Direct communication exists in all matters connected with the filling of orders, including billing and insurance, but not payment. The regional or home office is often kept informed.

4. Methods and terms of payment or intracompany settlement form part of lateral communications; they are either routine or negotiable. Headquarters is informed.

5. Full communication between supplying and receiving subsidiaries

resembles the relations between independent suppliers and their customers. In other words, there are no close intracompany links. This includes communications and negotiations covering inquiries, offers or bids, their acceptance, and execution.

6. A full relationship exists, as members of the same family with common interests. They include an exchange of information and lead to permanent close links, with visits back and forth on several personnel levels. Company headquarters, especially on the regional level, usually plays an active part in these lateral relations. They are particularly important in large companies making industrial products and in construction and engineering firms.

Cooperation between Subsidiaries

The existence of such close and well-organized lateral relations is of major significance in multinational corporations whose various European subsidiaries manufacture different parts of the end product. However, at the same time such a division of labor between units in different countries —often, but not always, within the Common Market—naturally leads to greater centralization and greater decision-making power on higher levels (regional or corporate).

One major U.S. corporation, for example, has three plants in Europe. The one in France now makes only farm machinery and parts of tractors, such as the transmissions. The German plant manufactures other parts of the same tractors—for example, the motors. The two factories then exchange their products (without paying duty) and each assembles the tractors. In addition to selling their tractors on the home market, both subsidiaries export them to assigned territories: The French, to North Africa, the German, to most of continental Europe. The company has a third manufacturing subsidiary in Britain that also makes farm equipment but different models. Both the British and French subsidiaries export their farm machinery throughout Europe. The company's construction equipment is not manufactured in Europe, and such orders are handled by a special export division at corporate headquarters.

A manufacturer of office machines and computers started the division of labor among its various European plants many years ago, in the immediate postwar period. It did so in order to balance imports and exports and thereby obtain the necessary import permits. It now has ten plants in Europe, of which some manufacture or assemble the complete machines, while others make component parts that are then shipped to the assembly plants. In emergencies, such as the long general strike in France in the spring of 1968, these parts had to be imported from the United States or by stripping inventories all over the world. This required a coordinated effort on a global basis.

A similar situation developed in several other large American companies in Europe during that period. One was a soap and detergent manufacturer that produces in France a special soap that it exports to Germany because the French factory has a larger capacity than is currently needed for the domestic market. When this plant was strikebound in May 1968, it was necessary to manufacture the product at a company plant in Italy. At the same time, both the Italian plant and another company plant in Germany worked overtime to produce large inventories of most company products for immediate shipment to France once the emergency there was over. This greatly reduced the losses caused by the lack of inventories in France. However, it was not entirely surprising that these emergency measures created disagreements between the French and the other subsidiaries, which had to give up a part of their own inventories and production capacities to help out, thereby disturbing their own schedules and planning. "The VP–Europe," commented a spokesman, "had to act as arbiter and *impose* on the other subsidiaries the assistance they were not fully prepared to give to the French subsidiary." Such strong action by regional or corporate headquarters can be the exception to the rule of local autonomy, it can be the usual company policy, or it can be an exception that, if repeated, will lead to a change of policy.

This last-named development is seen as unavoidable—and in the best interests of the company—by an assembling and semimanufacturing subsidiary's general manager. His company, which is in the conveyance industry, has recently established a European regional office. It split up the work done in its three major continental plants in France, Germany, and Italy, so that each now makes only specific parts: One manufactures motors; another, electrical parts; and the third, steel construction. This requires constant and precise coordination between the manufacturing and assembling subsidiaries. Again, difficulties arose during the French general strike, as they did when the German government imposed restrictions on truck traffic to ease congestion on the *Autobahnen* (expressways) and divert traffic to the federally owned railroads.

The Supplying Subsidiary

So far the problem of allocating sources of supply has been discussed mainly from the viewpoint of the receiving subsidiary, whether a marketing or a limited production subsidiary, and whether the import from another country unit is permanent or temporary. But the problem can also be looked at, in a slightly different light, from the viewpoint of the supplying subsidiary. In most cases, a manufacturing unit is eager to export its products to neighboring markets where no production facilities exist. This increases sales, profits, and the status of the subsidiary and its local management. It may also reduce manufacturing costs and thereby further increase profits or lower prices and improve the subsidiary's competitive situation. Such exports, furthermore, will always be looked upon most favorably by the government of the host country and improve the subsidiary's image with various government agencies. This can be valuable for permits, licenses, government orders, and allocations. There are situations, however, where the manufacturing subsidiary does not like to export, such as those emergency shipments mentioned previously, but normally a competition will develop for export markets among various supplying subsidiaries. Soon, headquarters will have to assign sales rights or sales territories to different subsidiaries and protect them. Then the problems are the way this protection is enforced and whether subsidiaries are allowed to accept orders from outside their own territory.

Most of the following rules apply not only to inquiries from marketing subsidiaries or distributors, but also to those emanating from large customers (including government agencies):

1. The manufacturing subsidiary is not allowed to accept or even discuss any inquiry or order outside its country, but must turn it over to the international division or to regional headquarters.

2. The manufacturing subsidiary has sales rights not only in its own country, but also in some other countries where no manufacturing or marketing subsidiary exists.

3. The manufacturing subsidiary has the right, and indeed the duty, to fill orders from certain pre-listed marketing subsidiaries, with or without previous or later notification to the home or regional office.

4. The manufacturing subsidiary has the right to negotiate with any marketing subsidiary and can accept their orders if prior approval by U.S. or regional headquarters has been obtained.

5. If the supplying subsidiary receives an inquiry or order from a customer or dealer in the marketing subsidiary's or licensed distributor's country, it must turn the inquiry over to them for approval or action.

6. If a direct inquiry or order comes from a country where a manufacturing subsidiary exists, it must be turned over to the subsidiary directly or by way of the regional or home office.

7. Such direct inquiries can be accepted after approval by an authorized local subsidiary or by headquarters.

8. In addition to approval of such direct orders by a local subsidiary—or a subsidiary that has local sales rights—or by headquarters, the supplying subsidiary must pay a commission to the authorized subsidiary.

There may be variants of these patterns for orders that can be filled from inventories as opposed to those that must be made to specifications or that are exceptionally large and complex. This applies also to single and repeat orders, to new and old customers, and particularly to orders that require the cooperative efforts of several manufacturing subsidiaries.

Illustrative Examples

The following description of various cases discussed in the author's many interviews will serve to illustrate and better explain what has so far been set forth in this section:

In a company making photographic equipment and film the marketing subsidiaries without manufacturing facilities purchase their requirements, according to estimates submitted in the annual forecast, either from the company's plant in England, France, or Germany, or from the United States through the international head office. These various sources of supply are determined by the home office because, while the products are uniform throughout the world, not every product is manufactured by every European factory. A manufacturing subsidiary must refuse any order received from a marketing unit not assigned to it as well as any order from a dealer outside its own country. In an extraordinary case—for example, if a manufacturing subsidiary should be out of stock—the marketing unit is allowed to buy from a subsidiary in another country making the same product. All that is required is that a special report be sent to the home office. If, however, a permanent change of supply sources or a change for a longer time period is desired, permission must be requested and the reason thoroughly explained. Such requests are not readily granted.

Almost exactly the opposite policy was found in the Spanish affiliate of a manufacturer of abrasives and adhesives. Because of its status as a joint venture, and also because Spain belongs neither to the Common Market nor to EFTA, the general manager of this local unit can change his source of supply for products not manufactured in Spain or for raw materials. But he has to give advance notice to headquarters so that the necessary adjustments can be made.

By contrast, the Austrian marketing subsidiary of a plastics manufacturer receives 90 percent of its supplies from the British plant (within EFTA, to which both countries belong) and 10 percent from a factory in Belgium that makes different models. Other manufacturing subsidiaries are situated in Spain and Greece. They offer no advantages, because they do not belong to EFTA, are far away, have inadequate transport facilities, and do not manufacture the whole range of products. The question of changing sources of supply therefore never comes up.

The Swiss marketing subsidiary of a very large company making household and industrial machines has a wide range of sources of supply since each manufacturing subsidiary makes different models in various price ranges whose parts are not interchangeable. This means that local management has no choice but to get *certain* models from Germany, where high duties must be paid. But because imports from Britain are duty-free, this subsidiary purchases its requirements from the United Kingdom whenever possible.

A Dutch manufacturing and marketing subsidiary that makes radiators and imports central heating and sanitary equipment from other company subsidiaries is so far quite independent in selecting its sources of supply. The local manager buys from whichever unit can furnish the material at the lowest price and with the fastest delivery, and he does this through direct contacts with his colleagues in the supplying subsidiaries. However, a regional office has been established only recently in Brussels, and it is assuming progressively greater responsibilities. The local manager in Amsterdam believes it inevitable that his freedom of decision in the matter of supplies will soon be greatly restricted, and he is objective enough to deem this to be to the benefit of the corporation as a whole. In fact, he thinks this is also in his own best interest. The European business of the company is growing, and growth must be accompanied by efforts to reduce production costs. For both reasons, production must be increased—and this can be done profitably only for the whole Common Market, not for the different countries separately.

In the business machines industry, the author interviewed representatives of several companies. Two of them had divergent rules for allocating sources of supply; the rules, not surprisingly, followed the general pattern of management control. In one company, the subsidiaries enjoy a great deal of autonomy that includes the free selection of their sources of supply. In another corporation, the national units simply send their orders to regional headquarters in Frankfurt, where they are processed and forwarded all the way to the international division in America. From there they go back to one of the European factories or, when necessary, to one of the American plants. The regional manager said he really does not care one way or the other as long as the goods are delivered on time; prices are uniform.

In the Geneva headquarters of a major electrical and electronics corporation it was explained that the policy in matters of supply is flexible and that the company does not like to impose strict rules on subsidiary managers. Thus in routine matters a marketing subsidiary is free to bypass the regional office and directly contact the New York export department to obtain fast action on deliveries. But if the subsidiary hears of a large public or private project from which an important order for a big installation could be obtained, it gets in touch with Geneva, where it will be decided which producing subsidiary is to do the bidding. Therefore, speedy routine orders are treated differently from large special installations.

The importance of speed was also emphasized in another electronics corporation. The manager of the Dutch subsidiary directly contacts one of the continental plants without going through the regional office because this would delay action in the highly competitive field of industrial products, where offers or bids must be made quickly and accurately. For consumer goods, however, the orders normally go first to the proper area office in Antwerp, from there to the European regional office, and finally to one of the factories, which ships and bills directly to the ordering unit. Because this system is slow, however, it can only be used for inventory orders or others where speed is not essential.

In one major automotive company the nonmanufacturing subsidiaries and licensed distributors, which may or may not have local assembly plants, sell mostly German-made or British-made cars. Ordering and buying by the marketing units from the German or British factories is almost like buying from independent suppliers, but prices set by the manufacturing subsidiaries are approved by the parent corporation and sales are, of course, made only to subsidiaries or licensees. There is a close and constant lateral relationship of the marketing and assembling subsidiaries with the two manufacturing subsidiaries in Germany and the United Kingdom. They correspond frequently, and numerous visits are arranged on various levels in routine matters without headquarters participation. Only in major actions or large programs is an approval from the U.S. office necessary. Otherwise, information through the normal reporting system is sufficient. Certain parts and auxiliaries are often made locally under the control of the marketing subsidiary.

One of the large tire and rubber companies has plants in several Common Market and EFTA countries, and the marketing subsidiaries usually obtain their supplies from the plants within their trading community. The selection of the source of supply within one or the other community—Britain or Sweden, France or Germany—is decided by the VP–Europe in Brussels. He will also accept or reject the request of a marketing subsidiary for a temporary change in the supply pattern. He will base his decisions on facts known to him but not necessarily to the various subsidiaries—facts such as orders and inventories on hand in the different plants, as well as plant capacities.

A special situation exists in the food-packing industry. The European subsidiaries that own and operate canning plants depend for their supply of tropical fruit on the company's plantations in the Pacific and on independent growers under contract. The subsidiaries submit forecasts specifying their needs for the coming year to company headquarters, where they are reviewed, revised, and approved and where allocations for supplies from the various sources are made. Since these supplies are limited and cannot be increased on short notice, forecasts have to be accurate. Sources of supply cannot be changed for at least one year. In fact, even medium- and long-range forecasting and planning must be much more exact than in most other industries because it takes several years for new trees to grow and bear fruit. The local manager's experience and forecasting skill are therefore paramount. However, in practice, the subsidiaries' estimates of future needs are always trimmed by headquarters because of production limits.

A few American companies still work entirely, or mostly, with independent importers and dealers who usually have exclusive sales rights either for the whole line or for certain categories of products—for example, according to different brands, qualities, or price ranges. In some countries the company may also have its own supervisors or sales managers who maintain contact with the various agents, receive their orders, and forward them to the home office or to a regional office. Billing and shipping is handled directly by the export department in the United States, as are collections and drafts. The local sales manager acts only in case of delinquent accounts.

Protection of Territorial Rights

Looking now at the other side of the coin, the territorial sales rights of subsidiaries and their protection, a variety of rules, methods, and patterns can again be observed.

The most common practice is that all sales outside the country (or the assigned sales territory) must be approved by the international division or by the regional office. This includes sales to other subsidiaries, to licensed distributors, and, where it is permissible, to outside customers. This avoids anyone's interfering with the company's international plans or commitments. In this connection it should be mentioned that sales from European subsidiaries back to the American parent company or its domestic customers are becoming increasingly important. This was exactly the development found in a U.S. tire company's Spanish affiliate. It now ships snow tires to America because the changeover from regular tires in the assembly line is much less costly in Spain than in the United States.

In one steel corporation, approval of outside sales does not come from headquarters but from the subsidiary concerned. The Spanish affiliate, for example, has sales rights only in Spain and Portugal, while Greece belongs to the Italian subsidiary. Sometimes, however, a customer may find it more advantageous to get a shipment of steel from Spain. In such a case, the Italian subsidiary must be asked to give its consent. It is supposed to agree if the reasons are valid and the order would otherwise be lost. This method of bilateral agreement has been worked out after some friction between various subsidiaries when similar cases were decided by U.S. headquarters. An electric company adheres to the same principle of bilateral negotiations between the subsidiaries involved, with the proviso that the matter must be referred to the regional office in London if no mutual agreement can be reached.

A large American corporation in the nonferrous metals field has an international office in Switzerland which has no jurisdiction over the company's various manufacturing subsidiaries, but gives them staff support for their marketing of U.S. products in their countries. These subsidiaries are completely independent in selling at home and exporting to other countries the products they manufacture. The main function of the Swiss office is the marketing of U.S. products in European countries where the company has only sales subsidiaries. The goods made in America and various European countries are not identical and therefore there is no direct competition between the various plants. The same policy prevails in the organization of a major competitor with the modification that all European plants and marketing units, including the one responsible for imports from the United States, report to a regional manager.

In the construction and engineering field, subsidiaries often work in each other's territory for various reasons, as when one unit is so busy with one or more major projects that it cannot take on an additional job—particularly while another subsidiary has manpower available. Furthermore, two subsidiaries sometimes cooperate in the execution of a job they undertake jointly either in one or the other's country or in a third country. In the Frankfurt office of a big construction firm the author was told that in such a common effort the two subsidiaries would decide practically everything between themselves, dividing the work, the manpower (engineering staff), the costs, and the profit. They would then ask the U.S. corporate office to do the intracompany billing and accounting.

In another construction company, the two European subsidiaries were originally formed to operate in the EFTA and Common Market countries respectively, but it did not quite work out that way, and frequently they had to work in each other's territory. A short time before the author's visit, the British subsidiary completed a job in Holland only 50 miles from the seat of the Dutch subsidiary. It was considered more practical to handle the entire project from England than to transfer many people and the administration from Britain to the Netherlands, where a severe shortage of living accommodations exists.

Engineering projects and installations for the Eastern European countries are also often transferred from the subsidiary that usually is assigned this trade to the unit in another country. This is because the client, a Communist state agency, prefers it that way for currency, trade agreements, and political reasons. Normally, the subsidiary that has sales rights will give assistance to the unit in the other country and be credited with a commission.

A multinational group of scientific research laboratories owned by an American foundation follows the same pattern as large worldwide industrial corporations. Each laboratory and "development office" has its assigned territory, but orders for research projects frequently come from other countries and must then be cleared with the laboratory that has territorial rights or with a European regional office in London. For research orders originating in Latin America, approval is given by the foundation's head office in the United States. There is no objection to having two laboratories accepting similar research orders if each is in a different country.

PROBLEMS OF LOCAL PRODUCTION

As more American corporations establish manufacturing subsidiaries abroad, or add production facilities to existing marketing subsidiaries, or convert assembly and semimanufacturing operations to full production, they come face to face with many new problems. These vary, of course, according to location, size, industry, and management patterns.

One of the most frequent problems involves manufacturing products for the local market that are different from those made by the company in the United States and in other European countries. The decision as to whether to allow or encourage purely local production and, if so, to what extent is not easy; it is a major policy decision practically always reserved to corporate top management. In times past, when the principal aim of European subsidiaries was simply to earn a good return, the answer to the question was usually yes. Nowadays, however, in spite of occasional protestations to the contrary, the local profit picture is no longer the exclusive yardstick and several global considerations have equal or greater weight.

In most modern industries, prospects for the long-range success and profitability of new products are uncertain if the products are confined to local markets—that is, if they do not have at least a regional or continental potential. Research and development, indispensable for contemporary industrial production, cannot be conducted in one small market alone. Advertising, too, needs a large market area, even if it has to be adjusted to national conditions. Corporate management is therefore reluctant to allow the manufacture of a new product for one local market only. Yet this general attitude often leads to a rigid rejection of *all* such efforts. The parent company, and especially middle management at the home office, has an inclination to take the easy way out, to judge all problems bureaucratically and indiscriminately according to a set of immutable rules. The problems frequently reach top management in a form that has been evaluated and prejudged by lower corporate levels, particularly where technical questions are concerned.

It should be clear that not all suggestions to manufacture some purely local products can be measured by the same yardstick. First of all, there is —or should be—a distinction between entirely different local products and those that are basically modifications and adaptations of items made or launched elsewhere. Second, not all new or modified products need special research and development, or widespread advertising. Third, sometimes local products can well be developed, manufactured, and introduced in conjunction with other more widely accepted products—and for this and other reasons they may not require major investments. Fourth, local production facilities that have been provided for an expansion yet to come may be partly unused or not used to capacity; local products can therefore fill the gap. Fifth, such stopgap production may well be only temporary, and the local products can be discontinued if and when they are no longer profitable or when full production facilities are needed for the manufacture of "authentic" corporate products.

It is always local management that presses for products that fit the local market, regardless of whether or not they can be sold elsewhere. It is nearly always the home office that opposes such moves or is at least reluctant to agree. The international division, frequently caught in the middle, usually leans toward local demands or a compromise solution perhaps suggested by regional headquarters. The corporate production or product development department and the product divisions are generally the most outspoken foes of localized production.

The trend among U.S. corporations engaged in manufacturing abroad is certainly toward centralized production. In fact, those subsidiary managers who informed the author that they produce items which can only be marketed locally were a distinct minority. This happens mostly in joint ventures, affiliates, and new acquisitions and in certain countries that still have some degree of protected national market, such as Spain. And it occurs only in subsidiaries with full independent manufacturing facilities. Wherever local management can initiate and execute the local manufacture of goods that are suitable only, or mainly, for its own market, it greatly strengthens its autonomy. Indeed it is only feasible where production is not too tightly controlled by headquarters. For this reason alone, some corporations are as a matter of principle opposed to localized products.

Manufacture in the Most Economical Location

In contrast, the more recent trend toward concentrating production of certain company products in one or two countries, and other products in plants situated in a third or fourth country increases centralized control because of the necessity of higher level coordination and planning. This system of manufacturing every product or component where it can be made best or most economically, again creates many problems. It is applied mostly within the Common Market, but sometimes it may even be more economical or more efficient to ship an item from France to Britain than to manufacture it in both countries. The biggest risk involved is that of local strikes or other interruptions of production. The problem can be solved only by larger inventories or by having more than one plant make the same item. Both solutions require considerable additional investments, and decisions concerning them, based as they are on complex calculations, must be made at corporate headquarters. The result, therefore, is stronger centralization.

Some voices can be heard in opposition to this theory of manufacturing a product where it can be done most economically. An Italian subsidiary manager pointed out, for example, that the saving involved in filling three million bottles in one country as against filling one million bottles in each of three countries is not as great as the "home strategists" may think, and that it can be wiped out by a single strike. And he saw a further reason. "It is only right," he said, "to manufacture in the country of consumption. Otherwise we are back again where we started, and one country feels discriminated against."

The concentration of production in certain plants and the unification of products obviously lead to stronger centralization. However, a crosscurrent, at present only in its infancy, can be discovered by the careful observer. A local manager in the nonferrous metals industry referred to it when he remarked that manufacturing in various European countries has to involve a constant exchange of ideas, methods, improvements, and inventions between the local plant and production headquarters and between the factories themselves.

The jurisdictional patterns in foreign production are extremely varied and depend on numerous intertwined factors, including historical, personal, geographic, organizational, industrial, and environmental conditions.

A local plant may be completely under the jurisdiction of the local subsidiary—it may indeed be its principal part and major field of activity —and the subsidiary manager can at the same time be in charge of plant and production.

The factory or the subsidiary's production department, however, often reports to the general manager of the subsidiary only in administrative, financial, or higher personnel matters. In all technical matters, such as production techniques, machinery, new products, and quality control or testing, the plant or production manager reports to the production departments at regional or corporate levels or both or to the product groups. He also gets directions, support, and assistance from the same units.

The plant or local production manager, or the subsidiary manager, if he is in charge of production, is under the jurisdiction of the regional office or, where none exists, under that of the international division or corporation. Where the responsibilities of the regional office do not include production matters, local plant or production management may report directly to the international division at corporate headquarters.

However, local factories, or for that matter the entire manufacturing subsidiary, may also be under the jurisdiction of the corporate production department or a product division, at least in technical matters. In other fields they may report through a regional office or directly to international.

Where the international operations have been reorganized along product lines, such dual jurisdictions have been eliminated and the manufacturing subsidiary reports in all matters to its product group. However, some corporations have several plants in larger countries, and while each reports to a different product group, all may be under the administrative jurisdiction of either a general national manager or the regional office.

Separate Subsidiaries in One Country

The structural relationships of several manufacturing and marketing subsidiaries in one country that report to various product divisions show many variations. They therefore merit more detailed treatment. They range all the way from close coordination under common administration to complete separation, indeed almost to alienation. The following seven examples offer a good cross section of this diversity.

1. Each of three Italian subsidiaries of the same corporation reports to the international division of a product group (pharmaceuticals, cosmetics, food products) in the United States, since there are no regional offices in Europe. The final decision in important matters rests with cor-

porate top management. There are only loose personal relations among the three Italian managers. One subsidiary was established by the parent company; another is a later acquisition that has been continued under its well-known Italian brand name and to a certain extent under the old management; the third is a joint venture with minority participation by another American company.

2. A large electronics corporation has four major product divisions covering different consumer goods and industrial products. In larger markets each of the four product groups has its own manufacturing subsidiary; elsewhere, one or the other of the product divisions may have only marketing subsidiaries. One of the four managers in one country has a dual responsibility. He is not only in full charge of his own unit, but is also responsible for administration, taxes, and other common interests for all four subsidiaries. As subsidiary manager, this executive reports to the divisional VP–International of his product group; as national general manager, he reports in important matters to the corporate VP–International. Since his product group has no regional office in Europe, both lines of reporting go directly to New York. But one of the other three local managers reports to a regional manager of his division in Rome. The general manager has no real line jurisdiction over his three colleagues, but rather coordinating functions. He is, for example, the chairman in regular local meetings, and directs certain overall administrative and financial matters discussed there.

3. One of the major oil companies has three divisions (oil, petrochemicals, and motels). In some important markets the corporation operates through two or three separate subsidiaries, each of which reports to its own regional headquarters in London or in Brussels. In small countries there is often a single subsidiary that reports in administrative, personnel, financial, and other general matters to the regional office whose products form the major part of its business. Meanwhile in technical areas and all others that affect one specific product group, the local unit reports to each of the three regional offices.

4. In another corporation, the author found that various subsidiaries in the same city, sometimes even in the same building, have no relationship with one another whatever. Each product group has its own European organization with its own regional patterns and lines of command, and these do not seem to converge anywhere except at the highest corporate level. But of this common pinnacle local management had no real knowledge. If it were not for the common corporate name, the subsidiaries might not know that they all belong to the same company.

5. A world-famous manufacturing company has only two major divisions: household items and industrial machines. Each division has an en-

tirely different international organization suitable for its particular distribution channels and types of customers and dealers. In smaller markets the corporation maintains only one marketing subsidiary, with dual reporting. In larger countries there are two subsidiaries, of which one or both may do manufacturing. Both divisions have regional offices in London, and in spite of almost complete separation they share a strong company spirit.

6. A corporation with divisions in the pharmaceuticals, cosmetics, and chemicals lines has a single international division handling all products. There is also a single European regional office to which all subsidiaries report. Again, in smaller countries only one local unit handles all lines, while in more important markets two or three subsidiaries work side by side reporting through identical lines of communication to the same upper management levels.

7. In an aluminum corporation, plants making different products are normally located in different countries. All these manufacturing subsidiaries report to one regional manager. All reports and communications, whether in technical, administrative, or marketing activities, are channeled exclusively through him and his office.

In this connection it is worth mentioning that wherever the regional manager is an engineer or technical expert, and especially where he was formerly a plant or production manager, his European headquarters exercises considerable authority over factories and production departments of local subsidiaries. This is only natural. By contrast, when the general manager of the regional office (or of a subsidiary) is a marketing man, a financial expert, or an administrator, he is usually bypassed—de jure or de facto—by factories and production departments. Therefore, if a company wants all activities, including production, to be under regional control (and similarly under the control of the local manager) it will probably appoint a technical expert, with European manufacturing experience if possible. This is not to say that a strong regional or subsidiary manager without technical experience cannot also exercise adequate control over manufacture. However, he will usually need a technical assistant for advice in production matters.

A certain degree of independence for plant managers is necessary because, while products may be identical to those manufactured in the United States, production methods and procedures can seldom be completely duplicated and unified. The American international manager of an electronics corporation who has his world headquarters in Italy commented that the Italian plant must be far more flexible in its operations than the company's American factories. It must above all "adjust its thinking to the smaller European markets." Since highly specialized machines cannot be amortized quickly enough before they become obsolescent, or only at prohibitive rates, specialization must be limited.

QUALITY CONTROL

Quality control of local production is in most U.S. corporations conducted or directed by corporate headquarters, but the manner and degree of central control vary greatly. The following general patterns can be distinguished:

- Local control left entirely to subsidiary (very rare).
- Local control according to strict instructions (manuals).
- Local control for certain products or parts.
- Local control with subsequent release of products for sale, followed *occasionally* by central control.
- Same, but *always* followed by headquarters control.
- Local *and* corporate control; products are released for sale by headquarters only; subsidiary must wait for cabled approval from home office.
- No local quality control, this being handled exclusively by parent company.

Testing Methods

Central corporate quality control is performed either through analysis, tests, or inspection of samples air-shipped—usually immediately after production—by the subsidiary, or else by dispatching specially qualified technicians for inspection on the spot. Which of the two methods is used depends on the nature, size, and weight of the products to be tested. In the pharmaceuticals, cosmetics, soft drink, and canned food industries, quality control by headquarters consists for the most part of checking samples shipped from local plants. To a lesser degree the same method is used by some textile, synthetic fiber, foundation garment, and other companies that manufacture small, light, easy-to-ship items. Some electronics, plastics, and precision instruments firms use the sample method for those of their products or component parts small enough to be air-shipped and use the local inspection system for heavier or more voluminous articles. It stands to reason that the machinery, business machines, automotive, and heavy equipment industries can perform quality control only through local inspection, except for some parts or accessories.

In one of the large automobile corporations testing of finished vehicles is done locally, but tires, batteries, and other accessories are sent to Detroit for testing whenever a new supply has been contracted for from an outside manufacturer. Here, another factor enters into consideration in setting quality control policies: complete confidence by the parent company in its own large, fully equipped, and expertly staffed plants—which are from time to time inspected by corporate experts—versus somewhat less confidence in local suppliers of components and accessories.

A parallel situation exists in the soft drink industry and some chemicals and pharmaceuticals companies, where the products themselves may be under various forms of local and central quality control, but where samples of new bottles or containers made by outside suppliers are always sent to headquarters for testing. Many corporations also require samples of raw materials to be tested by home office experts. New supplies of these items (components, containers, and raw materials) are normally not used by subsidiary plants until they have been approved by headquarters. In addition, performance samples are also occasionally sent to the parent company for testing. But the regular continuous quality control of bottles, parts, and raw materials is mostly a local responsibility.

With regard to samples of the finished product, pharmaceuticals, cosmetics, and soft drink companies often test or analyze not only samples airshipped by the subsidiary, but also other samples from retail and wholesale stores. They do not reveal the purpose of the purchase or the identity of the person who collects these samples. The reasons for this practice are threefold: to doublecheck on the performance of producers or bottlers, particularly when they are independent subcontractors; to test the shelf life of the products; and to see whether there has been proper closure or sealing, packaging, and labeling.

Local Autonomy

Sometimes quality control is left to local plants because it is not considered particularly important or because of already existing safeguards. Sometimes it must be handled locally. A Spanish subsidiary manager pointed out that, since most of his products are different from those made by the parent company's factories, the latter's technical personnel do not have the necessary knowledge to test them. In many companies central control measures extend only to products made in the United States as well as overseas; purely local products are tested locally.

While autonomous quality control is observed primarily in large manufacturing subsidiaries, located in the most industrialized European countries, the author did find at least one exception. In one of the smallest, least advanced European countries, a pharmaceuticals corporation's subsidiary manager stated that most of his quality control is done locally—in spite of otherwise strict centralization. He explained that the reason is simply that his market is "not important enough" for headquarters to bother much about.

Another pharmaceuticals company grants some of its subsidiaries authority to handle their own local quality control, but based on sound considerations. After a manufacturing subsidiary has undergone an "apprenticeship" period of about three years, the parent company gradually releases it from the strict obligation to send samples for home laboratory testing. It thus permits local quality control, though sometimes it does this in conjunction with another period of *occasional* corporate tests.

Central, Regional, and Local Responsibilities

In this company and in others, analysis and testing of samples is conducted mostly by a European central laboratory, often, but not always, located near the regional office and under its administrative jurisdiction. In technical matters, meanwhile, communication is established directly with corporate counterparts in the United States. Frequently, these regional laboratories are also in charge of picking up samples from the trade and of supervising and advising subsidiaries in quality control matters. When there is any doubt, however, whether a batch or group of tested products should be released, the matter is normally referred back to the parent company.

Technical and scientific responsibilities for quality control are quite often completely separated from normal reporting channels and control relationships. A local manager may not have the right to overrule his own quality control people when they reject a newly produced quantity of products. His only opportunity for redress may be an appeal to the corporate quality control department, which again is not ordinarily under the jurisdiction of the international division.

The most frequent method of quality control is dual: local *and* central, with varying degrees of frequency and of responsibility for approval. In a chemicals and pharmaceuticals company, for example, the rule for new products is that samples of the first three batches must be sent to the parent company after they are tested locally. Local tests are mainly chemical analysis, while headquarters tests also include animal experiments. Old products are tested only occasionally in the central laboratory, but every batch is always carefully analyzed locally.

In another pharmaceuticals corporation, central control is stricter:

Whether old or new products, samples of every batch must be sent to New York for analysis and inspection, and such products must not be sold until approved. In one cosmetics company the same rule prevails, but the local manager has the power to begin sales of a batch immediately after positive local tests if an emergency exists; specifically when inventories are exhausted and at least some small orders have to be filled. But this is a rare occurrence. The local manager took pains to point out that the requirement to send samples to the parent company really is a formality and an extreme precaution—his samples have never yet been rejected. By contrast, in a second cosmetics firm that also requires samples of every batch to be sent to New York, sales can always be made after favorable local tests without waiting for headquarters approval. Approval is thereby clearly defined as an additional safety measure, but it is not expected to change the results of the subsidiaries' own quality control procedure. Finally, in a third company, known for its extremely tight central control, New York approval of samples must always be awaited and there are no exceptions whatever.

Why are corporations that produce cosmetics and—to a slightly lesser degree—corporations that produce pharmaceuticals in the forefront of those practicing strict centralized quality control? First, most of them tightly control all other subsidiary activities. Second, they usually insist on product uniformity and want to insure not only satisfactory quality, but also identity of products. Third, there is the danger of injury and of subsequent customer claims and loss of consumer confidence, although it is noteworthy that pharmaceuticals, which are subject to the same dangers as cosmetics, are less tightly quality controlled. Fourth, these products are under stringent government restrictions and regulations and need a variety of health, import, and usage licenses. Fifth, pharmaceuticals and cosmetics require long, difficult, and expensive research and development, but are generally easy to produce.

By contrast, the conditions in the electrical-electronics, machinery, and instruments industries are, in many respects, the opposite. Manufacture is highly complex, requiring either identical or equivalent equipment and as highly skilled workmanship as at home. If a subsidiary succeeds in producing goods that meet all specifications, it can also be trusted with its own quality control. However, inspection teams from regional or corporate headquarters are often sent abroad. Usually, they examine not only the quality of finished products and component parts, but also the equipment, installation, and procedures. At the same time, they give technical advice to local technicians. All this is particularly important when a corporation has plants all over the world producing identical items whose parts must be interchangeable from one plant to another.

RESEARCH AND DEVELOPMENT

American corporations with subsidiaries abroad at first concentrated all their R&D at home. For several years after foreign manufacturing plants were established, the American research laboratories of major companies continued to function as they had in the past. Then the multinational corporation discovered that excellent scientific manpower was available in many European and some Asian and Latin American countries and that quite a few of these men had postgraduate training in the United States. Several large corporations began to import foreign scientists, and for a short time this stilled the complaints of certain European governments and writers that U.S. companies employed only lower level European manpower. But soon another, more vociferous, complaint was being heard: the brain drain of European talent by American business and universities. It was—and still is—true that European scientists were being lured to the United States, not only by higher compensation, but also by greater opportunities, wider recognition, and much better facilities. (Incidentally, a similar brain drain is being experienced by smaller European countries, whose young scientists and technologists are attracted by their larger and richer neighbors. Many talented Belgians go to France, Austrians to Germany, Danes to Sweden, and Dutchmen to France or Germany.)

In order to regain goodwill, several large U.S. corporations, which had already previously employed European experts in their laboratories at home, established their own laboratories and research centers in Europe and staffed them mainly with Europeans. But the integration of these research facilities in the corporate organization soon produced an exchange of men and ideas within the company between America and Europe. European critics, eager to attain equal treatment and full partnership within a multinational corporation, watch carefully to see how much research is done by U.S. companies on both sides of the Atlantic. They want to make sure that the new corporate research and development efforts in Europe are more than mere goodwill gestures. As it happened, other considerations contributed greatly to the European-American partnership: utilization of profits of European subsidiaries, the scarcity of American talent in some fields, and, above all, the cross-fertilization of ideas among scientists and technologists of various backgrounds.

One major U.S. corporation has only one of its four central laboratories in the United States. The others are in England, France, and Spain. Of the $62 million spent by the company in 1966 on R&D, 67 percent was spent in Europe.

Many American corporations, however, are not yet as advanced in European R&D. Some, which might be said to be in the first phase, still do all their research at home with American experts exclusively. Others are in the second phase, bringing a few European scientists and engineers to their U.S. research centers. Yet quite a few companies are now in the third phase: They have established laboratories in Europe, if only on a minor scale. Few have reached full parity.

The structural position of European R&D centers on the corporate organization chart and their relationship with the company's international operations depend mainly on this stage of development, as well as on the relations between geographic, functional, and product-group divisions. There is also frequently a marked distinction between basic and applied research, with the former usually still in an earlier, more exclusively American phase. Besides, the regional organization plays a major role. Where no European regional office exists, R&D is normally less developed in Europe and is entirely separated from international operations. The same situation can be observed in very large corporations, where R&D may be organized in a separate corporate division equal to and completely independent of the international division and the product groups.

One computer manufacturing company, for example, has a basic research laboratory in Zurich that is not linked with the European organization at all, but reports directly to central corporate R&D. However, there are also several applied research laboratories in various European cities which report to a research center in southern France, but are linked in administrative and personnel matters with the subsidiaries in the same countries. The research center reports directly to regional headquarters in Paris.

An important soap and detergent manufacturer also has several local laboratories and one research center near the company's regional office. A new product was recently developed by one of the local laboratories, then tested and improved by the central laboratory. It was test-marketed and introduced in certain European markets, and all research data went to the American R&D center for study before the product was allowed to be launched in America. This corporation has reached a historic stage of development: New products are sometimes elaborated by European researchers in European laboratories for European markets, but may be introduced in America and other parts of the world later. In spite of this decentralization in R&D—which is matched by decentralized production—line relationships, all the way down from corporate headquarters through the regional office to the subsidiaries, are rather strict.

In a plastics company that has no regional office in Europe, the only European R&D operations are concentrated in a Paris laboratory that has direct relationships with the various subsidiaries. It furnishes them with technical information, especially on new products, including such technical-commercial data as cost elements for local plants. This technical and research center is financed by direct contributions from all European subsidiaries, affiliates, and licensees.

Where products are usually not uniform, as in the food industry, R&D has to be decentralized. In one important food company, the largest subsidiary has its own laboratory under local jurisdiction, but exchanges information with the American research center. In this and similar cases, local research and development help the company adjust its products to different consumer preferences.

Thus, although many American companies in Europe have learned by trial and error and have grown by default, most of them have managed themselves well enough to benefit from their experience and to apply managerial concepts and practices relevant to their specific situation. By making an even greater effort to understand and relate to European market conditions and to the numerous other factors involved, they will be able to move one step closer to true multinationalism.